10 50

D0060159

BOOKS AND PLAYS *by Stanley Richards*

BOOKS:

The Best Short Plays 1972
The Best Short Plays 1971
The Best Short Plays 1970
The Best Short Plays 1969
The Best Short Plays 1968
Best Mystery and Suspense Plays of the Modern Theatre
10 Classic Mystery and Suspense Plays of the Modern Theatre
Best Plays of the Sixties
Modern Short Comedies from Broadway and London
Best Short Plays of the World Theatre: 1968–1973
Best Short Plays of the World Theatre: 1958–1967
Canada on Stage

PLAYS:

Through a Glass, Darkly
August Heat
Sun Deck
Tunnel of Love
Journey to Bahia
O Distant Land
Mood Piece
Mr. Bell's Creation
The Proud Age
Once to Every Boy
Half-Hour, Please
Know Your Neighbor
Gin and Bitterness
The Hills of Bataan
District of Columbia

Chilton Book Company

RADNOR, PA.

THE BEST SHORT PLAYS *1973*

edited and with an introduction by

STANLEY RICHARDS

BEST SHORT PLAYS SERIES

for TERESA MITCHEM

Copyright © 1973 by Stanley Richards
First Edition
All rights reserved
Published in Radnor, Pa., by Chilton Book Company
and simultaneously in Ontario, Canada,
by Thomas Nelson & Sons, Ltd.

Manufactured in the United States of America
Designed by Adrianne Onderdonk Dudden

ISBN: 0-8019-5589-0
Library of Congress Catalog Card No. 38-8006

Second Printing, September 1974

CONTENTS

INTRODUCTION

In the six years since I've undertaken the editorship of *The Best Short Plays* annuals, I have learned many things; most saliently, that the work of an editor, at least a conscientious one, is not quite as simple as it generally is assumed to be. To a good many people the prime requisite of an anthology editor is his adeptness with the paste-pot. In short, it is rather a common assumption that he merely gathers together a group of plays, pastes them onto proper manuscript pages and pilots them to the printer. The truth, however, is far removed from the theory.

To begin with, during the course of each year a vast amount of plays are submitted to me. These submissions emanate from a number of sources including authors, agents, publishers, college and university drama departments and theatrical managements. Each and every play is personally read and carefully evaluated and although a work may be rejected for one or more reasons, often there is a perceptible indication of the author's inherent talent. In such cases, I retain a special interest in the author and his future works for I firmly believe that there is nothing more rewarding for an editor than to discover and maintain a professional vigil over the development of a gifted new dramatist.

A creative editor (as opposed to the paste-pot genus) has certain obligations to his authors. First and foremost, he must present them to the reader (and subsequently, to producing groups) in the best possible fashion. For example, there is one play in this present collection that originally was sent to me several years ago. Although, at the time, I felt that the play needed additional work, it also was evident that the author had enormous talent and undeniably was worth close attention. With a few basic suggestions from this editor, the author eventually resumed work on the play and now it finally appears here in what I believe to be its consummate form. It also is a pleasure to add that he since has become an award-winning dramatist.

In another instance, a play came to my desk just as I had begun to work on *The Best Short Plays* series. Again, here was a play with strong potentials but riddled with an excess of verbiage and occasional structural deficiencies. The author, who was then unpublished, willingly came to discuss his manuscript with me. Point after point was taken and suggestions were offered, much as a director might impart to an author during the course of rehearsals of a new play. The young writer, fortified by these suggestions, returned to his typewriter and in less than two months emerged with an impressive play, one that, since its publication in 1970, has been presented on literally hundreds of stages as well as on national television. This then, to me, is an important facet of an editor: to have the ability and patience, the strong interest, to work closely with a writer when necessary. It is an historic axiom in the theatre that when a play needs work it needs work, regardless of whether it was created by a seasoned professional in a luxurious Manhattan duplex or by a newcomer in a cluttered dormitory room. A play when staged is a collaborative effort of author, director, players and designers. Equally, a new play can gain immeasurably when there is a creative affinity between the author and his editor.

Another factor that immediately springs to mind in the collaborative process of a play is, of course, the audience. Essentially, it is the same with the reader: for a collection of plays to be effectual it must have strong appeal and areas of involvement for a wide category of readers. As I have commented on a previous occasion: "Assuredly, not all of the selections will have appealed to everyone. But, just as assuredly, each play will have appealed to someone and, consequently, by diversifying my annual selections, hopefully we reach through to all types of audiences." A collection, therefore, should be well balanced, integrating different styles and categories of plays, yet all somehow must be rooted in the human experience and reflect the dramatic aspects of a changing society and world.

I once heard it argued that an editor must be impartial in his judgment. This, to me, seemed like rather a futile discourse for how exactly can an editor not have some personal preferences over others? Doesn't an architect, a fashion coordinator, a designer, an artist, or anyone for that matter, bring to a work or a product something of his own tastes? The objective of an editor, in my opinion, is not to impose his own tastes upon readers but, hopefully, to *share* them.

STANLEY RICHARDS
New York, N.Y.

Robert Anderson

DOUBLE SOLITAIRE

Robert Anderson

A leading American playwright, Robert Anderson was born in New York City in 1917, attended Phillips Exeter Academy, and was graduated from Harvard University in 1939. While at Harvard, he wrote and directed plays, did drama criticism, and taught drama and writing courses. He served as a naval officer in World War II, and during this period wrote *Come Marching Home,* a drama which won the National Theatre Conference prize for the best play by a serviceman on overseas duty.

Following his discharge from the Navy, Mr. Anderson buckled down to a writing career and turned out dozens of scripts for radio and television. In September, 1953, he made his debut as a Broadway playwright with *Tea and Sympathy,* directed by Elia Kazan and starring Deborah Kerr. Named a "best play" of the season, the drama ran for 712 performances and later reappeared as a successful film, for which Anderson wrote the screenplay.

Tea and Sympathy was the longest-running play in the twenty-one-year history of The Playwrights' Company. Just before the play opened, Mr. Anderson was invited to join the management of that noted production company, founded in 1938 by Robert E. Sherwood, Sidney Howard, S. N. Behrman, Maxwell Anderson, Elmer Rice and John F. Wharton ". . . to make a center for ourselves within the theatre, and possibly rally the theatre as a whole to new levels by setting a high standard of writing and production."

The organization produced his next two Broadway scripts: *All Summer Long* (1954) and *Silent Night, Lonely Night* (1959), the latter co-starring Henry Fonda and Barbara Bel Geddes.

In the season of 1965–66, Mr. Anderson's play, *The Days Between,* was chosen by the American Playwrights Theatre circuit for production in college and community theatres throughout the nation.

In March, 1967, Robert Anderson once again achieved extraordinary Broadway success with his program of four short comedies, *You Know I Can't Hear You When the Water's Running,* which entertained audiences for 755 performances.

His next Broadway venture was *I Never Sang for My Father,* an affecting drama performed in 1968 by a superb company headed by Hal Holbrook, Teresa Wright, Alan Webb and Lillian Gish.

The author's many screenplay credits include *The Nun's Story* (nominated for an Academy Award), *Until They Sail, The Sand Pebbles,* and his adaptation of his play, *I Never Sang for My Father,* which won the Writer's Guild Award for best screenplay (drama) and an Academy Award nomination in 1970.

Double Solitaire (with its companion piece, *Solitaire*) was initially presented at the Long Wharf Theatre, New Haven, and subsequently at the 1971 Edinburgh International Festival, Scotland, where it was hailed in the press as "a tremendous play, deeply moving yet deceptive in its simplicity." The production opened at the John Golden Theatre, New York, on September 30, 1971, and once again was greeted with critical acclaim. Clive Barnes proclaimed in *The New York Times* that it was "Mr. Anderson's finest achievement to date," while George Oppenheimer of *Newsday* found it "infinitely perceptive and deeply touching," a verdict generally shared by other first night jurors. Now, with its publication in *The Best Short Plays 1973, Double Solitaire* appears in an anthology for the first time.

Mr. Anderson, who is the incumbent president of The Dramatists Guild, is married to actress Teresa Wright and they live in a farmhouse, built in 1825, in Bridgewater, Connecticut.

CHARLEY

BARBARA

MRS. POTTER

MR. POTTER

SYLVIA

GEORGE

PETER

Scene:

A bare stage, except at stage left there is a round table with two chairs and at stage right a round table with two chairs. Slightly upstage center between the two tables, a screen or freestanding flat.

At the stage right table sits Charley Potter, age forty-three. At the stage left table sits his attractive wife Barbara, age forty-one.

Mrs. Elizabeth Potter, Barbara's mother-in-law, comes from the shadows to Barbara's table. She is seventy-one, patrician, a lady who has missed a great deal in her life and knows it but doesn't know just how it happened. She is a composed woman who speaks rather thoughtfully. A note of philosophic acceptance.

MRS. POTTER: Ernest is having a perfectly wonderful time trying to decide what we should all do for our fiftieth anniversary. He's like a little boy with a birthday party to plan. He consults me, of course, but it will end up being all his way. He says it's an old tradition that the wedding is the bride's party and the fiftieth anniversary, the groom's. Of course he made it all up.

He's decided to ask the guests to bring pictures of *their* weddings, and he's going to have several projectors and show the pictures on the four walls of the banquet room all at once. He says it's very modern. Perhaps it would be amusing to see the styles. But I tell him many of the husbands and wives are dead, and some are divorced. Ernest says they needn't bring *their* pictures.

He's so proud of the ones he took at your wedding. We ran through them the other night, and they are lovely. Except, of course, for the ones of me. Ernest has always managed to get me at a poor angle. I tell him it's subconscious hostility. (*She smiles*) I say to him that good photographers weed out their poor pictures. But not Ernest. He shows them all. If he dies before I do, I'm going to get rid of at least half of them. (*After a moment*) Your mother wore such a pretty dress . . . the blue lace with the picture hat. And you were such a lovely bride. I was so happy that day, though you wouldn't think so from looking at Ernest's pictures of me. Happy for both of you, but most especially for Charley. And was he happy! You haven't seen the pictures for a long time, but wait till you see his face, looking at you with such adoration. You know, Barbara, you were only his third girl. He never would play the field. There was Betty when he was seven—oh, yes, he started very young, head over heels in love. It's always had to be head over heels for Charley, or nothing. I used to say to him, when he couldn't get his special girl for a party, "Call up someone else. You don't have to marry the girl." But he wouldn't. He'd sit home and write the special girl a long love letter. I would have found it a great strain to have someone that devoted. Anyway, the sun rose and set with Betty. Then, at thirteen, it rose and set with Peggy. And then at nineteen, it rose and set with you—the best of them all. (*She pats Barbara's arm, and looks at her a long moment*) Ernest's next idea for the party is that he and I should renew our marriage vows. He's in a great dither now trying to decide how to work in both the projections of the pictures and renewing the vows. I told him I wouldn't be able to go through the ring ceremony because of arthritis. (*She holds out her hands*) I haven't been able to get my wedding ring off for five years. I couldn't divorce him if I wanted to. (*She laughs*) And I've wanted to—often. In every marriage more than a week old, there are grounds for divorce. The trick is to find, and continue to find, grounds for marriage. (*An almost imper-*

ceptible look at Barbara) It's a romantic idea, this renewing the vows. But then men *are* the romantics, so full of nostalgia for the past they thought was so happy. I remember my youth as rather miserable. Ah youth, that happy time when I was so sad! But they remember it as so happy. I imagine it has something to do with their sex drive. That's so important to them. I remember my fifties as being my happiest years. The children were grown, there were grandchildren whom I could cuddle for a few minutes and then thrust back into their mothers' aching arms. (*She laughs*) Another of Ernest's romantic ideas has always been to move to the country, to a farm. Get away from it all. The simple life. Family picnics under the spreading maple trees. Of course he forgets the mosquitoes. Men always forget the mosquitoes. I do hope they've removed Thoreau from school reading lists. The image of that dreadful shack at Walden has made more men unhappy and wrecked more marriages. (*A long moment*) One final thing—Ernest is going to talk to Charley and suggest that you and he stand up with us and renew your marriage vows too. (*She looks at Barbara for a long moment*) We renewed our vows on our twenty-fifth. Perhaps it helped, because here we are . . . and we have a good life. I have my garden, though I can't work in it as much as I used to. And there's the church . . . and I read a good deal.

And Ernest and I play cards. I always hated cards, but he finally persuaded me. We play double solitaire. You know, each one lays out his own deck, but you put the aces in the center as they come up, and each builds on them. The play of the cards is lively. We have little jokes about the game. I slap his hand when he plays on a card I was about to build on. And we laugh. And he teases me. It gives us something to do together. And I have my poetry readings. I'm reading at The Club next Tuesday if you're free—two-thirty. (*She recites, very simply*)

All, all of a piece throughout.
Thy chase had a beast in view.
Thy wars brought nothing about.

Thy lovers were all untrue.
'Tis well when old age is out,
And time to begin anew.

(*After a moment, as she draws on a glove*) Not exactly what the ladies want to hear. But I find those lines strangely comforting . . . there'll be coffee and sandwiches after. Rather better than you usually get at such affairs.

(*She reaches out and puts her hand on Barbara's arm and looks at her a moment and smiles. She moves back into the shadows. Barbara remains at her table. As Mrs. Potter walks into the shadows, slides of a wedding and wedding party start to show on the screen or flat in the center. And Ernest Potter, age seventy-five, enters. He is a gentleman of the old school, full of warm charm. Very handsome, and, for his age, jaunty and youthful in spirit*)

MR. POTTER: When I took that one, I was standing in the middle of your mother's flower bed. I got hell for it, but the shot was worth it. (*A shot or two of Barbara and Charley in the garden*) You can make a choice of those you might want to show at the party and keep them all. I always meant for Barbara and you to have them. They've stood up very well for twenty-two years. (*A picture of Mrs. Potter. Nothing too poor, but just not very good*) Not very good of your mother. But then, she doesn't take a good picture. I've tried my damnedest over the years . . . she's a beautiful woman, too! There's a couple along here I particularly want you to see.

CHARLEY: (*Turns away, obviously disturbed and saddened a bit by the pictures*) I'll look at them later, Dad. Thanks.

MR. POTTER: I showed them to Peter the other day when he was over. He was very interested in them. Maybe you'd like to show them to Mary, too. It's nice for children to be able to see their parents when they . . . uh . . . well . . . as they were then.

CHARLEY: Yes. (*The pictures stop for the time being*)

MR. POTTER: Now, Charley, see how this fits in with your plans for the party. I thought the first part of the evening we'd have festivities. There are going to be a lot of people who haven't seen each other for a long time, and they'll want to say hello and have a drink.

CHARLEY: There's a small room off the main room at the hotel, and we'll have a bar set up there, and a little music.

MR. POTTER: Then I thought we'd have dinner, and then right after dinner, your mother and I have decided we'd like to renew our marriage vows. We did it on our twenty-fifth, you remember.

CHARLEY: That's a nice idea, Dad.

MR. POTTER: And then after that, more festivities, and the slides and pictures.

CHARLEY: Maybe the vows should be before dinner.

MR. POTTER: I thought of that, but there'll be a lot of drinking then, and I thought maybe after dinner the food would have absorbed some of the champagne. We could do it before the dessert and champagne.

CHARLEY: Or you could do it before everything, so everything after would be party, the way it was fifty years ago.

MR. POTTER: Well, let's turn it over in our minds. Your mother will have some definite ideas about it, but if you and I stick together, we might prevail. She had it all her way the first time. (*Change of mood*) Now, Charley, I tell you what your mother and I would like . . . what would make our anniversary for us. It wouldn't cost you a penny. Your mother and I would like you and Barbara to stand up and renew your marriage vows along with us. (*Charley's smile sets*) It would give us great pleasure, old man. (*Charley's mouth opens, but for a moment nothing happens. Then he licks his lips and goes on*)

CHARLEY: I . . . uh . . . well . . . this is your party, Dad . . . and. . . .

MR. POTTER: Your mother has talked to Barbara about it, and you can discuss it, but I can't tell you what it would mean to us.

CHARLEY: Dad, it's . . . well, we'll think about it.

MR. POTTER: It would be good for you, too, Charley. It

helped your mother and me on our twenty-fifth. There's something reaffirming about the ritual . . . to stand in the presence of God and your friends and your family and say, "To have and to hold . . . in sickness and in health . . . for better or for worse. . . ."

CHARLEY: Dad, you know neither Barbara nor I are very religious any more. There would be a certain . . . hypocrisy.

MR. POTTER: I don't look upon it as a religious ceremony, Charley. It's . . . I don't know. There's something about standing up there, in the face of all the unhappy marriages, the divorces, the whole mess out there, to stand up there and say, "We made it!"

CHARLEY: We'll think about it, Dad.

MR. POTTER: Maybe while you're going through the ceremony, we could flash one of the pictures on the wall. (*He flips through a couple of shots, and ends with a close shot of Charley and Barbara, embracing. Pantomime of Charley shutting off the projector*)

CHARLEY: (*Smiling at his dad's efforts to show the films*) Later, Dad . . . I'd like to look at them later on. Slowly. You know?

MR. POTTER: (*After a moment*) Charley?

CHARLEY: Yes, Dad?

MR. POTTER: Your mother's worried about you.

CHARLEY: (*Smiling*) Why, Dad?

MR. POTTER: She's a very wise woman. She senses something, and I think she just may be right.

CHARLEY: About what?

MR. POTTER: Charley, you're only going through what every couple in the world has gone through.

CHARLEY: Come on now, Dad . . .

MR. POTTER: Damn it, Charley, I didn't give you much advice about things—women and sex and all that—when you were growing up. I assumed you were learning it some place. But now, Charley, what the hell's the use of what I know and have learned if it can't help you? They used to call them The

Dangerous Years . . . hell, every year of marriage can be dangerous if you want to make it that way. If you're not committed.
But if you're committed, you get by them, by them all. You just
bite the nail and hang on.

CHARLEY: Dad. . . .

MR. POTTER: Renew your vows, Charley! I put great store
by form and routine and ritual. They sound dull, but they carry
you along. A lot of times in my life, I haven't felt like doing a
thing. I didn't care if school kept or not. But I went ahead and
did whatever I was supposed to do. And often I'd get a surprise.
Halfway through, there suddenly was some feeling. Presents I'd
give your mother. Hell, sometimes it starts out as a perfunctory
note from my secretary: "Don't forget your wife's birthday." And
I've got no interest in it. And very little love for her on that
particular day. And then I make the effort and don't just send
my secretary out for something. And before I've finished selecting
the present, I can't wait to get home and give it to your mother.
And at that moment I love her.

CHARLEY: You're an old campaigner, Pop. An old soldier.

MR. POTTER: Bring home some flowers unexpectedly, for
no reason at all. Whisk her away on a trip on the spur of the
moment. Your mother keeps telling me, "You can't play the show
over again." But it never hurts to try. (*A better idea*) Take her
for a night to a hotel here in your own city. There's something
very exciting about that.

CHARLEY: (*Smiles*) Did you do all those things, Dad?

MR. POTTER: (*The old sport*) Most of them. And a few
more. Your mother wouldn't go for the hotel. She said it was
ridiculous for us to go to a hotel when we had our own apartment. Your mother sometimes lacks the light touch. That's not
meant as a criticism. Just an observation. She's a fine woman
. . . Look, Charley, someday someone's going to come up with a
better set-up. They haven't yet. So the answer is accept the situation and find your own way to make it work . . . and don't ask
too many questions. And I've got to tell you, old man, it gets
worse. But a man doesn't whine. A dog whines, but a man

doesn't whine. Wait till she goes through The Change. Women are impossible in that period. And at least for your mother, it was the end of . . . (*He makes a gesture, knowing Charley will understand*) I mean, finished! Without any "I'm sorry's" or "What are you going to do?" And the thing is so damned delicate. Naturally you don't bring it out in the open and discuss it. You just let it ride. Oh, a more aggressive man might have made a big issue of it and blown the marriage sky-high, made the wife think she was some kind of monster. I mean, I didn't think very pretty thoughts when I finally realized what had happened without any mention of *my* problem. But I didn't say anything to her. You don't say everything you think . . . and I'm still a vigorous man in that area. (*He smiles jauntily*) So you should be, too. They say it's a matter of inheritance.

CHARLEY: (*Amused at the old fox*) I look upon that as my most valuable inheritance, Dad.

MR. POTTER: Of course I don't do anything about it, out of respect for your mother, who is a fine woman. I know she needn't have known. But *I* would have known. I hear about all these people sleeping around, and I ask myself, "If I had gone to bed with this or that woman. . . ." And I've had the opportunity!

CHARLEY: I'm sure you have, Dad. You're a charming man.

MR. POTTER: You pulling my leg?

CHARLEY: No. I mean it.

MR. POTTER: Well, some women have found me attractive. And on trips, in the course of my business, sometimes it almost seemed harmless. But your mother is a fine, clean woman, and I couldn't have come back to her if I'd done that. (*He has said this with great force, as though someone had been arguing with him*) Now, your Uncle Philip . . . he's played fast and loose with woman after woman. *Now* where is he? No children. No family. Lolling away his life on a beach down in Florida. Nothing accomplished. We wouldn't let him bring his women to the house because of the effect it might have on you and Ruth when you were children. Perfectly beautiful women, laughing all the time. . . .

CHARLEY: I was always fond of Uncle Philip.

MR. POTTER: Well, you were too young to know the truth. I don't know how he does it . . . where he gets his money. . . . But he'll come whining in the end for a handout. Or he'll be lonely. *Something* will happen to him. It's *got* to! (*He has said this with determination. The man just can't get away with it! . . . and then he relaxes*) So, Charley, you coast . . . as I said. Just be happy you can get from one end of the week to the next. Join some clubs. Find some committees. All those committees I'm on. Scenic Preservation, Museum of Natural History, Boys' Club, you don't think I'm really interested in all those things? But they have meetings. And I've got my hobbies. Shot an eighty-six yesterday. And my cameras. You started me on that interest, Charley. Saved my life! Then there's the Board of Education, YMCA. . . . We go to the movies at least once a week, and one night in my darkroom. . . . Time passes. (*He looks at Charley for a moment, then gets up, preparing to leave*) When this anniversary business is over, let's us go off fishing together. Get a boat, and go out in the middle of a lake and get to know each other.

CHARLEY: That's a good idea, Dad.

MR. POTTER: (*Puts his hand on Charley's shoulder*) Just remember . . . bite on the nail.

(*He pats his son and moves off into the shadows. From the shadows comes Sylvia, an extremely stylish woman around forty. She talks as she moves to Barbara's table*)

SYLVIA: I wouldn't marry again for a million dollars. I was a very boring wife. I came to know exactly what I was going to say on every occasion and said it. Oh, I read all the books on how to be a thousand different women for your husband . . . on one occasion I even suggested an innovation or two in our sex lives, which had the unfortunate effect of blocking him completely for two weeks. So I finally persuaded him to divorce me—sans alimony, of course. I have my own shop, and I wasn't going to fleece him because I was a frumpy bore. I lost ten pounds and immediately became more attractive and interesting—at least to myself.

"Don't you get lonely?" they ask me. Who has time to be lonely? "Who do you see?" My God, I see their husbands. Not my friends' husbands, of course. I use some discretion. And it's not all sex, or even mostly . . . I find that every man has enough interesting happen to him in a week to fill one evening's conversation.

Mondays I see this movie bug. He has to sit near the screen, and his wife has to sit far back. For years they compromised and sat in the middle and spoiled it for both of them. Also, she is an easy weeper and cries at almost everything, which annoys him and makes him feel insensitive. And he laughs easily, which makes her feel she has no sense of humor. So. . . . Tuesdays I see this man who loves games, particularly Scrabble. His wife thinks games are frivolous, and besides she can't spell. Wednesday is matinee day, and there's this sweet older man. He doesn't like to sit up late, so we have an early dinner after the matinee and I go home and get to bed early. A-lone. He's just had a heart attack, so that's why I'm free today. Thursdays I have lunch with this nice homosexual boy. That takes care of my mothering instincts. Thursday nights there's this man who likes to come and sit in my neat, pretty, attractive apartment. His sexual relations with his wife are marvelous, but she's a slob about her house. So he just comes and sits in my apartment and we talk. Each time he comes, he walks through my rooms and looks at them, shaking his head. Friday and Saturday nights are heavy date nights. Sundays I have the *New York Times,* and I do my other reading to keep up with the various interests of my dates—*Scientific American, Art News, Cahiers du Cinéma, Fortune, Sports Illustrated.* . . .

Now and then, of course, one of them asks me to marry him. A kind of conditioned reflex learned at mother's knee . . . to make an honest woman of me. I find they usually ask at just about the time they're getting tired of making an effort. They're ready to take me for better or worse and for granted. I much prefer to be a visitor in a person's life. I get treated with much more consideration.

Of course it gets lonely on Mother's Day and Christmas and other tribal times when families rush off to graduations and weddings, Bar Mitzvahs and circumcisions. But what the hell. I have a little warm dog who sleeps in my bed—when no one else is there, naturally. Some men are really thrown by having a dog stand there watching them. (*She laughs*) They say I'll be lonely when I'm old. Well, I can always take a few pills or cut my throat. I mean, life was meant to be lived, not just endured.

(*And she drifts off into the shadows. As she leaves, George comes down to Charley. George is a man in his late forties, a man of great experience, rough-hewn, warm and charming. His most characteristic attitude towards things is expressed by laughing and shaking his head sadly at the same time, muttering, "Sad . . . Sad." He is paternal towards Charley in a nice way*)

CHARLEY: (*Intense*) My father expected me to say right out, "Sure, great." And I opened my damned mouth to say it, and nothing came out. And that's all I've been able to think about since.

GEORGE: (*Laughs*) God, it's sad.

CHARLEY: I haven't discussed it with Barbara. She hasn't discussed it with me. We each know the other one's been asked, but neither of us is saying anything. (*George laughs. This sort of perverse situation delights him*) What I'm talking about is me sitting there with my mouth open and nothing coming out. Like finding yourself unable to function with a girl when you want to, or think you want to. You have every intention, but something inside you that knows you a lot better shouts, "You're a damned liar." And doesn't let you do what you think you want to do. And then you start to sweat and ask questions—like "If you can't feel that way about her, what are you doing married to her?" It's been a rough few days.

GEORGE: (*Asking the obvious but inappropriate question*) So, what are you going to do, get a divorce? (*Charley looks at him as though he were crazy*) Well, you can't just sit there and say, "It shouldn't be this way."

CHARLEY: (*Loud*) It *shouldn't* be this way! (*Then he smiles*)

GEORGE: You know, Charley, your reaction to things like

this always reminds me of a guy with a football. He starts running down the field, and he suddenly sees a lot of tacklers in the way. He says to himself, "God damn it, they shouldn't be there. According to The Book, the interference should have taken them out." You get mad and run right into the tacklers and get thrown for a loss. You've got to learn to . . . improvise.

CHARLEY: George, how the hell have we been friends all these years? You think I'm a sentimental dope . . . naive. . . .

GEORGE: And you think I'm a cynical old bastard.

CHARLEY: Sometimes I've envied you your cynicism.

GEORGE: Sometimes I've envied you your . . . what? . . . your ridiculous battle with the inevitable. I'm not cynical. Just seven years older than you. Look down and you'll see my footprints in the sand—slightly bloody.

CHARLEY: (*Smiles*) Barbara hates for me to spend time with you. She says you give me wild ideas. She says I always come home restless and grind my teeth in my sleep. (*Back to his problem*) Damn it, George, the thing itself, renewing the vows, is not that important, but it's set up a whole chain of reactions. By realizing I don't feel the way I should to stand up there with deep commitment and conviction, I suddenly got a terrible sense of the absence of that feeling in my life. And I was, and am, scared to death.

GEORGE: (*Be reasonable*) Well, Charley. . . .

CHARLEY: I know. But it suddenly made me hungry for it. Desperately hungry for that intensity.

GEORGE: I'll have my book finished in a week or so and turn it over for your blue pencil. That'll keep you busy and take your mind off it.

CHARLEY: I don't seem to want to take my mind off it. It's made me put my mind *to* it. (*Suddenly intense*) Christ, George, do you know there's nothing I'd die for. (GEORGE *just looks at him, taken aback a little, and touched by the flat-out nature of the statement*) It's an over-blown way of putting it. But these few days have made me wonder, "Jesus, what do I feel strongly about?" I whip up some passing superficial enthusiasm. But not enough to march or even sign my name to a protest. My life seems to be spent in discussing the day's news and the latest movies—entirely superficial. God, you're the only one I ever talk to like this. The rest of my friends would be embarrassed. And I don't know anything about where they *really* live. I used to talk to Barbara, but.... (*He shrugs*)

GEORGE: Yes, I know. Frighten her to death. The dark side of a husband's soul is too threatening for a wife to take seriously. I told Doris once about a kind of homosexual dream I had had. It had bothered the hell out of me for days, and I wanted to talk about it to someone. She laughed and said, "You, George! Ha-ha." And the next time we were together, she said, "Well, this is better than little boys, isn't it?"

CHARLEY: (*Smiles and shakes his head*) Suddenly I'm examining everything I do and feel, and so much of it seems too damned pointless. I mean, yesterday I'm up there making out the monthly checks, and I found myself stopping and asking, "Which of these damned things I'm paying for do I really care about?" ... and I went through an unconscious withdrawal into a kind of fantasy. I wanted the house to burn down. Or maybe I wanted my whole life to burn down. And then I'd sit in a bare white-walled room, and anything or anyone who wanted "in" to that room or my life would have to pass the most rigorous test for meaningfulness. And I would want to start in that room with a woman, because I'm no good as a swinging single. A woman about whom I could feel and continue to feel with such intensity that my whole life would take on meaning ... because that's the way it was when Barbara first came into my room. I was nothing ... (*He stops, then after a moment, starts to smile*) Then, of course, I start coming to. I realize that she would need clothes, and that I'm easily bored in one room, and we'd want children, and ... and ... and ... and I join the human race.

GEORGE: You want too much, Charley. (*Then in a lighter tone*) Get an accountant to make out your checks.

CHARLEY: (*Smiles*) Remove myself from all points of contact with my life, the points that let me know what I feel—my checkbook, sex. Someone else to pay the bills. Someone else or me-but-not-really-me to sleep with my wife. Cool. That would scare the bejesus out of me, George. I sense something about myself—that I could be the damnedest most detached person, and I could freeze to death somewhere out there in the cool world, without this connection with life through my feelings for someone. That's why this blandness terrifies me. I feel my spiritual temperature dropping, and I get scared, and I reach out desperately for some saving intensity and intimacy. (*He pauses for a moment, then . . .*) Barbara and I achieve this intensity and intimacy sometimes in sex. There can be nothing, and then . . . something. Primitive. A connection and intensity. And it dissipates this blandness and emptiness for a while. It used to be a joke, when I was in college. I always fell in love with anyone I went to bed with. Fortunately, it still works—even when all the other lines of intimacy and communication are blocked.

GEORGE: I have my work. Maybe that's what I'd die for.

CHARLEY: You're lucky. Much as I enjoy editing you and some of my other authors, it's not that meaningful to me. And my own writing—I'm afraid by being cowardly about my commitment to that years ago, it's no longer that fulfilling or urgent. Two roads diverged in a yellow wood, and I . . . I didn't take either one of them but slogged into the middle of the woods, trying to keep an eye on both roads, hoping they might eventually come together. Son of a bitch, George, *what* do you do? My father sensed I was upset. He suggested I bring home some flowers unexpectedly. (*They both smile at this*) Or take her to a hotel right here in New York, where we have our apartment. He says that's very sexy.

GEORGE: I never tried that one. I did the flowers, of course, and then a slightly too-expensive present for no reason at all. It didn't have the desired effect. Doris was sure I'd been cheating on her.

CHARLEY: Had you?

GEORGE: Not yet. I was going through the same period you're going through now. Depressed as hell, scared because I didn't feel "that way" about her, and trying to rediscover it. Doris and I hadn't been dancing for ten years, and I took her dancing. After the first set, her feet began to hurt and my bursitis was getting me in the right arm, and so we huddled in the corner by the candlelight and ordered champagne—which I hate—and tried to be romantic for a while. Then we both felt foolish and talked about the children.

CHARLEY: (*Smiles*) I did something. . . . When I came back from the service, I'd gotten into the habit of wearing my skivvies, my underwear, to bed. One time, I started wearing pajamas instead—just the tops. And I started shaving before going to bed. And I cleared all the magazines from my night table, and I just lay there waiting for her as she came out of the bathroom.

GEORGE: (*Laughs*) Jesus.

CHARLEY: It terrified her. She began to take longer and longer before she came out. And she took to wearing older and older nightgowns, and she finally came to bed with a ratty old tennis sweater over everything. I went back to wearing my skivvies.

GEORGE: How did the kidnapping bit work out? (*Charley looks at him*) Dragging her off on the spur of the moment to some romantic weekend spot. (*Charley looks at him, pained and amused*) You don't think I did that? You think I'm some unfeeling monster? We all do that. The whole damned thing is a cliché. That's what makes art and literature possible. Where'd you take her?

CHARLEY: I've got this thing for beaches. We were together first on a beach at Ipswich.

GEORGE: I took Doris to Pennsylvania—Bucks County. No luggage, no nothing. I just grabbed her one summer evening, shoved her in the car, and went. We had to stop in the village down there to get a bathrobe, because she said what if the john were down the hall? And while we were buying the bathrobe, we got a sweater and skirt because it was turning chilly, and under the circumstances I wanted her to be happy. Anyway, the whole damned thing turned into a shopping expedition. You see, Charley, it's to laugh.

CHARLEY: Yeah.

GEORGE: You think I'm cynical—my women, my girls, the way I carry on. I wasn't cynical when I married Doris. I was sick with love for her. Do you imagine I'd have even thought of laying a hand on another girl? Hell no! And that was beautiful. But, man, you can't keep it up, and I tried. And she tried. So, you go underground, keep your own confidence, be careful, discreet . . . and . . . a little sad. If you don't, you get a lot of divorces, which makes everyone unhappy. Marriage isn't long for this world, Charley. The women are saying they're fed up with it. The men will finally get honest and say they don't like it. The kids won't have it. They're getting rid of all that bullshit. My youngest son tells me, "We're reexamining all your institutions to see if they suit us." I can't wait for them to hit marriage. We're transitional figures, Charley. And it's rough to be a transitional figure.

CHARLEY: I *like* marriage. I thought. I hate the old bastard for disturbing my sleep.

GEORGE: (*After a moment*) Charley, we've asked each other a lot of dirty questions over the years. Let me ask you one now. Would you feel this . . . hypocrisy if you were standing up there at this make-believe altar with Maria? (*Charley smiles at him*) Have you been in touch with her?

CHARLEY: Not for a long time. We wrote for a while after I came back from California. Then. . . .

GEORGE: She just got divorced.

CHARLEY: (*Smiles*) Yeah. I heard about it. It's been coming for a long time.

GEORGE: You "heard" about it. So my question stands. If I ever saw a man in love, you were in love with Maria. You came back from California raving about her poetry, this beautiful new poet. I don't think anyone was deceived. (*Charley smiles*) Which came first? Your father's suggestion about renewing your vows, or your hearing of Maria's divorce?

CHARLEY: My father on Monday. Maria on Wednesday.

GEORGE: I would say she timed her divorce with a total lack of consideration for you.

CHARLEY: My thing with Maria was more or less a one-way

street. I was crazy about her, but she was . . . oh . . . it was hard to tell how she felt about me really. She was having a rough time with her husband. (*Shrugs*) But you're right. That's part of the last few days—the way I felt when I heard that. I walked the streets like a caged tiger. I tell you those two things coming together. . . . I worked out a dozen schemes to take me to California. Young authors we publish who need checking on. Wild-goose chases to sell another of my stories to the movies. I wrote Maria a dozen letters in my mind. I was alive, I didn't have a drink all day. I didn't need one. At the end of the day I found myself in a flower shop ordering her favorite flowers. I wrote out five different messages to go with them. And then I finally said, "You can't go this route," and I picked out some other flowers and took them home to Barbara.

GEORGE: (*Shakes his head and smiles sadly*) God. . . .

CHARLEY: We both got a little high and we had a good time. And just before I fell asleep, she said, "Charley, do you have to be high to make love to me?" (*George shakes his head*) I copped out by pretending to be asleep. But I didn't sleep that night, thinking about that . . . The next night I didn't have a drink before dinner or after dinner. And I was very conspicuous about not having one. And I started to make love to her—as a kind of answer. But she was tired. So . . . it isn't true . . . really.

(*But he still wonders*)

GEORGE: (*After a moment*) I understand Maria's on her way to London. Going to stop off in New York to see shows . . . and old friends. (*He looks at Charley*)

CHARLEY: (*Smiles, shakes his head*) No.

GEORGE: I've heard that from alcoholics and chain-smokers.

CHARLEY: No. It took me three months to stop thinking about her the last time. I had to stop writing her, ask her to stop writing me. I thought I could go on pouring out my heart to her in letters and still keep on with Barbara—on another level. Again, keeping my eyes on two roads. I shocked myself one morning, writing an adoring letter to Maria after having made love to Barbara the night before. I felt like that man—you remember, your friend . . . the man whose wife caught him in bed with another woman, and he jumped up stark naked yelling, "It's not me. It's not me." (*He smiles at the picture, then*) But it *was* me —sleeping with Barbara and writing the letters to Maria. And I desperately longed to be just one "me." So I quit writing.

GEORGE: (*Smiling*) And immediately she vanished from your mind.

CHARLEY: How the hell do you keep your feelings straight with your various girls?

GEORGE: The difference is I'm not in love with any of them. I don't want to write letters of undying love to any of them. I don't seem to have your need to adore. (*There is a note of sadness in all this*) I'm my own man, in sickness and in health, for better or for worse—till death do part me from myself. (*After a moment*) You want too much, Charley. What right have you got to have things simple?

CHARLEY: (*Smiling, acknowledging*) The motto of my family is *Dum spiro, spero*—While I breathe, I hope. (*Then seriously*) I asked Barbara to go to the Bahamas with me for a quick week—one of the outer islands—to get away from it all.

GEORGE: Once more onto the beach, dear friend. (*He shakes his head*)

CHARLEY: She said she was too busy with the preparations for the party.

GEORGE: Perhaps just as well. I have friends who wrangled along in the city, always with the illusion that if they could get away from the clutter of their lives and be alone in the country, things would be better for them. When their kids left home, they took to the woods and looked at each other across the uncluttered space and promptly got a divorce. I try to confront my illusions as rarely as possible.

CHARLEY: She'd go if I insisted. (*They look at each other a long moment—the unstated statement, "Why haven't I insisted?"*)

GEORGE: (*Puts his hand on Charley's shoulder*) Keep breathing, Charley.

(*He moves off into the shadows. Charley runs a few slides*

of the wedding. At about the third slide, Peter, age twenty-two, appears in the shadows, looking at the slides. He is very youthful and attractive, wears sweater, jeans, sneakers)

PETER: Dad?

CHARLEY: Oh, yes, Peter.

PETER: You wanted to talk over my plans.

CHARLEY: Yes. Come in. (*Peter comes to his father and kisses him on the cheek*)

CHARLEY: You've seen these, I think.

PETER: Yes. Grandfather showed them to me. (*They look at two or three more*) They're nice. (*It is obvious he thinks them rather painful, but he feels he has to say something*) The color has stood up very well.

CHARLEY: You've heard your grandfather's plan. The guests to show pictures of their weddings on all four walls simultaneously.

PETER: (*Smiles*) Melinda and I took him to The Electric Circus. That's probably where he got the idea.

CHARLEY: (*Stops the projector*) I'm surprised he hasn't persuaded you and Melinda to get married as part of the festivities. (*Peter smiles a little uncomfortably*) You mean that gracious, charming old couple walking hand in hand into the sunset doesn't persuade you of the joys of matrimony? (*Peter smiles again*) Tell me your plans.

PETER: Well, I've told you I've got this short film I made—about three minutes. I brought it to show you.

CHARLEY: Good.

PETER: Melinda and I thought we'd go abroad with it. Try to show it around at some of the small film festivals, and just wander around Europe.

CHARLEY: Sounds great.

PETER: After that, well, I just want to make films and be with Melinda. I've been getting along on fifty bucks a week, and I can always pick that up anyplace. And Melinda speaks perfect Italian and French, and she can always work as a tutor. And that's all we need—if we don't get involved with things.

CHARLEY: (*Smiles*) Lots of luck.

PETER: Well, I mean, what's the point of it?

CHARLEY: Somehow things accumulate without your noticing.

PETER: (*Very serious*) We always want to keep it very—you know, very simple. You've seen how we live now. A bed, our books and records.

CHARLEY: You know, your mother dreads it when I go to visit you and Melinda. I get painfully nostalgic for all that—and I come home with a tremendous desire to simplify my life. I start throwing everything away. I know it's none of my business, but what about children?

PETER: (*Knew this would come up*) No.

CHARLEY: I sense a lot of thinking behind that "No."

PETER: (*Gestures with his hands. He is uncomfortable*) We've talked a lot about it. I guess we're being selfish, but we don't want to have children unless we're married, and we don't want to be married—that is, legally—to be tied down. (*Tries another way of putting it*) I mean, I love coming home to Melinda now. You'll see it in the film. We've promised each other that if either of us, well, stops feeling that way . . . (*In his difficulty, he gets direct and specific and slightly accusing*) I don't know . . . I just don't ever want to have to swill a pitcher of martinis before I come home to my wife. (*He looks at his father a moment, embarrassed at the accusing tone*) I don't mean you. But I've seen it.

CHARLEY: Don't exclude me. There have been times. Maybe not a pitcher, but a few.

PETER: (*Worked up, as though he were being attacked*) It's just not going to happen to us! I can't imagine, we can't imagine—I mean, my feeling for Melinda has made all the difference in my life. You saw it. I was nothing before she came along. All right, so they tell us it can't last. We don't believe that. We believe we have something quite special, and *if we watch it*. . . . But, if it doesn't last, neither of us can imagine living without that . . . (*He searches for the word "intense" but his tension expresses it*) . . . feeling for *someone*. We've promised each other . . .

(*He half-kiddingly raises his hand to take an oath*) To love, or.... (*He shrugs*)

CHARLEY: "Split"? (*Peter acknowledges the word is right*) Rocks split. Wood splits. People tear and usually rather painfully. I'm sorry to sound so wise ... to be so sententious. It comes with the role. You want absolute freedom, Peter. I'm not so sure there is such a thing or even if it's entirely desirable. You know, commitments have their surprising rewards.

PETER: We're committed to each other now. We understand that.

CHARLEY: I don't want to embarrass you, but your mother and I never had more pleasure in sex, and I mean in every way, than when we decided to stop taking precautions and tried to have a child. You. It surprised the hell out of us.

PETER: That's nice. I'm glad you told me that.

CHARLEY: And we keep getting surprised. You must know, Peter, that life is not a continuing peak experience. It's often giving up intense heat for continuous warmth. It's sex often as an act of compassion and comfort and not just adoring desire. It's on occasion to have a few martinis and come home, even though it's the last thing in the world you want to do. (*He looks at his son's small and slightly sad smile*) I don't persuade you.

PETER: Do you persuade yourself?

CHARLEY: (*A long pause. Shakes his head*) Not entirely.

PETER: Thanks. The other night Melinda and I were at a party at her parents'. One hour into the party and half the guests were pushing the other half into the pool with their clothes on—all loaded. And God knows which wife belonged to which husband. Melinda and I held each other very close when we got home and she said, "Dear God, let's never let that happen to us."

CHARLEY: (*Smiling*) Your generation presumably advocates anarchy. At the pool there, that was their small fling at anarchy, which enables them to go back to work Monday morning. You know, Peter, the best most of us can manage is to preserve some little anarchy within the shape and form of our lives.

PETER: (*After a moment*) Where's the little anarchy in your life, Dad?

CHARLEY: (*Looks at him a long time, knowing he is near the truth, then passes it off*) Haven't you noticed that occasionally I wear loud bow ties? And when things get really rough, I go to some far away beach and walk naked.

PETER: And the joy? Where's that? Pure sensual joy? (*Charley just looks at him. His son is needling him where it hurts*) Wearing bow ties and walking naked on a beach are not going to be enough for me. (*Moving on, more daring, and more loving*) May I say something else?

CHARLEY: Sure.

PETER: I think you're too reconciled in your life and in your work. I wrote a paper on you once in college, on your short stories. Do you realize that every single one of your couples gets back together again in the end? Half of them don't belong together. But you bring them crawling back as though you had invented marriage and had to justify it under all circumstances. You and Mother would have been much better off divorced years ago.

CHARLEY: Now, Peter. . . .

PETER: (*Running right over*) But you stayed together, I suppose for us children.

CHARLEY: Come on, Peter, stop it. It's simply not. . . .

PETER: (*Pressing on*) What's real in those stories, Dad, is the ache and longing and pain. Sometimes I don't know how Mother could read your stories, the pain is so real and obviously personal.

CHARLEY: (*Trying to be patient*) Peter, my sister and I also thought our parents should have been divorced. No children think their parents love each other as children understand love.

PETER: Dad, how many of your friends are faithful to the wives they presumably love? God, I can't imagine being unfaithful to Melinda. It would make me sick to even think of it.

CHARLEY: I'm glad. I'm very glad. But you mustn't be so contemptuous of the way other people manage their lives. Life is just not that simple, Peter. It is for you now, and I'm glad, and I envy you, and I wouldn't have it any other way. But you must understand we all felt much the same way when we were your age.

PETER: You couldn't have!

CHARLEY: (*Flaring a moment*) You know I get very tired of being told what I felt or didn't feel at your age! I'm sorry, but my college notebooks were full of wonderful quotations. Hemingway: "A woman should be adored or abandoned." Someone else: "Let it be high noon, and then let it be midnight." I spent a night in jail for rioting in college, protesting the firing of a liberal professor. It enrages you to think that we could have been the same. Because if we were and ended up as we have, there's more than a chance you'll end up the same way. (*Peter is cowed by his father's "sounding off." Almost has to look at the sight indirectly, not straight on*) Therefore you must desperately insist that you are different. Therefore you will end up different. Look, I hope to Christ you do. But you do not have a patent on the search for meaningfulness in life or love and the frustrations resulting therefrom. The middle-aged man is much more fed up with things than you are. And he's in a much worse spot, because he can't feed himself simple solutions, because he knows they won't work. He's got the same anguish, but no clear answers, and time is running the hell out on him. And while he's desperately trying to salvage something before it's too late, the kids sneer at him and say, "You sold out. You blew it." And then he says to them, because he's hurt, "Wait till it's your turn!" And then . . . (*He stops himself. He realizes he has given away more of his true feelings than he meant to*) I'm sorry.

PETER: (*Different meaning*) I'm sorry too, Dad.

CHARLEY: I hope you make it. I'll do whatever I can to help. But don't get the idea I'm not trying to make it too. Show me your film.

PETER: Joy, Dad. That's all. Think about it.

(*Charley looks at him a long time and nods his head. The film begins. For a few moments they watch it together. Then Peter leaves.*

The title: "I'm Home!" Then, "A Film by Peter Potter."

The film is a lyrical evocation of a young man's coming home in the evening to the girl he loves. We start with his getting off a bus, weaving and skipping his way through the crowd of other people coming home from work.

He stops and buys an evening newspaper. He jogs to his next destination, a fruit and flower stand, where he buys a loosely wrapped small bunch of flowers—very cheap. And he continues on his way, breaking into a trot as he turns into his own street: a street in the Village, spring, a few trees out, flowers on the window ledges, people sitting on the stoops.

On the run, he turns into his own quaint building, looks for mail, sees none, goes in. He bounds up the stairs, opens his door, enters his apartment, which is only one large room with just the essentials. He calls out for Melinda (silent film). "I'm home." Sees a simple table, simply set. Looks in the tiny kitchen, but she isn't there. He shucks off his coat and proceeds to the bathroom, where the water is running. He goes in.

It is a large old-fashioned bathroom. Melinda is taking a steamy bath. She drapes a wet washcloth across her breasts in pretended modesty. He presents her elaborately with the flowers. She laughs and reaches out for them (playacting). He kneels down beside the tub and kisses her. The washcloth slips into the water. He continues to kiss her while she's holding the flowers, giggling, not having any place to put them. He starts to stroke her wet breast, still kissing her and enjoying her awkward protests. His hand goes under the water, shirt-sleeve and all, and she laughs as his mouth goes to her neck. As she laughs delightedly, she lets go of her flowers and they scatter on the water. We draw back quickly and stop action on the scene: the girl in the tub, the young man kissing and fondling her, and the flowers floating on the surface.

End of film. Obviously the film has had a deep effect on Charley. He looks over at Barbara at her table. She looks at him. They hold the look for a very long moment. Then . . .)

CHARLEY: *(Indicating the view offstage)* Marvelous spot, isn't it?

BARBARA: Yes, beautiful.

CHARLEY: All that ocean. *(He gets up, moves his chair towards the open space in the center)* Reminds me of the beach at Ipswich.

BARBARA: *(A small smile)* All beaches remind you of the beach at Ipswich. *(She gets up and during following moves her chair towards center, also a small stool which has been at her table)* But this Godforsaken shack. "Fully equipped."

CHARLEY: *(Determined not to be put off by anything)* Well, it's fully equipped with the sun and the sea and the beach, this deck and a double bed. What else do we need?

BARBARA: *(Arranging her chair and stool before she sits in sun to rest)* Have you sat on that double bed? *(Barbara is on edge, but succeeds in being bantering)*

CHARLEY: Well, we'll drag the mattress out here on the deck and sleep under the stars. We've done that before. *(He makes a big gesture)*

BARBARA: When we go into the village, remind me to get some ammonia. I want to scrub this place down. And some ant powder. How much are we paying for this place? *(In a sense she is trying to de-fuse the situation with down-to-earth concerns)*

CHARLEY: *(Lounging in his chair next to hers)* I don't remember. I don't care. We didn't come down here to keep house.

BARBARA: That's fine for you to say. But I can't prepare meals in that grime.

CHARLEY: We'll get a charcoal broiler, and I'll cook out here. The simple life.

BARBARA: If we're going to sleep out here and cook out here, there's no reason for us to have paid a fortune for this shack.

CHARLEY: We're paying a fortune for the chance to be alone for the first time in God knows when. I put my watch in my suitcase. And I'm not going to look at it again for a week. If we're hungry, we'll eat. Whenever. If we're sleepy, we'll sleep. Whenever. If we want to make love, we'll make love. Whenever. (*He nuzzles her neck playfully*)

BARBARA: Well, I'm sleepy. So I'll sleep.

CHARLEY: Let's take our clothes off and go swimming skinny.

BARBARA: Oh, now, Charley. Come on. There are people.

CHARLEY: There are no people. I asked the man for a place on a deserted beach where I could make love to my wife for a week.

BARBARA: And he's probably lying up there in the long grass right now with binoculars. A few minutes ago there was a boat out there. And there are planes.

CHARLEY: (*Looks up*) What the hell can they see?

BARBARA: They can see.

CHARLEY: You overrate the size of my cock, dear girl, if you think they can see it from up there.

BARBARA: Shhhhh. They can see.

CHARLEY: You think they can hear too? (*He holds her hand for a moment, then moves it towards his crotch*)

BARBARA: (*Drawing her hand away*) Come on now, stop it. You're some kind of maniac. No sooner do we get inside that door this morning than you start pawing me and wanting to practically rape me on that filthy floor. And now you want me to sit around and admire your amazing virility.

CHARLEY: It's not amazing. I just want to show you what you do to me. You and the beach. (*She looks at him, "Tell me another." He leans close to her*) Do you remember the first time at Ipswich?

BARBARA: Come on now, Charley. I want to rest. I've had a hell of a rough time trying to get ready for the anniversary party. It was crazy coming down here just before it, but since we are here, let me get some rest—first. I'll make a date with you for later.

CHARLEY: (*Playfully*) Remember what the doctor said to

you before we were married. It's a fleeting impulse. I.O.U.'s are not much good.

BARBARA: You know, Charley, you've become a damned chatterer.

CHARLEY: Become? I've always been. Just keeping contact. Nature abhors a vacuum. Remember when we went to Europe on our honeymoon and we saw all those middle-aged couples sitting at tables and staring into space and saying nothing? And you reached over to me and said, "Promise me, Charley, you'll always keep talking. Anything. Something. Just keep talking to me."

BARBARA: (*Smiling*) Yes. I remember.

CHARLEY: But that's all right. You just rest a while, and I'll sit here doing nothing. (*After a moment, he puts his hand on her, just to keep contact*)

BARBARA: That's not doing nothing.

CHARLEY: Just keeping contact. (*He is quiet for a moment. Then*) You know we've never been together on a piano bench. George says that's very exciting.

BARBARA: I'm sure George has had more girls in more bizarre places than the piano bench.

CHARLEY: You're not above some bizarre places yourself! George said the only advice he gave his son when he got married was to save doing it from the chandeliers until they are forty. For weeks after he told me that, I looked at every chandelier and tried to figure out how you'd manage it. Have you any idea how you'd do it?

BARBARA: It doesn't interest me enough to try to figure it out—and with your arthritis I suggest you forget about it.

CHARLEY: Women, by and large, have very little curiosity about those things, don't they? Men have much more fun with their feelings of sex than women do.

BARBARA: Oh, I don't know.

CHARLEY: Like I remember at my fraternity house in college, there was a guy who always got the most incredible erection after a good meal. It became the pride of the fraternity.

We used to invite people to dinner just to show him off. (BARBARA *smiles and shakes her head*) Just from eating a big dinner. Bill . . . Bill. What the hell was his last name? I wonder if it still happens to him.

BARBARA: What are you going to do, write him and ask him?

CHARLEY: Maloney, Bill Maloney. Actually quite a small guy otherwise.

BARBARA: You sound like a bunch of kids with a toy. Look at my Yo-Yo.

CHARLEY: Did I ever tell you I had my first orgasm while I was taking a math exam at prep school. There I was trying to figure out the square root of some damned number, and bam!

BARBARA: You told me. On our first date.

CHARLEY: (*He kisses her hand, and keeps holding it*) When we first met, when I'd have to go to New York to see my folks and then come back to you in Boston, I used to start getting excited around New London and stay that way till after we'd been together in your apartment three hours later.

BARBARA: You used to say it was Stamford and four hours.

CHARLEY: Well, I'm getting older and three hours seems like a more reasonable time. You'd be there waiting and all bathed, and if it was winter, a fire going . . . wearing that wonderful red flannel robe and nothing else. Whatever happened to that robe?

BARBARA: The moths got it.

CHARLEY: Thanks.

BARBARA: Well, you asked.

CHARLEY: It was a rhetorical question. When François Villon asked, "Where are the snows of yesteryear?" he didn't want some smartass to say, "They melted." (*Close to her*) Let's make love now. Then take a nap. Then go swimming skinny and make love in the water. You taught me that. Then come back and eat . . . and . . . see what happens.

BARBARA: (*Less kidding—but saying it—but without annoyance*) Not now, Charley.

CHARLEY: Men are much more easily put off than women. Kinsey says that a woman can talk to her three best friends on the phone without breaking stride.

BARBARA: Your mind is full of the damnedest most useless sexual information.

CHARLEY: You used to love to have me chatter away about sex. Shock you, amuse you. You used to laugh so much. It used to excite you, me going on with nonsense like this.

BARBARA: It amused me.

CHARLEY: It excited you. I proved it to you once with unmistakable evidence. Just by talking to you. No hand

BARBARA: Well, thank God I don't remember.

CHARLEY: It was a motel outside of Marblehead, July 18, Sunday, 3:33 in the afternoon. And what I was saying was . . . (*He leans towards her*)

BARBARA: I don't want to hear it. I'm a middle-aged matron now. Old enough to be the mother of the girl you were talking to.

CHARLEY: (*That she should think this is infinitely sad to him*) You don't look any different to me. Someone once said, "Men are only boys grown tall." I look at so many women, and I can't see any "girl" left in them—where they were ever girls. I have no trouble seeing it in you. (*She is touched by this, but still defensive*) That's one of the great things about you.

BARBARA: Name another.

CHARLEY: Well . . . (*He pauses a moment*)

BARBARA: Time's up.

CHARLEY: (*Can she really feel so unappreciated?*) Come on. Lots of things . . . a lot of things. (*A small touch of reassurance, he almost absent-mindedly strokes her wrist, then kidding*) That used to drive you crazy.

BARBARA: It still does when I'm trying to sleep.

CHARLEY: (*Stops stroking, but leaves his hand on hers*) The new thing, I understand, is vibrators. (*She shudders at the idea*) Feathers, they say, can be exciting. (*He reaches up and casually rubs his finger over the lobe of her ear*) That was never one of your spots. I'm sensitive on the back of my knees—some

days. Some days I'm not. (*He touches the back of his knees*)
Today I am, if you'd care to try. (*She doesn't care to try*) The
kids say pot makes it something extra—I'm willing to try anything. Maybe when I'm fifty. Chandeliers at forty-five. Pot at
fifty. Vibrators at fifty-five. Group gropes at fifty-eight. Though
I can't imagine anyone wanting to grope me at fifty-eight. I
speak for myself. You will remain eternally gropable. (*He looks
at her a long time. The game is over. Finally he speaks*) Barbara?
(*There is no answer*) What's the matter? (*She just looks at him*)
What?

BARBARA: I don't know.

CHARLEY: (*Gently, wondering*) We haven't been together
in weeks.

BARBARA: I know. (*Evasive*) All the preparations for the
anniversary . . . I've been . . . tired.

CHARLEY: That's why I thought if we got away. . . .

BARBARA: I'm sorry. (*She looks at him a long moment, a
sad frown on her face*) I've been terrified of this trip, Charley.

CHARLEY: Why? (*He moves comfortingly towards her*)

BARBARA: (*Shies away a little*) I don't know. The whole
thing. It's such a set-up. (*She looks at him, hoping for help*)
Your sentimental and nostalgic presents every fifteen minutes on
the plane. Then this shack, miles away from anyplace.

CHARLEY: I'm sorry it's so. . . . (*He gestures "ratty"*)

BARBARA: There's something so desperate about it. (*She
looks at him, questioning. He won't admit it*) As though we
were taking some kind of exam, and I know I'm going to flunk
it. (*He makes another comforting gesture towards her*) We're
down here, aren't we, trying to see if there's any reason for
renewing our vows?

CHARLEY: (*Uncomfortable*) Oh, come on now, Barbara.
We're just having a vacation, at last.

BARBARA: Charley, let's be honest. We're not going to
come out of this alive, so let's be honest.

CHARLEY: (*Making a warm, reassuring move towards her.
His response is always to touch, to give physical comfort*) Barbara.
. . . (*He stops*)

BARBARA: I just feel it's so desperate and so sad. Not just this. But the way it's been for so long. I tried to say it last time we made love. I asked you if you could only make love to me when you were a little high. I was a coward. I waited till you were asleep, and then I only whispered it.

CHARLEY: I wasn't asleep.

BARBARA: You didn't answer.

CHARLEY: I. . . .

BARBARA: (*Cutting him off*) I don't want an answer. It's just that lately I get the feeling that we're not just making love. We're trying to prove something. "I do love my wife, and I'm going to prove it by making love to her. See how much and how well I'm making love to her."

CHARLEY: Barbara. . . .

BARBARA: (*Running on*) Only you have to have a couple of drinks to make a quick connection, to by-pass all we really are till our bodies take over.

CHARLEY: Barbara, that's not so.

BARBARA: (*Hardly listening or hearing. She has been wound up for a long time, and she's going—but just spilling, not vindictive, almost fearful that if she stops, she'll be horrified at what she's been saying*) We used to go through all we really are and end up making love. Now it's nostalgia and martinis. Oh, I'm saying terrible things I never thought I'd say, and I'm jumbling them all together. But we are here . . . (*Suddenly loud, blurting it out*) . . . and I must say these things! (*Charley realizes that it is not the time to question or challenge. This may be irrational, what she's saying, but it's the truth of how she feels. He moves again to hold her, she shies away*) I have the feeling that we're two systems of nerve ends, which we manipulate expertly, desperately. Your hands and mouth are everywhere, expertly playing the instrument. But where are you? Where's Charley? And where am I? You move on, desperately trying to reestablish some intimacy. But not with me, Barbara. One night, so long ago, I said while we were making love, "Oh, I love you so." You should have seen your eyes. Your body and your arms responded tenderly, but your eyes opened in shock and fright at that kind of intimacy. I can't tell you how indecent I feel sometimes in bed with you. We've glided by each other for days or weeks, never touching. I don't mean physically. And then suddenly there we are in bed, naked, servicing each other. And I sometimes feel like a whore with a stranger—a stranger who then suddenly tries to prove he's in love with me. But I can't respond, except physically, because I don't know anything about him. Oh, I'm sorry. (*She puts both her hands over her mouth, shocked that she has said all this*)

CHARLEY: Barbara, you make me sound completely insensitive.

BARBARA: Oh, no, love, you're not that. And I didn't mean that. I'm saying it all wrong. No wonder you never want to talk. What do I mean? I know you don't always have to be high, because sometimes we make love in the morning—but why do I have these feelings?

CHARLEY: (*Gently*) Each time—most times when I make love to you, I feel closer to you—more intimate, more deeply connected, after. It is a way of reestablishing intimacy, contact. It is not the only way. But it *is* a way.

BARBARA: I guess I sense you would feel this way with any woman.

CHARLEY: I might. (*She looks at him*) But the point is that it is with *you, Barbara, my wife,* I am feeling it. And so I feel closer to *you*—and to myself for a while.

BARBARA: So often I feel more lonely after. Once in a restaurant, I saw you at one of those tables in the corner with a lovely woman, perhaps one of your writers. And you were talking, talking. I couldn't hear you, but I could see. The way we used to talk. Your eyes were looking at her, into her, not just towards her. And I said something to myself, and it shocked me. I said, "I wish he'd go to bed with her and talk to me." (*Saddened by this, Charley moves again to hold her*) No, please. I want to talk.

CHARLEY: (*Harsh*) I want to hold you, for God's sake! Let me touch you. I just want to hold you! (*The tone shocks her. Is this what he has been talking about? His instinctive need for physical intimacy and communication through bodies. They sit together, huddled, his arm around her)*

BARBARA: *(After a long moment)* I hate marriage. I hate what it has done to me. I'm not me. I'm a nice person, loving, warm, generous, understanding—when I'm not married. We used to share our loneliness, our miseries. Love each other for the sharing. But now we cause each other some of the loneliness and misery. How can we tell each other that? When you were going through that thing with Maria, and I knew it, the unmarried part of me said, "He's torn and miserable. Why doesn't he come and tell me, and I'd comfort him the way I used to, and he'd love me for the talking?" The married part of me hated you and her. Who do you talk to these days, Charley? *(He smiles)* You hate marriage too, Charley.

CHARLEY: No.

BARBARA: You like the idea of marriage. But you hate what it turns out to be. I've wanted to shout at you, "For Christ's sake, be a good sport! This happens to everyone. Settle! Don't always be considering the alternatives!" I envy you your longing to be in love, intensely, adoringly. I don't seem to feel that need, and I can't respond to it. It makes me feel ridiculous. Grotesque. A couple of times I wished I were dying because I thought it might give you that intensity of feeling you want. I fantasied it for months once. And I wondered why you weren't nicer to me when you knew I was dying. *(She smiles at the ridiculousness of the concept)* You've wished me dead sometimes, haven't you, Charley?

CHARLEY: Come on.

BARBARA: I've wished you dead. It seemed the only way we could ever get out of this. Lovers are lousy husbands. That's not fair. You're a good husband in many ways. But that unhappy, disappointed lover keeps messing up the works.

CHARLEY: You seem so—I don't know, so intent on killing his passion.

BARBARA: Oh, God, I know. You've thought me a cold bitch.

CHARLEY: No. But I've wondered so often when you turn

away. I've wondered about . . . about your insensitivity. (*Quickly*) Not to my feelings or needs, but to both our feelings and needs. As though something within you had said, "No, I'm a grown woman. That's all over." One of the great things about us when we were starting out was our accessibility, our availability to each other—in every way. *I* don't always feel like making love. But I do feel the need to be closer to you, somehow, some way. We've been so distant I begin to feel I'll freeze to death without some contact. And I know that in a few moments, I *will* feel like. . . . You don't seem to want to give the moment a chance. When you reach for me, I find it tremendously exciting, immediately exciting. But when I move towards you, so often it. . . . (*He stops. He has said all this most gently, tentatively*)

BARBARA: I don't know. I guess I'm unconsciously trying to flag you down. To shout, "Hey, Charley, it's me. Barbara. Age forty-two. Not your girl." You scared me because I knew I couldn't be your girl—your bride. All brides die, Charley. I felt it was fantasy time. Charades. (*They sit quietly for a moment*) I've thought about divorce a lot, Charley. Seriously. Why the hell should two people stay together for twenty-three years? Why should two people go along like two goddamned railroad tracks side by side into eternity? I don't think we're the least bit compatible any more—practically nothing in common. Your mother suggested we take up double solitaire. I almost laughed in her face, because what else have we been playing these last years? Charley, if you're staying with me because you're afraid it will break me up if you leave—don't. You've seemed so unhappy sometimes that I've wished you would get up the courage to call it quits. Just when I've thought you might, you start making that desperate love to me. I won't fleece you, because I have money of my own, and Sylvia says she'll take me into her shop, and . . . and I can take care of myself. I may be a little lonely, but not as lonely as I've been these last goddamned years. (*She breaks down and starts to cry, sobbing. Charley holds her tighter, pained, comforting. He kisses her hair*) Don't! Go away! (*He just holds her comforting. His eyes closed at the pain—*

*hers and his. At the moment he feels infinitely tender towards
her. As she subsides, he moves closer to her, touching her face,
caressing—a mixture of compassion and passion. Draws into herself)* No. *(She frowns)* Why?

CHARLEY: *(Calmly)* Because I want to.

BARBARA: Why?

CHARLEY: I don't know.

BARBARA: What'll it prove?

CHARLEY: Nothing.

BARBARA: I want to talk.

CHARLEY: We've talked.

BARBARA: I've talked. Are you afraid that if you talked
it would be too awful? *(He smiles sadly at the idea, and continues to touch her)* Dear Charley, two years from now, if we
stay together that long—and at this moment I'm not sure I
care if we do—you'll drag me down here to try to recapture
whatever it is we've got at this moment.

CHARLEY: Maybe.

BARBARA: I'm telling you now, I won't come. *(Charley
starts to unbutton her blouse. She looks at him, smiling sadly.
She touches his head)* You won't find anything there you haven't
found a thousand times before. *(He smiles, as he continues. The
lights slowly fade on them.)*

Michael Frayn

CHINAMEN

Michael Frayn

Michael Frayn makes his initial appearance in *The Best Short Plays* annuals with his ingenious and often hilarious comedy, *Chinamen*. Part of a bill of four short plays (for two players) by Mr. Frayn, with the overall title of *The Two of Us*, the production was first presented at the Garrick Theatre, London, on July 30, 1970. Its leading (and only) performers were Lynn Redgrave and Richard Briers who in *Chinamen* "brilliantly impersonated between them host and hostess, two shrill children and a quantity of guests all embroiled in a disastrous dinner party." The play, published here in an anthology for the first time, was described by *Plays and Players* magazine as "a devilish farce that has wit, brisk pace and close observation . . ."

The author was born in London in 1933 and educated at Kingston Grammar School and Emmanuel College, Cambridge. He became a reporter for *The Manchester Guardian* and eventually came to write the *Guardian*'s "Miscellany". column. In 1962, he moved over to *The Observer*, London, where he wrote a random column that became instantly popular and attracted a large readership.

His first novel, *The Tin Men*, was published in 1965 and won for Mr. Frayn the coveted W. Somerset Maugham Award. Among his other published novels are: *The Russian Interpreter* (awarded the Hawthornden Prize in 1967); *Against Entropy; Day of the Dog;* and *A Very Private Life*.

In addition to *Chinamen*, the other plays that constitute *The Two of Us* are: *Black and Silver; The New Quixote;* and *Mr. Foot.*

Characters:

STEPHEN
BARNEY } The actor

JO
BEE } The actress
ALEX

Scene:

The dining room of Stephen and Jo's house, with the table laid for six. There are three doors leading off: one into the kitchen, one into the living room, and the third into a corridor which gives access to lavatory, stairs, back door, etc. There is also a window overlooking the street. It is dark outside.

Jo enters hurriedly through the corridor door, still struggling into her dress. She begins to check the dinner table, balancing on one evening shoe and counting the cutlery with the other.

JO: (At speed) Knife knife fork fork spoon, knife knife fork fork spoon, knife knife fork fork spoon . . . soup spoons! Oh, my God! (She hobbles hurriedly out to the kitchen, holding her unzipped dress up)

GIRL CHILD: (Off) Mummy, can we come down and just say hello to all the people?

(Jo at once comes out of the kitchen, shouting in the direction of the corridor door)

JO: No! Go to sleep, both of you!

(She shuts the corridor door firmly and hurries back into the kitchen. As she does so, Stephen hurries in from the living room, carrying another dining chair to add to the four around the table)

STEPHEN: It's ten past eight, Jo!

JO: Don't tell *me* it's ten past eight! (*He puts the chair down and heads back at once towards the living room*)

STEPHEN: John and whatsit always arrive at eight-fifteen sharp for eight o'clock. Oh God, I've forgotten her name again! (*He goes out into the living room. Jo re-emerges from the kitchen, carrying soup spoons*)

JO: *Laura!* It's getting the children to bed that does it— we'll *have* to get another *au pair*, Stephen. Oh, not that one— that's the one with the dicky leg.

(*She picks up the chair which Stephen has just brought in, and hurries it out to the kitchen, still holding spoons, shoe, and dress. As she does so, Stephen hurries back in from the living room carrying another chair*)

STEPHEN: Laura, Laura, Laura . . . my block about names gets worse and worse every day!

JO: Get another chair out of the living room, Stephen. I'm putting the dicky one in the kitchen so no one can sit on it by mistake. (*She goes out*)

STEPHEN: (*Putting down the chair he is carrying, and heading back for another*) David and *Laura!* David and *Laura!* David and *Laura!* (*He goes out into the living room as Jo returns from the kitchen*)

JO: *John* and Laura! *John* and Laura! For heaven's sake get it straight, Stephen. We've known them for ten years! (*She starts hurriedly distributing soup spoons, as Stephen hurries back in with another chair*)

STEPHEN: I can't really tell our friends apart, that's the trouble. John and Laura, John and Laura, John and Laura. They're all exactly the same—same age, same number of children, same sort of job, same income, same opinions. . . .

JO: (*Surveying table*) Zip me up, will you?

STEPHEN: (*Zipping her*) They even look alike! It's like looking at Chinamen. Nicholas and Jay—Simon and Kay— Freddie and Di. . . .

JO: No doubt they think the same about us. Have you put the ice out for the drinks?

STEPHEN: Yes. Good God, *we*'re not like that! Are we?

JO: Now, John can sit at the head of the table. . . .

STEPHEN: John and Laura, John and Laura, John and Laura.

JO: Then Laura can sit *here*.

STEPHEN: (*Indicating*) Bee next to John. John and Laura, John and Laura. Barney over there. At least I won't forget *their* names! Barney and Bee, my God!

JO: (*Gazing at him, appalled*) Not Barney and Bee, Stephen!

STEPHEN: What do you mean, not Barney and Bee? Of course it's Barney and Bee!

JO: Stephen!

STEPHEN: Barney and Bee! Barney and Bee! I might forget David and Dora, but *Barney and Bee*. . . .

JO: Stephen, she's left him! Bee's left Barney!

STEPHEN: No!

JO: I *told* you!

STEPHEN: I don't remember that.

JO: She couldn't stand it any longer! She just quietly left, without any fuss, about a week ago, and went off with a man called Alex!

STEPHEN: (*Rubbing his chin and struggling to focus his mind*) Oh . . . some faint memory does stir. A singer, or something, wasn't he?

JO: He runs one of those psychedelic discotheque places.

STEPHEN: So it's not Barney and Bee any more?

JO: No, darling. Alex and Bee.

STEPHEN: Alex and Bee. It doesn't sound very convincing somehow, does it?

JO: Well, that's what it is. You won't forget again, will you, Stephen?

STEPHEN: Alex and Bee. Alex and Bee. Thank God you told me! So Barney'll be coming on his own tonight?

JO: No, no, no—it's not Barney who's coming! It's Bee, and she's bringing Alex, so that we can meet him. Oh God—no napkins!

(*She runs out to the kitchen to fetch them. He stands gazing after her, the ramifications of the situation slowly dawning on him*)

STEPHEN: (*Appalled*) Alex and Bee are coming here tonight?

JO: (*Running back in with the napkins*) Yes, *Alex* and *Bee*. Do get it straight, darling. (*She rapidly distributes the napkins as Stephen gazes at her*) Well, at least Alex will make a change from all the Chinamen. According to Sara Dolomore he's about nineteen, with hair down to his shoulders, and strings of beads and dingle-dangles all over him. What are you looking like that for, Stephen?

STEPHEN: Jo, I've done a terrible thing!

JO: What do you mean?

STEPHEN: Well, I ran into Barney at lunchtime today. I'd entirely forgotten about Bee leaving him . . . .

JO: (*Despairingly*) So you asked after her? You said, "And how is your very lovely wife?"

STEPHEN: No. I said, "See you this evening, then."

JO: Stephen, you didn't!

STEPHEN: And he said, "This evening? What do you mean?" And I said, "You're coming to dinner this evening!"

JO: And he said, "No, I'm not. You must have mixed me up with Simon, or Mark, or Nicholas." I bet you felt a fool!

STEPHEN: No, he said, "Thanks, Stephen. You don't know how much that means to me just at the moment." I thought at the time it was a slightly odd thing to say.

JO: Oh, my God!

STEPHEN: Anyway, so I said, "Eight o'clock, then!" And he said, "Eight o'clock!" (*They both look at their watches, and then stare at each other*)

JO: (*Wildly*) Well, ring him up! Stop him!

STEPHEN: It's no good ringing him at quarter past eight! He'll be on his way—he's probably on the doorstep now!

JO: What a bloody stupid thing to do!

STEPHEN: Bloody stupid thing inviting your lot, if it

comes to that! Fancy inviting Bee without Barney and not telling me!

JO: I did tell you! You just weren't listening, you stupid oaf!

STEPHEN: Well, fancy not making sure I was listening! Anyway, I *was* listening. I wasn't remembering, that's all.

JO: You weren't remembering!

STEPHEN: Oh, for heaven's sake don't waste time arguing!

JO: I'm not the one who's wasting time!

STEPHEN: (*Shouting*) All right, then! So let's decide what we're going to do before .... (*The front door bell rings. They gaze at each other*)

JO: Don't let them in!

STEPHEN: We've got to let them in! Anyway, that'll be David and whatsit, David and Nora.

JO: John and Laura. (*As she speaks she goes to the window and tries to see them through the crack in the curtains*) But we mustn't let *anyone* in till we've thought out what we're going to do.

STEPHEN: Oh, for heaven's sake! They'll all be meeting on the doorstep!

JO: Well, at least if they meet on the doorstep we shan't have to watch.

STEPHEN: Perhaps the first thing is to decide exactly what we're trying to do. Why are we so frightened of them meeting? Are we trying to spare their feelings, or is it just our own embarrassment that we're worried about?

JO: I've a good mind to walk out the back door and leave you to get on with it.

STEPHEN: My God! If anyone should be walking out it's me! I mean, let's reason this out one step at a time. (*The bell rings again. They stare at each other, undecided. Then Stephen gives in*) Oh!

(*He hurries out through the living room. Jo rushes to the window for another look through the crack in the curtains, then runs to the mirror and has a last quick look at herself. Then she goes to the living room door and opens it a crack, listening to hear who it is*)

STEPHEN: (*Jovially, off*) No, no, no, not late at all. Just right. Come in and sit yourselves down. (*She shuts the door, hurries to the table, and distractedly dabs at the cutlery. Stephen reappears from the living room, still speaking to John and Laura as he turns to shut the door*) Excuse me a moment. One or two little ... you know ... (*He nods jovially to complete the sense, then shuts the door and turns tensely to face Jo*) David and Dora.

JO: John and Laura.

STEPHEN: What are we going to do? (*He opens the door again and calls jovially off to John and Laura*) Fix yourselves drinks, will you, um?

JO: John.

STEPHEN: John. (*He shuts the door and turns back to Jo*) We must have a clear and definite plan of campaign. (*He opens the door and continues jovially to John and Laura*) Over there! On the side! Right ... (*He shuts the door and turns back to Jo*) We can't just stand here and wait for it to happen.

JO: No, well, look ... (*She beckons him urgently over to the window to show him what she has in mind*) You go down and wait outside the front door, and when Barney arrives, get rid of him.

STEPHEN: Get rid of him? How?

JO: I don't know. Make something up. Tell him the children are infectious. Tell him the pipes have burst. Tell him the truth, why not? We've known him for long enough. He'll see the funny side of it.

STEPHEN: "Barney, a rather amusing mistake has occurred! We didn't really mean to invite *you* at all—it was your wife and her new boy friend we meant!"

JO: (*Bundling him towards the living room door*) Tell him something else, then.

STEPHEN: He's going to be terribly hurt whatever I tell him. He was setting so much store by this.

JO: If the worst comes to the worst, take him out to a restaurant, and I'll tell the others you've been called away on business.

(*Still extremely reluctant, he allows himself to be bundled through the living room door. As it opens they both compose their faces for their guests*)

STEPHEN: (*Jovially, to John and Laura*) Got drinks, then? Good, good, good. Sit down and relax—I'm just passing through. (*He disappears*)

JO: Hello! Hello! No, don't get up! I'm just putting my head 'round the door! I've got one or two . . . you know . . . (*She gestures vaguely behind her*) In the kitchen . . . and the children . . . terrible muddle . . . completely disorganized, I'm afraid! Anyway, I'm glad you managed to get here all right. (*She smiles reassuringly, and shuts the door. Then she runs to the window, draws the curtains back, and looks out. She opens the window, calls to Stephen in a stage whisper, enunciating carefully*) Stephen! If Alex and Bee arrive first, I'll let them in. You hide behind the dustbins, and wait for Barney. (*She draws the curtains again and goes back to the living room to address a few more words to her guests*) All right still? Good. You will keep helping yourselves to drinks, won't you? Oh, that reminds me . . . (*She shuts the living room door and hurries back to the window. She draws the curtains back and calls to Stephen*) Have you got any money on you, if you have to take Barney out? *Money!* Hold on, then . . . (*She hurries back to the living room and opens the door*) How are you both these days? I don't think I ever asked you. (*She makes a brief foray into the living room as she says this, and continues without pause as she emerges holding her handbag*) Do pour yourselves another drink. I've got to pay the milkman. (*She shuts the door and returns to the window, where she throws the money out to Stephen*) Here you are. Five pounds, all I've got. (*The corridor door opens, and Barney looks in. Jo is still leaning out of the window*) But don't take him if you can possibly get shot of him by any other. . . .

BARNEY: (*Tapping with belated discretion on the door*)

Anyone at home? (*Jo spins guiltily around, drawing the curtains behind her*)

JO: Barney!

BARNEY: I came the back way, I hope you don't mind. There's some rather thuggish-looking customer lurking about on your front doorstep. Drug-addict, probably, looking for money. (*He kisses her*)

JO: (*Confused*) Barney, I was just going to. . . . We were just thinking. . . .

BARNEY: I hope I'm not too late. (*He hands her his briefcase and umbrella*) Been sitting in the pub ever since six o'clock. Couldn't face going home to an empty house. Just waiting for the moment to come round here. Then when the time came, I thought I'd just have another drink first. You know how it is, when you're just killing time.

JO: Barney, there's something I've got to tell you right away, before you come in.

BARNEY: Thanks, Jo—but let's not even talk about it. I know how you feel.

JO: I'm terribly sorry about Bee leaving you, Barney. I really am. Look, I don't quite know how to put this, but. . . .

BARNEY: I know—you just don't know what to say to someone when something like this happens, do you? I don't know what to say about it myself. Ten years, and then—woof! It's quite a shock.

JO: Yes. But the thing is, Barney. . . .

BARNEY: She's gone off with a pouf. Or so I gather. Did you know that? I'm told he wears earrings—got hair halfway down his back. I mean how does that make me look? It makes me a complete laughingstock, doesn't it?

JO: Yes, but listen, Barney. . . .

BARNEY: I haven't so far had the pleasure of making his acquaintance. I'm about the only person in town who hasn't, I may say. Do you know what she's done? She's wheeled him 'round to meet all our old friends, to get them all on her side! Wherever I go I find people have just had them to dinner! Then when I turn up, they're embarrassed. They don't want to know me. People who have been friends for years!

JO: Barney....

BARNEY: I mean, I take it you haven't just....

JO: No, no, no. But....

BARNEY: It's always the same when a couple splits up. No one wants to take sides, but everyone does.

JO: Yes, but....

BARNEY: I was just going to say, that's why I'm so very touched to be invited here tonight. Sorry, you were going to say something. (*She looks at him as if she is, then changes her mind*)

JO: No, no. Just that . . . it's very nice to see you.

BARNEY: (*Putting his arm round her, and leading her towards the living room*) Bless you, Jo. You really find out who your friends are when something like this happens. Where's Stephen? In here?

JO: (*Stopping short*) Oh, my God, I'd forgotten all about him! He's just . . . fixing something outside. I'd better give him a call. (*She leads Barney firmly towards the kitchen*) Now why don't you sit down quietly in the kitchen for a moment? Then we can have a little chat about things together while I'm getting the dinner.

BARNEY: (*Turning at the kitchen door*) Jo, you're a real brick. You and Stephen—don't you ever....

JO: No, no.

BARNEY: I mean, old Stephen's like me. He may not seem very exciting and so on, but....

JO: Don't worry, Barney.

BARNEY: You're still . . . ? (*He links his little fingers together and pulls, in a gesture indicating solid attachment*)

JO: Yes.

BARNEY: (*Patting her on the shoulder*) Good girl.
(*She at last manages to get the door shut on him and at once hurries across to the window. Just as she is drawing the curtains back, Barney puts his head out from the kitchen again*)

BARNEY: (*Wagging his finger*) I'm serious about that, Jo.

JO: (*Whirling round to face Barney*) Yes. Stay there, Barney. I'll bring you a drink.

(*He goes back into the kitchen, leaving the door open. Jo opens the curtains with great precaution, and, glancing anxiously over her shoulder at the open kitchen door, mouths silently to Stephen*)

JO: Barney's here! Come back! (*She pantomimes desperately, pointing at the kitchen and indicating that he should return. At last, evidently satisfied that he has understood, she closes the curtains and goes to the kitchen*) What would you like— whisky? (*She hurries to the living room, addressing John and Laura as she dives briefly in and emerges again holding up a bottle of whisky*) How's Midge enjoying school? Need a drop of whisky for the soup—there's another bottle on the side. Do keep helping yourselves. (*She shuts the living room door and hurries to the kitchen, where she hands the bottle through the open door to an arm which emerges to take it*) Fix it yourself, will you, Barney? There's ice in the fridge. (*Having taken the bottle, the arm takes her hand, drawing it off, evidently to Barney's lips. There is the sound of a kiss*) Oh, Barney! (*She flutters her eyelashes, in hurried appreciation*) Anyway, make yourself at home. I've just got to . . . you know . . . this and that. . . .

(*She shuts the kitchen door. As she does so, the living room door opens and Stephen enters, talking jovially to John and Laura*)

STEPHEN: That's right! Ships that pass in the night! Anyway, pour yourselves another drink. (*He closes the door and turns to face Jo*) What is it?

JO: He's here! Barney! He came in round the back.

STEPHEN: Oh, my God!

JO: I've put him in the kitchen.

STEPHEN: In the kitchen?

JO: In case Alex and Bee arrived before I could warn you.

STEPHEN: (*Irritated*) You should have got rid of him.

(*He goes to the kitchen, turning instantly jovial as he opens the door*)

STEPHEN: Hello! Barney! Nice to see you!

BARNEY: (*Off*) Stephen!

STEPHEN: (*Emerging again, still holding Barney's hand*) Don't get up! Stay where you are! Got something to keep you occupied, have you? Anyway, pour yourself a drink. Oh, you have. That's the spirit! (*He smilingly disengages himself, shuts the door, and turns furiously upon Jo*) Why didn't you get rid of him?

JO: Oh, Stephen, I couldn't! He kept thanking me for inviting him. He thinks we're the only friends he's got left. He made me feel such a heel for inviting Alex and Bee.

STEPHEN: Oh, for God's sake! We can't start being sentimental at this stage!

JO: (*With asperity*) Well, *you* get rid of him!

STEPHEN: I can't get rid of him *now!* Now you've set him up in the kitchen with a bottle of Scotch!

JO: Well, we'll just have to get rid of Alex and Bee instead.

STEPHEN: How?

JO: I suppose you'll have to go down and wait outside the front door again. (*Stephen compresses his lips with reluctance*)

STEPHEN: Supposing they come round the back, like Barney?

JO: (*Pushing him towards the living room door*) Keep an eye on the back as well! Patrol back and forth! Good heavens, you were in the army—you know how to guard things. (*But just as he is about to open the living room door, he rebels*)

STEPHEN: Look, I can't just walk straight past David and Nora *again!*

JO: John and Laura. Well, go out the back way, then! (*Jo urges Stephen towards the corridor door*) Just get out there fast, that's all that matters, because any moment now they're going to be ringing that. . . .

(*The front door bell rings. Stephen and Jo, already hold-*

ing the corridor door open, freeze. They gaze at each other in silence for a moment)

STEPHEN: *Now* what are we going to do?

JO: Well, we'll just have to . . . I don't know . . . shout at them out of the window.

STEPHEN: Shout at them out of the window?

JO: Explain what the situation is. Tell them to go away.

STEPHEN: Go on, then.

(Jo crosses to the window, and looks out through the crack in the curtain, irresolute. She makes as if to shout, but gives up)

JO: Or we could just pretend not to be here. How about that? (*The bell rings again. As they stand undecided, the kitchen door begins to open. They notice it at once*) Barney!

STEPHEN: (*Hurrying to bundle Barney back into the kitchen*) Sit down, Barney! Have another drink! (*He goes into the kitchen, while Jo hovers anxiously at the door*)

BARNEY: (*Off*) I just thought you might like me to answer the bell, Stephen.

JO: No, no, no, no!

STEPHEN: (*Re-emerging*) No, no, no, no!

JO: Just sit down and relax!

STEPHEN: We'll be out there to chat in a minute. (*They close the kitchen door, and look at each other. The front door bell rings again*)

JO: You'll *have* to answer it. Just open the door and send them away. (*She urges him toward the living room*) Just open the door and explain everything quietly to them in the hall. They're reasonable people. They'll understand. Well, Bee's a reasonable person. She'll understand.

STEPHEN: (*Hesitating, his hand on the door handle*) Bee? She's one of the least reasonable people I've ever come across.

JO: Well, whatever you tell them, do it quickly, before they've got their coats off.

(With the utmost reluctance Stephen opens the door, switching on his jovial manner as he does so)

STEPHEN: Here I am again, then! (*His face falls*) Bee! (*He turns to exchange one brief horror-stricken glance with Jo*) They're in! (*He at once turns back towards his guests, reassembling his face even as his head turns*) Bee, how lovely to see you! And this must be Alex! (*Stephen advances into the living room. Jo closes the door behind him, in a state of shock*)

JO: Oh, my *Gawd!*

(*At once the living room door reopens, and Stephen emerges, smiling jovially back at Alex and Bee*)

STEPHEN: Well, sit down! Make yourselves at home! (*He shuts the door, and turns haggardly to Jo*) Dick and Dora let them in!

JO: John and Laura.

STEPHEN: They've got their coats off! They're sitting down making themselves at home already! (*He opens the door and calls jovially into the room*) Pour them drinks, will you, um?

JO: John.

STEPHEN: John. (*He shuts the door*) You were quite right about that Alex man. I've never seen anything like it! I can't imagine what Bee was thinking of. Well, what are we going to do? We can't go and chuck them out now they're sitting down with drinks in their hands, talking to Thingummy and Whatsit, can we?

JO: No. Well, I suppose they'll all three of them just have to be very adult and mature about it and face facts.

STEPHEN: You mean, face each other?

JO: Well, there's nothing else for it, is there?

STEPHEN: This Alex lad doesn't look very adult or mature to me. I don't think his voice has broken yet.

JO: Well, Barney and Bee will just have to be adult and mature about it.

STEPHEN: Bee's got her funny tense look on. At the slightest provocation she's going to burst into tears or start playing Truth or Dare.

JO: We'll have to tell them Barney's here, Stephen. There's no other way out of it.

STEPHEN: Well, I refuse. Point blank.

JO: I'll do it, then.

STEPHEN: All right.

(*Jo goes to the door and stands for a moment, thinking what she is going to say, trying out various social faces. Then she turns briefly back to Stephen, who is watching her anxiously*)

JO: You go and prepare Barney. (*Then she turns back to the door, puts on her social face, and at once throws the door open*) Bee! How lovely to see you! *Super* dress!

(*She advances into the room, closing the door behind her. Stephen grimaces after her, then reluctantly addresses himself to the job in the kitchen. He hesitates outside the kitchen door, thinking how he's going to broach the subject, then flings it open with determination and a jovial smile*)

STEPHEN: How are you doing out here? Plenty to drink? Good . . . er. . . . (*He holds a sustained middle "er," as if trying to remember what he is going to do next. Then, as if he has remembered and discovered that it lies elsewhere, he concludes the "er" with a brisk "ah," and shuts the door. He has another think, drumming his fingertips on his front teeth, then resolutely flings open the door again. He repeats the sustained "er," exactly as before, then notices Barney's briefcase and umbrella. He hands them into the kitchen, as if this had been his intention all the time*) Your stuff! (*He shuts the door. As he does so, the living room door opens, and Jo comes out, laughing, and still talking to the occupants of the room*)

JO: Of course not! I've been wanting to meet Alex for— oh, a week now! Pour yourselves another drink. (*She closes the door and turns to face Stephen*)

STEPHEN: Well, what did they say?

JO: (*Gloomily*) I didn't tell them. What did Barney say?

STEPHEN: I didn't tell him.

JO: It would have been one thing if Barney had just happened to be in the room when they'd come in. But you can't just say brightly in the middle of the conversation, "Oh, by the way, we've got your husband out in the kitchen!"

STEPHEN: That was where it all went wrong, putting Barney in the kitchen.

JO: It just doesn't seem natural. It's either got to happen naturally or not at all.

STEPHEN: It was your fault, putting him in the kitchen. I can't think what you were up to.

JO: It seemed perfectly logical at the time.

STEPHEN: Anyway....

JO: Anyway, we'll just have to find another way of doing it. We'll have to feed them separately, that's what it comes down to. We'll serve all this lot dinner in the living room, and we'll give Barney his dinner in the kitchen. I think that's the answer, isn't it? (*She hurries to the dinner table, and sets to work to off-load one complete place setting on to a tray*)

STEPHEN: But just a moment. Where will *we* have dinner —you and I? With Barney or with the other lot?

JO: Well . . . we'll rush back and forth between the two.

STEPHEN: They'll think that's a bit odd, won't they?

JO: I don't see why. The host and hostess are always rushing in and out at dinner parties. I'll run backwards and forwards with the food. You run backwards and forwards with the wine. (*Jo hands Stephen the loaded tray*) There, that's for Barney. We'll be one short in there, but I don't suppose I'll have time to sit down, anyway. Now, just give me a hand with this table. (*He puts the tray aside, and helps her carry the table to the living room door*) Oh, come on! Don't look so doom-laden about it! We've had awkward situations at dinner parties before, haven't we? If you give a dinner party you expect something like this to happen! We'll cope. It's always been all right before!

STEPHEN: I sometimes wonder if life is worth living. (*He opens the door and backs into the living room, addressing the occupants jovially*) Here we are, then! Meals on wheels! (*He disappears from view. The table is edged slowly through the door*)

JO: I thought it would make a change to eat out here for once! It gets such a bore, always using the dining room for dining, and the living room for living. (*Further progress is halted by some obstacle off, so that Jo remains on stage holding her end of the table, edging it up and down and back and forth as she speaks*) Mind the lamp, darling! John, would you move that china albatross thing before Stephen . . . (*There is a crash of breaking china*) Never mind! I always hated it! Just kick the bits under the sofa. Darling, we can't stand here all night! Well, lift your end *over* John's head. (*The offstage end of the table goes up, so that everything on it begins to slide towards Jo. She desperately raises her end*) Down! Your end down! (*The offstage end goes down, so that everything slides the other way. She lowers her end*) Sorry, John! Was that your head under there?

BARNEY: (*Emerging from the kitchen, holding his glass of whisky*) Jo, is there anything I can do?

(*Jo desperately shoves the table out and slams the door on it*)

JO: No, thanks, Barney! Just getting the place straight. You go back and make yourself comfortable in the kitchen. (*She tries to urge him along, but he stands his ground. He is now quite noticeably drunk*)

BARNEY: It's awfully lonely in the kitchen, Jo. I've got no one to talk to out there.

JO: I'll be out there in a moment. Have another drink.

BARNEY: I've had another drink. I've had several drinks. Ah, Jo! (*He looks round the room sentimentally*) This room brings back memories! All the times Bee and I have been here, all the happy times we had together . . . This used to be the dining room. You used to have a dining table in here . . . (*He crosses to where the dining chairs still stand, marking the spot from which the table went. He sits down on one of the chairs, as if he were at the table, while Jo shoots anxious glances in the direction of the living room*) You and Stephen, Bee and me, Simon and Kay, Nicholas and Jay, the glasses gleaming in the candlelight. . . . We used to talk about our children, do you remember? The little tricks they'd been up to—the funny things they'd said. And where we'd been on holiday, and what John and Laura were doing these days. Now it's all over. Even the table's gone. (*Jo hands him the tray with the single place setting on it*)

JO: There's a perfectly good table in the kitchen, Barney. Now you take this along with you, and I'll be out there to give you some soup in half a tick.

BARNEY: (*Taking the tray, and looking at it suspiciously*) I'm not going to be eating all on my own, am I?

JO: No, no, no. That's just to be starting with. I'll bring the rest of the stuff in a minute.

BARNEY: (*Holding the tray with one hand and putting the other arm round Jo*) Don't you leave me, Jo. You're the only friend I've got left in the whole wide world. Well, there's Stephen. Where is Stephen? Why's he never around when anyone wants him? Every time I come in, he goes out! I don't think Stephen likes me.

JO: Of course he likes you, Barney. Now, come on, this way. . . .

BARNEY: I probably shouldn't say this, Jo, but you're wasted on Stephen. Do you know that? I've always thought so. Time after time I've sat at that table . . . (*He attempts to return to the site of the table, but she restrains him*) . . . and thought, my God, fancy a marvelous girl like Jo being married to a man like Stephen!

JO: Now, come on, Barney. . . .

BARNEY: I mean, old Stephen . . . well, he's a bit of a stick, isn't he? Not really your type, I should have thought. Not *my* type, I can tell you that.

JO: I thought you thought he was just like you?

BARNEY: Do you really think so? If I'd been around at

the right time you wouldn't have thought that! Old Stephen wouldn't have stood a chance. I've always been secretly in love with you, Jo. It's not just something I'm saying because Bee's left me. Left me for a bloody pouf, did you know that?

JO: Yes. In here, Barney.

BARNEY: (*Suspiciously*) How do you know that?

JO: You told me.

BARNEY: Just walked out without a word. Last Wednesday evening. Hair down to here, by all accounts. Well, I ask you, what sort of position does that leave *me* in? (*She at last manages to push him into the kitchen*)

JO: Now you just sit down and relax, and . . . well . . . pour yourself another drink.

(*She shuts the door firmly, hurries across to the dining chairs, and takes the first two to the living room door. She is just about to open the door when the kitchen door bursts open again, and Barney comes out*)

BARNEY: (*Shouting furiously*) But if I ever get my hands on the little fairy I'll shake him till his wings drop off!

JO: (*Hurrying across to put him away again*) Sh! You'll wake the children!

BARNEY: (*Contritely*) Oh, the children . . . yes. Sorry, Jo. Sorry. (*She pushes him back towards the kitchen*) Let me give you a kiss to show I'm forgiven.

(*Barney kisses Jo clumsily as she bundles him away. She shuts the door, then returns to the chairs. She brings the remaining four down to the living room door. The kitchen door opens again. Jo turns upon it, raises her finger sternly and says "uh!", as if to make a dog sit down. The door closes again. She opens the living room door and begins to move the chairs inside*)

JO: (*Merrily*) Chairs! I knew I'd forgotten something! You're all very quiet in here! Stephen, are you making sure everyone's got plenty to drink? (*As she hands in the last chair, Stephen emerges, calling back jovially over his shoulder*)

STEPHEN: David, pour everyone another drink, will you?

And do sit down! Bee, you be mother and arrange everyone. (*He closes the door, and turns anxiously to Jo*) What's going on? Where have you been? They're all just getting silently plastered in there, waiting for something to happen.

JO: I've been dealing with Barney. He's just getting noisily plastered in *there*. Thinks he ought to have married me.

STEPHEN: David and Laura shut up like clams at the sight of Alex. Alex hasn't said anything yet, and Bee just keeps looking at him anxiously, as if he might disappear in front of her eyes. For God's sake let's start to eat, before something happens.

JO: I'll get the soup, you get the wine.

(*She goes out to the kitchen, he to the living room*)

STEPHEN: (*Jovially, as he enters*) All right?

JO: (*Likewise*) All right?

STEPHEN: That's right.

JO: All right.

(*They both reappear immediately, he with a bottle of wine which was previously on the table, she with a tureen of soup*)

STEPHEN: (*To the occupants of the living room, as he leaves*) Just got to put some wine in the soup.

JO: (*To Barney, as she leaves the kitchen*) Just got to put some soup in the *au pair*.

(*They cross at speed*)

STEPHEN: (*Furiously*) But why does it always happen to us?

JO: Stephen, it's going to be *all right!*

(*Stephen goes into the kitchen, she into the living room*)

STEPHEN: (*To Barney, as he enters*) Wine that maketh glad the heart of man!

JO: (*To the occupants of the living room, as she enters*) Soup! Soup! Beautiful soup!

(*They reappear almost at once, Stephen still holding the bottle of wine, Jo now holding a single bowl of soup.*)

STEPHEN: (*To Barney, as he leaves the kitchen*) Don't worry—I'll be back. Just got to give the *au pair* a drop.

JO: (*To the occupants of the living room, as she leaves*)
Yes, I'll be sitting down in a moment. Just got to drop this in on
the *au pair*.

(*They cross at speed again*)

STEPHEN: By God, you're right! He's as pissed as a newt!

JO: Some of them are pretty glassy-eyed in there.

(*Jo goes into the kitchen, Stephen into the living room*)

STEPHEN: (*To the occupants of the living room, as he
enters*) Wine that maketh glad the heart of man!

JO: (*To Barney, as she enters the kitchen*) Soup of the
evening! Beautiful soup!

(*They reappear at once, Jo empty-handed, Stephen carrying the breadbasket*)

STEPHEN: (*To the occupants of the living room, as he
leaves*) No peace for the wicked!

JO: (*To Barney, as she leaves the kitchen*) A woman's
work is never done!

(*They cross at speed*)

STEPHEN: (*Desperately*) They're not saying anything!

JO: Say something yourself, then! Make conversation!

(*Jo goes into the living room, Stephen into the kitchen*)

STEPHEN: (*To Barney, as he enters*) You know where
Simon and Kay say Nicholas and Jay are going this year?

JO: (*To the occupants of the living room, as she enters*)
Have you heard that story of Nicholas and Jay's about Marcus
and Poo?

(*They re-emerge almost at once, Stephen still carrying the
bottle of wine, Jo empty-handed*)

STEPHEN: (*To Barney, as he leaves*) . . . and was last seen
walking stark naked down Kensington High Street carrying a
garden sprinkler and a double bass!

JO: (*To the occupants of the living room, as she leaves*)
. . . to which she replied, "But, Mummy, if you put some toys in
your tummy too then he won't *need* to come out"!

(*They close their respective doors and lean wearily against
them as they catch each other's eyes*)

STEPHEN: Not a flicker.

JO: Heavens, we've got a slow house in here tonight!

STEPHEN: It's playing these audiences of one out in the sticks that depresses me. How many more courses?

JO: Only three. (*She indicates the living room*) You go and sit down in there and talk to them while they have their soup. I'll just get the next course out of the oven, and then I'll join you. (*Stephen crosses wearily to the living room. She kisses him in passing*) Pour yourself a drink. Just relax and enjoy yourself! (*He gives her a hopeless look. She opens the door for him, and without breaking step he is transformed into the jovial host again*)

STEPHEN: (*To the occupants of the living room*) Did I ever tell you that story of Nicholas and Kay's about Simon and Sue?

(*Jo shuts the door behind him and crosses to the kitchen*)

JO: (*To Barney, as she enters*) Shall I tell you where Simon and Kay say Nicholas and Jay are going this year? (*She backs out again hurriedly*) No, Barney! Now just sit down like a good boy and eat up your soup. I haven't come out here for fun and games. I've just come to fetch the casserole. (*She goes in again, and emerges hurriedly once more, now holding a hot and heavy casserole dish away from her, looking as if she is trying to avoid having her bottom pinched. She turns to face him and addresses him as if he were one of her children*) No, Barney! No, it's no good looking at me like that, either. I'm not amused. (*She sets down the casserole so that she can close the door*) Now just you stay here and eat up all your soup and don't come out until I tell you. (*She shuts the door, picks up her casserole, and takes it across to the living room. She is just opening the door when she realizes that the kitchen door has opened again. She closes the living room door with weary patience*) Now, Barney, what is it? I thought I told you to stay there and finish your dinner.

BARNEY: (*Emerging, and raising his hand*) Please, miss, can I be excused?

JO: (*Sighing impatiently*) Well, I suppose if you must, you must. (*She nods at the corridor door*) Through there, turn left, second door on the right.

BARNEY: Thank you, miss. (*He turns towards the corridor door*)

JO: But straight back to the kitchen when you've finished!

(*She takes the casserole into the living room, trying simultaneously to smile at the occupants and to make sternly sure that Barney is not looking in. As soon as the door shuts Barney stops, in fuddled indignation*)

BARNEY: Turn left, second on the right! I've been here once or twice before, you know! I'm an old friend of yours—remember? It's the same story everywhere. They all say how sorry they are, and then they don't want to know you. But this is a new one, I must say, inviting you 'round and then leaving you to eat on your own in the kitchen, without even the *au pair* girl for company! It's not catching, you know! My God, when I think of all the dinner parties Bee and I gave for *them!* All the ghastly evenings I've spent *here,* sitting at the table in this very room! (*He goes toward where it was, shaking his head*) Now even the table has gone. (*He stops in his tracks, his lachrymose mood dispelled by astonishment*) Now even the *chairs* have gone! (*He gazes round in bewilderment*) What's happening here? They must have. . . . They must have taken them out for spring cleaning. Or perhaps they took them out and *sold* them! Well, poor bloody old Stephen and Jo! On their uppers and never said a word about it! Gave me a bowl of soup when they can't even afford to eat themselves! What a couple of real bricks they are! I must say, you really find out who your friends are when this kind of thing happens. Jo! Stephen! Where are you? (*He goes towards the living room door*) There's no need to hide yourselves away! I know what's going on! (*He stops, with his hand on the door handle, as another thought strikes him*) Oh, I was just going to have a pee, wasn't I? (*Barney crosses to the corridor door, turning as he goes out to call reassuringly back towards the living room*) Don't worry—I'll be right back! What a couple of bricks!

(*He goes out. As he does so, the living room door opens, and Alex enters. He is a beardless young man with a great mop of frizzy hair and bell-bottomed trousers and is hung about with chains and dingle-dangles; almost completely ambiguous as to sex and class. Jo's hand shoots out of the living room door, catches him, and pulls him back)*

JO: (*Off*) Alex! Where are you going?

ALEX: (*Reappearing*) I'm just looking for, you know, the gent's.

(*He shuts the door and crosses to the corridor door. Not seeing what he wants out there, he tries the kitchen door. He is just about to open it when the living room door is flung open, and Stephen rushes out, still clasping the bottle of wine*)

STEPHEN: (*Urgently*) *Alex!* No! (*Alex abandons the kitchen door as if it had been suddenly electrified, and starts back. Stephen hurriedly closes the living room door and runs across to interpose himself bodily between Alex and the kitchen door*) Not in there, Alex!

ALEX: Oh, sorry. I was just looking for, you know, the kind of, you know. . . .

STEPHEN: Well, you won't find it in there!

ALEX: (*Staring at the door curiously in spite of himself*) Oh, sorry.

STEPHEN: This is the kitchen.

ALEX: Sorry.

STEPHEN: (*Steering him towards the corridor door*) No, no, no—my fault. I should have shown you where it was in the first place.

ALEX: Well, you know, I didn't want to sort of, you know, put you sort of *out*, like.

STEPHEN: No, no, no—very remiss of me. (*He opens the corridor door*) It's just that you looked so much at home here that I'd forgotten you hadn't been to the house before.

ALEX: Oh, well, you know. . . .

STEPHEN: But I hope we'll be seeing a lot of you and Bee in the future. In a few months time you'll be able to find the way to the john here in your sleep.

ALEX: (*As he is gradually edged through the door*) Oh, well ... yeah, that'd be nice.

STEPHEN: Turn left, second on the right. (*He closes the door, hesitates a moment, and then opens it again*) You'll be all right? Shall I wait for you? I mean, you can find your way back, can you? It's the door immediately opposite, not the one 'round to the left. That's the kitchen. (*Stephen closes the door reluctantly again. He goes to the kitchen door to listen. Apparently reassured, he hurries back to the living room, resuming his story to the occupants as he enters*) Yes, so anyway, the upshot of it was that Nicholas had to go to the Ambassador's dressed as a horse! (*He closes the door behind him. At once Alex reappears from the corridor door*)

ALEX: It's locked! (*He realizes that Stephen has disappeared*) Oh ... (*He looks round the room in despair and spots a vase of flowers. He crosses to it, looks round the room to make sure no one is coming, then takes the flowers out and retires with the vase behind the window curtains. At once the lavatory flushes off, and Barney comes back through the corridor door. He goes to the kitchen door, then hesitates*)

BARNEY: Just a moment. What was I going to do? Oh, find poor old Stephen and Jo. (*He crosses to the living room*) Come out of there! No need to hide from me!

ALEX: (*Putting his head round the curtain*) Sorry! I'm just in the middle of something. (*Barney stops, and gazes at Alex in astonishment. Alex disappears again*)

BARNEY: So they have got an *au pair* girl after all! (*He pulls the curtain back and reveals Alex*)

BARNEY: Hullo!

ALEX: Oh ... hi.

BARNEY: What's your name, then?

ALEX: Er ... Alex.

BARNEY: Alex. That's a very pretty name.

ALEX: Oh . . . glad you like it. (*He moves towards the living room door*)

BARNEY: Well, don't rush off, Alex, now you're here. Stay and talk for a bit—I'm all on my own.

ALEX: Oh! Right.

BARNEY: Doesn't it get you down, looking after the children all the time?

ALEX: The kids? No. I don't get much trouble. There's the usual business about, you know, pot.

BARNEY: They still use the pot, do they?

ALEX: Oh, yeah, most of them.

BARNEY: That must make a lot of extra work for you.

ALEX: Oh, I just try to stop them getting busted.

BARNEY: The pots?

ALEX: The kids. I mean, you know, I try to sort of keep the fuzz off their necks as much as possible.

BARNEY: That's a problem, is it, the fuzz on their necks?

ALEX: Oh, you get the fuzz 'round, you know, twice a night, sometimes.

BARNEY: It's funny, Alex—I feel I can talk to you. I feel we somehow understand each other. Do you feel that?

ALEX: (*Politely*) Oh ... well ... you know ...

BARNEY: (*Putting his arm around Alex*) I mean, I expect I seem rather old to you, don't I?

ALEX: No, no.

BARNEY: You're probably thinking, who is this terrible dirty old man, coming and putting his arm round me like this?

ALEX: No, I mean, you've got to be, you know, sort of open-minded about this kind of thing, haven't you?

BARNEY: I expect you're wondering if I'm married.

ALEX: No, honestly, I'm not wondering anything.

BARNEY: Well, I wouldn't. tell this to anyone else, Alex, but she's walked out on me. My wife. Without so much as a by-your-leave. One moment she was there, and the next—woof! she was gone. But do you know who she's gone off with? She's gone off with a pouf! What do you think of that?

ALEX: (*Obviously unable to decide what he is supposed to think of this*) Oh ... well. ...

BARNEY: I mean, she used to try and tell me I was a bit obsessional. But she! She's a complete raving neurotic! You ought to meet her, Alex!

ALEX: Yes, well, there's this bird I'm, you know, going around with at the moment. . . .

BARNEY: You . . . go around with birds, too, do you, Alex?

ALEX: Yeah. I mean, birds are more, you know, my thing. I mean, no offense.

BARNEY: No, I admire you for it, Alex! It's this tremendous broad-mindedness, this wonderful openness to experience that my generation lacks. I mean, take my wife. She's just a mass of repressions and inhibitions. That's why she's so neurotic.

ALEX: Yes, well, this bird's like that. This bird I'm—you know—going 'round with. Thinks everyone's getting at her all the time.

BARNEY: My wife—exactly the same!

ALEX: Oh, they're all the same, in my opinion.

BARNEY: I mean, we'd go out to dinner somewhere, and I'd put my arm 'round some girl I'd known for donkey's years—just like I'm doing now, just the same, nothing more in it than that—and I'd look 'round, and my wife would have disappeared. And do you know where she'd be?

ALEX: In the bathroom, crying her eyes out.

BARNEY: (*Agreeing, wonderingly*) In the bathroom, crying her eyes out!

ALEX: I mean, so *jealous!*

BARNEY: My God, it's marvelous meeting someone who *understands* like this!

ALEX: It's fantastic being able to—you know—sort of get it off your chest, at last, isn't it? I mean, this bird I'm talking about. . . .

BARNEY: (*Interrupting*) Would you like a drink, Alex? I've got a drop of Scotch out here. Yes, go on.

(*He goes into the kitchen. Alex follows him as far as the door, and stands talking there as a hand first holds up the bottle of whisky, then a moment later proffers a full glass)*

ALEX: I mean, I can see why she's so, you know, hung up. She's married to this bloke who's even nuttier than she is. Thanks. They'd go out to a party, or something, and the first thing she knew she'd find him out in the kitchen, feeling up the bird who was giving the party and telling her that it was her he'd really meant to marry all the time. Well, it would make anyone insecure, wouldn't it? And you know what he did once? *(The hand reappears holding a second glass of whisky, clinks it against his, and disappears. Alex raises his glass)* The same to you. *(He drinks down the whisky)* He got so, you know, stoned, he went out to the kitchen and started feeling up the bird's husband by mistake, and telling *him* the tale! *(The arm appears and ushers him into the kitchen. The door closes. At once the living room door opens and Stephen comes out, still holding the bottle of wine, and addressing the occupants)*

STEPHEN: . . . but above all, surely, it's a question of setting the present economic crisis within the context of European cultural structure. *(He closes the door, and looks anxiously round the room, calling in a stage whisper)* Alex? Alex! *(He crosses to the corridor door, and calls off)* Alex! Are you all right! *(There being no answer, he goes out to investigate and returns an instant later, baffled. He notices that the curtain is disarranged, crosses to it, and finds the vase behind. Frowning, he replaces the flowers. As he does so, the kitchen door opens, and the broken remains of the dicky dining chair are thrown out. He spins 'round, and picks the chair up)* Barney! What have you done with this chair? *(He tries to open the kitchen door, but it is locked)* Barney! Barney? What's happening? Why won't this door open? Why have you locked the door, Barney? And what have you been doing to this chair! All right, the leg was loose— but to get it into this condition you'd have needed two people sitting on it or something! *(The implication of his words strikes him. He turns back to the door)* Barney! Barney!

(The living room door opens, and Bee enters. She is wearing some astonishing minimal see-through type of outfit, more suitable to someone ten years younger)

BEE: (*Anxiously*) Stephen....

STEPHEN: (*Whirling round, and attempting to hide the very existence of the kitchen door*) Bee!

BEE: Where's Alex?

STEPHEN: I'm not quite sure, Bee. Around somewhere.

BEE: Perhaps he's in the kitchen.

STEPHEN: (*Guarding it*) No, no, no! I've looked. There's no one there. He went to the loo, originally.

BEE: He can't still be in the loo, can he?

STEPHEN: (*Urging her*) Why don't you just go and look?

BEE: I mean, I don't want to fuss. He can't stand me fussing.

STEPHEN: But all the same....

BEE: All the same, if something had happened to him....

STEPHEN: (*Holding the corridor door open for her*) First on the left, second on the right.

BEE: Oh, I expect he just got bored and went home.

STEPHEN: (*Seizing on this explanation with relief*) Yes, he did!

BEE: (*Surprised*) He did?

STEPHEN: Of course he did! I forgot to tell you. He said he had a headache, so he was going home. He just slipped quietly out the back so as not to break up the party. How stupid of me to forget! (*Bee gazes at him for a moment, and then suddenly gives a loud despairing wail and bursts into tears*) What? What is it, Bee? What's the matter? (*He puts a baffled protecting arm around her, looking back anxiously over his shoulder at the kitchen. She seizes him gratefully and cries into his chest*) Sh, Bee! What is it?

BEE: Don't you see? He's left me!

STEPHEN: Left you?

BEE: I *knew* he would! I *knew* it couldn't last!

STEPHEN: He hasn't left you, Bee! He's just gone home with a headache!

BEE: Headache!

STEPHEN: He said he'd ring you tomorrow. (*But this makes Bee give a cry of fresh pain and weep more bitterly still*)

No, he said he'd ring you *tonight*. (*But this makes it worse still*) He's going to ring you the moment you get in! So you see he hasn't left you, has he, Bee!

BEE: (*Bitterly*) He wouldn't have to ring me if he hadn't moved out, would he? (*She wails more loudly than ever*)

STEPHEN: No, well, I've got that wrong. (*He looks round anxiously at the kitchen door*) I didn't mean he was going to *ring* you exactly. I meant ...

BEE: Oh, shut up, Stephen! You're just making it worse!

STEPHEN: No, what I meant was. ...

BEE: Oh, Stephen! You're the only friend I've got left in the world! Don't you leave me!

STEPHEN: No, I won't, but. ...

BEE: Alex has walked out on me. Barney hates me. All my friends have turned against me because of Alex. All Alex's friends treat me as if I were his mother. Jo's afraid I'll have an affair with you next. You're the only person left, Stephen! I've always felt you were the one man I could really talk to. If only we'd met earlier, it could all have been so simple! (*She embraces him hysterically. He looks wildly from door to door, uncertain as to which he would less welcome intervention from*)

STEPHEN: Sh! Sh! Calm down now!

BEE: Oh, Stephen!

STEPHEN: (*Disengaging himself with difficulty*) Now, you just wait here, and I'll go and fetch you a nice stiff calming drink.

BEE: (*Seizing him again*) Don't leave me!

STEPHEN: I shan't be a minute. You just sit down and re-lax. (*He attempts to set the broken chair for her, then realizes what he is doing and picks it up again*) I mean, you just stand up and relax. (*He goes out through the living room door, re-suming his conversation with the occupants as he does so*) ... and, of course, of setting European cultural structure within the context of our repressed sexual fantasies. ...

(*He disappears and shuts the door. At the sight of the door shutting Bee gives way to a new burst of despair*)

BEE: Now they've all gone! They've left me! I've no one to turn to! (*She in fact turns towards the kitchen door and leans against it in melodramatic despair, in the attitude of Love Locked Out*) No one! No one! (*Suddenly she stops crying and lifts her hand from the door. She listens, frowning, then puts her ear to the door and listens again, puzzled*) Alex! That's Alex's voice! (*Bee turns away from the door, opens her handbag, and hastily begins to refurbish her appearance*) Oh God! Mustn't let him see I was worried. Cheerful smile, knew he was there all the time. . . . (*As she finishes this task the door opens, and Barney comes thoughtfully out. She closes her bag and turns to him, smiling*) Alex!

BARNEY: (*Putting his arm 'round her confidentially*) Jo, there's something I think you ought to know about that *au pair* girl of yours . . . (*His voice dies away as he gets his gaze properly focused on her. She is staring at him, transfixed with astonishment.*) Bee!

BEE: Barney!

(*For a moment they just stare at each other, still embraced. Then, abruptly, Bee breaks away and opens the kitchen door to see who is inside. Hastily Barney pulls it shut again*)

BARNEY: Friend of mine, that's all.

BEE: You and Alex?

BARNEY: We were just having a friendly conversation—nothing more to it.

BEE: (*Wildly*) You and Alex—having a friendly conversation? It's a conspiracy! Getting together behind my back! (*She turns and rushes off, weeping, through the corridor door*)

BARNEY: (*Following her as far as the door*) No, Bee, listen! Stop! (*He is going to pursue her further, but at that moment the kitchen door opens. He runs back to it*) Now you keep out of this! You've caused enough trouble already! (*He puts his hand 'round the door and takes the key out of the lock on the other side*) *Au pair* girl! My God, I knew young people were confused, but I didn't know the rot had gone this far! (*He *slams the door shut and locks it. Then, pocketing the key, he runs back to the corridor door)* Bee! Listen! Let me explain! *(He seizes the handle of the corridor door and pushes, assuming in his anxiety that it opens the same way as the kitchen door. But it doesn't. He calls imperiously)* Open the door! Come on, open the door! *Open this door! (He hammers on it, then suddenly drops his commanding manner, and becomes pleading instead)* Look, Bee, it's all a misunderstanding! You looked in there, you thought it was the *au pair* girl, didn't you? I thought it was the *au pair* girl! But listen, Bee, you open this door and I'll tell you an astonishing fact. Bee! *(He turns away from the door for a moment, amazed at himself)* Though why the hell *I* should be excusing myself to *her!* *(He addresses himself furiously to the door again, hammering and shouting)* Open this door at once! I know what you're doing—you needn't think I don t! You're in the bathroom, having a good old weep!

GIRL CHILD'S VOICE: *(Calling, from off)* Mummy! Mummy! There's a lady crying in the bathroom!

BARNEY: *(Shouting at the top of his voice)* Look, *stop* crying in the bathroom, and come down and open this door! *(He rains a frustrated fusillade of blows upon the door, then stops, realizing that someone else somewhere is hammering on a door. He runs furiously across to the kitchen, and shouts through the closed door)* Stop that noise at once! I can scarcely hear myself knock! *(There is another salvo of bangs from the kitchen, to which he bangs furiously back)* One more bang out of you, my girl, and I'll put the police on to you, my lad! *(He runs furiously back to the corridor door and thunders on that one again)* Come downstairs this instant and open the door!

(Barney shouts and thunders. Alex thunders, too. There is a sudden brief lull, during which the living room door opens, and Jo enters, holding a nice stiff calming drink and talking back over her shoulder to the occupants of the living room.)

JO: . . . in which case, so much for European cultural structure . . . ! *(She closes the door)*

BARNEY: (*To Jo, in furious explanation*) She's in the bathroom, weeping!

JO: Stephen said she needed a stiff drink.

BARNEY: She'll need more than a stiff drink if I ever get my hands on her! (*He whirls back upon the door, pounding on it and shouting at the top of his voice*) Can't you understand? I'm trying to tell you I love you!

JO: Why don't you go up and tell her at slightly closer range?

BARNEY: Because the little bitch has locked the door! (*He hurls his weight against it to demonstrate*)

JO: It opens this way.

BARNEY: (*Almost too furious to comprehend*) What?

JO: Pull it.

(*He pulls it violently. It opens without let or hindrance, sending him reeling back into the room. As he picks himself up there is another salvo of knocking from the kitchen*)

JO: What's that?

BARNEY: That's your friend Alex. I've locked him in the kitchen pending his arrest on a variety of serious charges. All right! I'm coming! (*He rushes out through the corridor door. There is the noise of heavy feet thundering up the stairs, then of rending wood, and then of glass objects smashing. Calmly, Jo goes over to the corridor door*)

BOY CHILD'S VOICE: (*Calling, from off*) Mummy! *Mummy!* There's a lady and a man fighting in the bathroom!

JO: Go to *sleep,* dear! I don't want to hear another sound out of you two—you know we've got people to dinner. (*With philosophical calm Jo closes the door to deaden the continuing noise. There is another salvo of blows from the kitchen. She raises her eyebrows wearily, notices the nice stiff calming drink still in her hand, and drinks it down stoically. As she finishes it, the living room door opens, and Stephen creeps quietly out, looking anxiously back over his shoulder and smiling benignly. He shuts the door behind him. Jo reports the situation to him with calm detachment*) Barney and Bee are fighting in the bathroom.

Alex and the rest of dinner are locked in the kitchen. The children are awake.

STEPHEN: David and Dora are asleep.

JO: John and Laura. Are you sure?

STEPHEN: They hadn't said anything for quite a while. I don't know whether you'd noticed.

(*Jo opens the living room door. She and Stephen both gaze off at John and Laura. Bursts of noise from bathroom and kitchen continue intermittently*)

STEPHEN: It was the economic crisis that finished them, I think.

JO: I knew we should have kept off politics.

STEPHEN: They look quite peaceful.

JO: I *think* they quite enjoyed the evening, didn't they?

STEPHEN: Oh, I think everyone did, all things considered.

JO: I think it all went off reasonably well.

STEPHEN: Jo, I'm sorry I shouted at you earlier.

JO: I lost my temper, too. It always gets a bit tense when people are coming to dinner. You always think everything's going to go wrong.

Curtain

Jason Miller

CIRCUS LADY

Jason Miller

Rarely has a young dramatist earned such a cascade of superlatives from the critics or has flashed as meteorically from near anonymity to the forefront of American writers as did Jason Miller with his play, *That Championship Season*. The drama, which deals with the twentieth annual reunion of a high school basketball coach, now retired, and four members of the team that he guided to the state championship two decades earlier, originally opened on May 2, 1972 at the New York Shakespeare Festival Public Theatre. In September, it transferred to Broadway where it has settled into a lengthy run at the Booth Theatre. Described by the press as "a drama of searing intensity, agonized compassion and consummate craftsmanship" and its author as "a towering new dramatist," *That Championship Season* won the 1972 New York Drama Critics' Circle Award as the best play of the year while Mr. Miller garnered a Drama Desk citation for outstanding playwright of the year. The play is scheduled for early filming with the screenplay to be written by Mr. Miller.

Prior to the opening of *That Championship Season*, the author was represented Off-Broadway in 1970 by *Nobody Hears a Broken Drum*, which tarried briefly, and a bill of three short plays bearing the overall title of *The Circus Theatre*. One of the latter was *Circus Lady*, here published for the first time in its final version.

Another of Mr. Miller's short plays, *Lou Gehrig Did Not Die of Cancer*, is included in this editor's forthcoming anthology, *Best Short Plays of the World Theatre: 1968–1973*.

Jason Miller was born in Scranton, Pennsylvania, in 1939. While a student at the University of Scranton, he began writing plays and winning prizes for his efforts. He then became interested in acting, which he pursued as a graduate student at Catholic University. He subsequently appeared at the Champlain and Cincinnati Shakespeare Festivals as well as Off-Broadway in *Subject to Fits* and in Washington, D.C. with Helen Hayes in *Long Day's Journey Into Night* and Geraldine Fitzgerald in *Juno and the Paycock*. Presently, he is starring as Father Karras in the film version of William Peter Blatty's novel, *The Exorcist*.

The author, his wife and three children now live in Neponsit, New York.

Characters:

MARIE PEREZ
JOHN PEREZ
WELFARE MAN
RUTH
MAN

Scene:

A fourth floor apartment in one of the Puerto Rican Negro ghettos of the East Bronx, New York. The apartment faces the street. Visible is a living room and stage right, behind beaded curtains is a bedroom. The only entrance is a door stage center. The apartment is incredibly cluttered and unkempt; clothing lies in various piles throughout the room, newspapers, magazines, empty TV dinners, stacks of hard-covered and paperback books lie everywhere. The furniture is lumpy and stained, covered with dust. The apartment smells like a pet shop.

John is standing with a shoe in his raised hand. John is about eighteen. Dark, slim and taut. Although he is half Puerto Rican, his features have a distinct American look. He is dressed only in black chinos.

JOHN: (*Slamming shoe on the floor*) Ahhh!

MARIE: (*From bedroom*) John, is that you? Answer me, John, is that you, please! (*Very loud*) John, is that you?

JOHN: Yeah, it's me.

MARIE: Do you have to make all that noise? What are you doing?

JOHN: Killing a cockroach. (*He scrapes cockroach off floor with paper, goes to window and drops it out*)

MARIE: There's some Wheaties in the cupboard and a banana on the sink. See if there's milk.

JOHN: I'll eat out. (*He searches through a pile of clothes for some socks*)

MARIE: I don't buy groceries so you can go and eat out. The welfare check doesn't come until tomorrow, remember that.

JOHN: I'll eat out, I said—someplace where there's no cockroaches for company.

MARIE: Where is there a place like that, John? Where is there a place like that around here, without cockroaches? Cockroaches come here when they die; this is a cockroach heaven. (*She laughs*) It's easier to get rid of people around here than it is cockroaches.

JOHN: Come on, get out of bed. The welfare investigator is supposed to come today. We got a letter, Ma, so get up.

MARIE: What time?

JOHN: Two o'clock.

MARIE: Are you dressed? (*No answer*) Have you got your pants on, John?

JOHN: (*Looking for a clean shirt amid a pile of clothing*) Yeah!

MARIE: Are you sure?

JOHN: Yeah! I got my pants on 'cause they're the only thing that's clean.

(*Marie enters. She is in a slip. Marie is about 5'2" and she weighs about 250 lbs. She is enormous. Like a great amoeba, she oozes through the apartment. Her weight has physically and mentally incapacitated her, and the disorder in the house is a reflection of the chaos in her own mind*)

MARIE: You're too old to walk around naked anymore, even in front of your mother.

JOHN: I don't walk around naked.

MARIE: You might as well be naked, walking around in them little jockey shorts.

JOHN: So, you walk around in your slip.

MARIE: Honey, if I arouse you, you got problems. Believe me, you got problems.

JOHN: The welfare man is coming, remember?

(*Marie sits in a chair*)

MARIE: Won't he be surprised!

JOHN: Christ, Ma, you're a mess. You smell! You smell worse than that pile of clothes. It smells like a pile of. . . .

MARIE: I don't like that language. (*Smells her underarms*) It's been worse! It's the heat—but you're right, I need a bath or something.

JOHN: Well, take one, go in and take one.

MARIE: Takes too long. Maybe you could take me to the car wash and just roll me through. (*Laughs*)

JOHN: The welfare man will be here in fifteen minutes.

MARIE: Give me the spray. (*John takes a bottle of deodorant from the bureau and gives it to her. She sprays underneath her armpits*) Just like a big bouquet of roses, now—honeysuckle rose. I'll just sweep that welfare man right off his feet.

JOHN: Feet. Look at your feet, they're black. Let me wash them. (*He goes off and gets wash rag*)

MARIE: John, when I heard you slamming around in here before, I thought it was him knocking again. I just lay there sweating in terror.

JOHN: (*Washing her feet*) He won't bother you. I need a wire brush, I need a pick and a wire brush to get these feet clean.

MARIE: Don't be unkind, John. Don't be angry at me. I just can't bend down that far anymore. Just look at my toenails now, they look like the heads of rusty nails. Years ago I used to wear sandals and paint each toenail red—that was the style then, sandals and each toenail painted bright-red. Your father used to say my feet were pretty.

JOHN: Yeah, he loved your feet so much he went back to Puerto Rico.

MARIE: He voyaged across the seas, as they say in books, yes, he did.

JOHN: One day I'll go to Puerto Rico, find him and . . . cut his cojones off.

MARIE: Don't talk like the streets in here, John! He's

probably not there now. Your father was a traveling man, just like you, made for the road, not the home.

JOHN: Done. (*Finishing her feet*) Like new.

MARIE: Well, now you can distribute the loaves and the fishes. (*Laughs*) Loaves and fishes? (*John picks up four or five shirts, smells each one to test their cleanliness*) Don't forget how to laugh. You can't endure without laughter, John.

JOHN: I can't endure without a clean shirt, either. It smells like a cat pissed all over them.

MARIE: That language is not necessary. You're not talking to one of your street whores now, and don't you forget it.

JOHN: At least street whores have clean clothes. They take a bath once in a while.

MARIE: Don't you dare talk to me like that, I'm still your mother. (*A knocking is heard outside, it could be a knocking in the walls or it could be a knocking on Marie's door*) John, it's him. It's him! Don't answer it! Stay where you are. He'll go away like he did yesterday. (*John goes to the door*) John, don't open that door. (*He opens it, there is no one there*)

JOHN: I told you it's in the walls. It's the hot water pipes in the walls.

MARIE: Tell Mrs. Gonzales that. She lives on the first floor. Tell her it's the pipes, because he knocked on her door and she opened it and he raped her three times. Go down and tell *her* it's in the walls. Read it. It's in the papers. He's in this building. He knocked twice yesterday when you were out. He's here somewhere in this building. God almighty, the world's turning into an insane asylum—a great big outdoor insane asylum.

JOHN: Listen to me, will ya. There was only Mrs. Gonzales raped in this building, no one else.

MARIE: John, don't go out. I need someone here to protect me.

JOHN: There was only one woman raped in this building, Ma, come on.

MARIE: But he got two up the block. Two in the same day. One right after the other. The man knows no fear; it's in the papers. He raped two women on the same day, one right after the other, and played music on the radio while he did it.

JOHN: Ma, he is not going to rape you, believe me. He's not going to climb four flights of stairs just to rape you. You're safe.

MARIE: He's a maniac, don't you understand? Give me the papers over there. Listen to this, just listen. "Police found a note pinned to one of the victim's bed sheets. It read 'I come in the darkness of the night, I come like a thief in the night, bringing love and holy light' . . . signed, Mr. Lord Byron." Does that sound like a normal man? He's a maniac.

JOHN: Still, he is not going to write any poems to you, not you. People don't rape people like you. You'll never get raped.

MARIE: Mrs. Gonzales has one breast. The other one was removed and he raped her. So why not me?

JOHN: Because he didn't know Mrs. Gonzales had only one breast until he raped her.

MARIE: But it didn't stop him; he kept right on going. Don't you see, don't you see the pattern? He likes . . . deformed women. There are men like that. I read about these men. They only like something that's . . . abnormal. He was out there and he heard your voice and he went away, but he'll be back.

JOHN: Ma, look, I have to go up to the job center and see if the telegram came. I'll be back soon.

MARIE: They'll send the telegram here.

JOHN: Or up there.

MARIE: Can't you wait until next spring before you go away for the training?

JOHN: Ma, we went through this before. I may not get a chance to go next spring. These programs aren't reliable. Read the papers, they die every day.

MARIE: Why can't they train you in New York? Chicago is a million miles away.

JOHN: I don't know why it's Chicago, but it is.

MARIE: You're not mature enough to go to Chicago. Chicago will eat you up.

JOHN: I had no trouble taking care of myself so far.

MARIE: Oh, big tough guy. You weren't so tough when I bailed you out of the reformatory two years ago. You cried like a baby. Remember that, muscles? You were like a little boy, afraid of the dark.

JOHN: And you're like a record that keeps going and going and going.

MARIE: You're my life line, John. What will I do without you?

JOHN: You got Aunt Ruth. You can live with Aunt Ruth in Queens.

MARIE: They don't want me. She has three children and you know her husband's no friend of mine. You know that.

JOHN: Ma, I got a break, a real break. The man says I have natural intelligence. It's not like I'm going to be gone forever. After the training I'll get a good job and get you out of here.

MARIE: Out of sight, out of mind. You'll go over the horizon like your father, and never come back.

JOHN: Look, the welfare and Aunt Ruth can take care of you until I come back. It's that simple.

MARIE: It isn't that simple. It isn't simple at all. The welfare isn't my son. The welfare doesn't talk to me. The welfare doesn't wash my dirty feet. The Welfare Department gives out checks and smiles and says goodbye and closes the door.

JOHN: It's after two, I gotta go.

MARIE: You're always going someplace. Always on the go. I sit up here all day and all night listening to the world outside going someplace, everybody going somewhere except me, John.

JOHN: I'll be back soon. Anyway, I thought Aunt Ruth was coming here today. She'll be here all afternoon.

MARIE: She's not reliable. Sometimes she comes, sometimes she doesn't. Can't you at least wait until the investigator comes?

JOHN: No, I can't.

MARIE: I need protection with that maniac roaming the building. You know you'll just talk to those bums on the corner all afternoon.

JOHN: I'll see you later.

(*He exits. She gets up. She wanders aimlessly about, finally picks up a box of candy. Sits down again eating candy. She lights a cigarette, picks up a book and begins to read. After a few moments a knocking is heard on the door, or maybe it's just the pipes in the wall*)

MARIE: Who is it? Who's there? I'm going to call the police if you don't say who you are! John, come out of the bathroom. John, my eighteen-year-old son, come out of the bathroom and see who's at the door. (*There is no answer. After a few moments, Marie gets up and sneaks cautiously over to the door; bending, she tries to peek through the keyhole. As she is peering out someone knocks loudly on the door. Marie is startled and screams out*) Who is it?

WELFARE MAN: It's the Welfare Department.

MARIE: Prove it!

WELFARE MAN: I assure you it's your investigator. Please open the door.

MARIE: Show me some identification. Slip some identification under the door. (*He does. Marie picks it up*) Mr. Steen?

WELFARE MAN: Mr. Stein.

MARIE: How tall are you, Mr. Stein?

WELFARE MAN: Five nine, Mrs. Perez.

MARIE: What color are your eyes?

WELFARE MAN: Brown.

MARIE: How much do you weigh?

WELFARE MAN: 170 pounds.

MARIE: (*Opens door*) Come in.

WELFARE MAN: (*He sees she is only in a slip so he retreats to the hallway. It suffices to say, Mr. Stein is a new investigator*) I'd appreciate it if you'd put something on, Mrs. Perez. It's against procedure for me to come in, otherwise.

MARIE: (*Taking a shirt*) Oh, I'm sorry. I'm a little upset and I forgot about my slip.

WELFARE MAN: It's just a little thing, but the department is very strict about little things. (*Comes in*)

MARIE: Sure, I know. Just sit anywhere. I haven't started

my spring housecleaning yet, as you can see. I've been sick—my heart.

WELFARE MAN: Don't apologize, I understand.

MARIE: I wish you were here before I took sick. It was spotless; you could eat off the floors. I come from a clean family, Mr. Stein, and this simply turns my stomach, believe me.

WELFARE MAN: May I ask what that was all about at the door just now?

MARIE: There's a rapist around here; he preys on this block. Lady downstairs with one breast was raped, can you imagine that? He leaves poems behind him. Honest to God, poems.

WELFARE MAN: Oh, Lord Byron. *Post* had a story.

MARIE: That's him, the nut.

WELFARE MAN: I didn't know one of his victims lived here!

MARIE: This building is his playground, for God's sake.

WELFARE MAN: Well, you're certainly doing the right thing by not opening your door to just anyone. They'll probably catch him soon.

MARIE: I hope so. I'm a nervous wreck.

WELFARE MAN: Well, I don't think you have anything to worry about. (*Marie looks at him*) I mean, the man will be caught and your fears will be over.

MARIE: Would you like some candy, Mr. Klein?

WELFARE MAN: Stein. Not right now. It looks good though.

MARIE: I really shouldn't be eating it but . . . .

WELFARE MAN: I don't think a few pieces will hurt.

MARIE: Yeah, but I'll eat the whole box by four o'clock.

WELFARE MAN: Oh. Now the reason I'm here. (*Leafs through his field book*) I've only been working for the department for two weeks now, so, bear with me if I make any stupid mistakes, alrighty?

MARIE: You know, I've had about ten investigations.

WELFARE MAN: According to your case record, you've been on welfare almost eighteen years.

MARIE: Eighteen! That must be some kind of record. Time just sweeps along, doesn't it?

WELFARE MAN: As I said, I was looking through your case record from the very beginning, almost eighteen years ago, and I found a minor discrepancy that I'd like to clear up now. When you first applied for public assistance, you stated that your husband abandoned you and went to Puerto Rico. Now I can't understand why at least one of your many case workers did not check on your husband's whereabouts in Puerto Rico, because he still, legally, must support you and your son. So, I sent a W-304 to Puerto Rico to check on him. And I sent a M-344 to his last place of employment to see if he left a mailing address. And I discovered that your husband is not in Puerto Rico. I then checked with the office of Puerto Rican affairs and I discovered that your husband never left this country at any time.

MARIE: Are you saying I lied on the welfare forms?

WELFARE MAN: I'm sorry you're taking this attitude, Mrs. Perez.

MARIE: You called me a liar, what other attitude am I supposed to take?

WELFARE MAN: I have to clear this up for state review.

MARIE: My husband left me . . . .

WELFARE MAN: It's all here in black and white.

MARIE: (*Pause*) I lied on the welfare forms.

WELFARE MAN: Is there a reason why you falsified the information?

MARIE: Yes, I wanted to protect my son. Do I have to tell you?

WELFARE MAN: I'm afraid you do.

MARIE: My husband committed suicide when I was a very young girl and my son was just a baby.

WELFARE MAN: Oh, I see.

MARIE: He committed suicide by filling the tub with hot water. Then, getting into the tub, he opened these two veins right here with a razor blade and just drifted off into eternity. I found him when I came home from work. I was working then—nights, as a waitress at the Plaza Diner. I was much thinner then. Oh, I was still what they call plump, but I had a nice shape if you know what I mean. My breasts and hips were in proportion even though I had just had a baby. I remember the short order cook, Mike, always offered to take me for a drink after work. He was a big Polack with a shock of . . . but I didn't go with him because I loved my husband and I loved my baby and I had a lovely smile because I was happy. You see, Mr. Stein, I had to work because my husband couldn't get a decent job. My husband had dark skin and spoke in a strange language, but my husband was a proud man, maybe too proud. He was more than a dishwasher, Mr. Stein, but that's all they let him be. And so one night, without warning at all, he killed himself. And that's the story.

WELFARE MAN: I'm sorry, Mrs. Perez.

MARIE: I blamed myself for a long time. I still blame myself because something should have warned me. There was something unspoken between us that I should have seen. He was a nervous, moody man, but his friends told me that everyone that came from his hometown in Puerto Rico was jumpy and moody like he was. Isn't that silly, a whole town of nervous, jumpy, moody people? But I believed it because I guess I didn't understand him and I needed to believe something.

WELFARE MAN: I will have to place this information in the case record, Mrs. Perez.

MARIE: Just as long as John doesn't find out. I don't want him to know how his father died. John is like his father, moody and jumpy. And that could even hurt John's chances for a good job if people knew about his father—do you follow me?

WELFARE MAN: Yes, I do.

MARIE: And now my son is going to leave. The poverty program is sending him to Chicago for training.

WELFARE MAN: Yes, I know the program. He's very lucky to get into it. The quota is almost filled.

MARIE: He is a very intelligent boy. He's waiting for the telegram with the bus ticket. That's how they do it, you know.

WELFARE MAN: Then you'll be all alone here, Mrs. Perez?

MARIE: Yes, I'll be alone. I don't know if I can sit here day after day watching the wildlife playing on the walls, knowing John won't be coming home at night. He's my life line, you know. Mr. Stein, I'm not an old woman. Maybe I belong in a circus. Maybe I belong in a side show, but I still need the sound of human voices in the next room.

WELFARE MAN: I understand, Mrs. . . . .

MARIE: No, you don't. How could you? Do you know I haven't been out of the house for six months because I'm afraid I can't get back up the steps without my heart exploding? I'm ashamed to walk the streets, because I'm afraid of the laughter. Mr. Stein, I'm a freak. My son can't bring anyone home here. And when he's really mad at me, he says he's going to charge admission and bring people up here and charge them a quarter to see the fat lady that got fired from the circus because she ate more than the elephants. Isn't that funny? It's true, that's why it's so funny. (*She breaks down laughing and crying*)

WELFARE MAN: It's all right Mrs. Perez. It'll be all right. Can I get you some water or something?

MARIE: There's some gin in the kitchen, just put it in some water.

WELFARE MAN: Certainly!

MARIE: Take a slug yourself.

WELFARE MAN: Well, it's not . . . I think I will.

(*He exits, comes back with two glasses of gin. Hands one to Marie*)

MARIE: Thank you. (*Takes a drink, offers him some candy*) Candy?

WELFARE MAN: Gin and candy are a little too much for my stomach. In view of the circumstances, I think we'll have to get you a first floor room somewhere.

MARIE: A room?

WELFARE MAN: It will only be until your son comes back, you understand.

MARIE: *If* he comes back. A room.

WELFARE MAN: He won't leave you here alone.

MARIE: His father did.

WELFARE MAN: Well, that was different.

MARIE: No, his father escaped. He left it all behind him, and that's what John is trying to do now. And I can't blame him if he went all the way to the Pacific Ocean and never looked back.

WELFARE MAN: Well, right now we have to get you situated and that's going to take some time.

MARIE: I couldn't live alone in a room, Mr. Stein. I'm an invalid. I'm a prisoner inside all this fat. My sister is supposed to come today. Maybe I can live with her while John's away. Maybe she'll understand.

WELFARE MAN: I'll try and rush things through for you, Mrs. Perez.

MARIE: I know you will.

WELFARE MAN: I also would like you to go to a mental health clinic and see . . .

MARIE: No! I will not have my mind tampered with. The lady next door went to your mental health clinics and they put her away. She came back, and she can't remember anybody's name. She's like a zombie.

WELFARE MAN: It won't happen to you, I promise.

MARIE: No, I don't believe you.

WELFARE MAN: I think you need help, Mrs. Perez.

MARIE: I know I need help, but I don't need that kind of help.

WELFARE MAN: Maybe if your son comes back—I mean as soon as the training is over—you'll calm down a little.

MARIE: I'd rather be crazy than lonely, Mr. Stein.

(*There is a loud knock on the door and a voice says:*)

RUTH: Open up the door, Marie. It's me, Ruth.

MARIE: Would you open the door? It's my sister.

WELFARE MAN: Certainly. I'll be going now. I'll be in touch with you soon.

MARIE: All right!

(*He opens the door. Ruth comes in. She is a tired-looking*

woman in her mid-forties. Her voice has a flat monotonous whine that gives an unconscious understatement to just about anything she says. Her sometimes cruel frankness to her sister is, nonetheless, motivated by a genuine concern for Marie)

RUTH: Hello! Is this your investigator?

WELFARE MAN: Yes, I'm Mr. Stein.

RUTH: Sending boys to do men's jobs! I brought you some gin, Marie. What are you going to do about her—five more pounds and she's going to explode. The place smells like a pet shop. Why they never put elevators in? My legs are killing me. (*Sits down*)

WELFARE MAN: Mrs. Perez, I'll get on that right away. You'll hear from me soon.

MARIE: All right. 'Bye.

(*He exits*)

RUTH: My God, what can a child like that do for the problems around here? He's probably still a virgin! I'll fix the gin. (*Goes to kitchen*) These varicose veins are killing me, Marie.

MARIE: What did the doctor say?

RUTH: Operate, like he always says. "Operate," I said, "I'll pay you on the installment plan then," I said. Now he gives me pills.

MARIE: I've been feeling terrible myself.

RUTH: It's no wonder, it's no wonder. You'll die of a heart attack some day. All that weight will kill you.

MARIE: Let's not start on me today, Ruth. I haven't seen you in a month.

RUTH: (*Handing her a drink*) I'm worried about you, Marie. This place is a pigsty. You've got to pull yourself together.

MARIE: How's the kids?

RUTH: Terrible! Ruth is running with a fast crowd. One of her girl friends got pregnant last week—fifteen years old and she's pregnant. It's a sin I tell you.

MARIE: It happened to all of us.

RUTH: It didn't have to happen, is all I'm saying. And Paul wants to go to college, but he's not too bright, Marie. He's too slow for college. But you can't tell his father that. He thinks he's some kind of genius. I want him to go to the army and get it over with. Jim's sick, too. It's always something.

MARIE: What's the matter?

RUTH: Piles. He's got piles as big as grapes.

MARIE: That's too bad.

RUTH: It's the season for them, you know—hot, muggy. The doctor says operate. These doctors love to cut you up.

MARIE: (*Pause*) I might have to move.

RUTH: Well, for godsake move to a first floor apartment. The steps just kill me.

MARIE: John is leaving, you know.

RUTH: Where's he going?

MARIE: To Chicago for job training.

RUTH: Well, you knew he was going to leave someday, didn't you?

MARIE: I didn't think about it.

RUTH: That's always been your trouble. Mama always said you'd sooner look the other way. She always said you'd rather close your eyes and pretend it didn't exist, remember?

MARIE: Mama and I weren't friends.

RUTH: She never got over it. Marie, you know that?

MARIE: She never even came to see her grandson. What kind of a mother was that, tell me, Ruth.

RUTH: You married a foreigner who couldn't even speak the language, my God, a man who wasn't even white.

MARIE: Are you people going to punish me for the rest of my life? You don't need God around here with you and your husband and mama. Mama's dead, so forget it.

RUTH: All right, it's forgotten. (*Knocking is heard*)

MARIE: Don't move! Don't say anything—it's him!

RUTH: Who?

MARIE: A rapist! He saw the investigator leave. Ruth, he's been trying to get in here all day.

RUTH: You're out of your mind. Somebody's at the door.

MARIE: (*Knocking stops*) He's gone away. He heard you.

RUTH: Marie! It's knocking in the wall, rapist! (*Knocking begins*)

MARIE: Don't open the door!

RUTH: You're crazy. (*She opens door. A man is standing there. Both women scream and shut door*)

MAN: Hey, this is Western Union and I have a telegram for John Perez.

RUTH: (*Opening door*) What's the matter with you, scaring the life out of people?

MAN: Nothing's the matter with me, lady. What's the matter with you two? Just sign here lady and I'll be off.

RUTH: (*Signs*) There . . . I don't have any change. (*Shuts the door*)

MARIE: I can hardly get my breath.

RUTH: I feel sick to my stomach. You and your rapist! Where's the gin? Here. (*She hands telegram to Marie and exits. Marie opens telegram and a check falls out*)

RUTH: (*Handing Marie a drink*) Here . . . who's it from?

MARIE: They want John to report Monday to Chicago. They sent him money for transportation.

RUTH: Marie, the boy deserves a life of his own.

MARIE: I know. I know, but it hurts Ruth, and I'm tired of pain. Awful tired.

RUTH: You have to pull yourself together. Rapist running through the building? Jesus, don't start getting delusions.

MARIE: It's not a delusion. Three women have been raped on this block in the past week. Read the papers.

RUTH: I don't read the papers anymore; they depress me. I don't know, the world is going mad. Rapers and killers. And they don't kill just one person anymore because they'll just get electrocuted. They kill five or six and get put away in a nice hospital and get served breakfast in bed. I don't understand anything anymore, I really don't.

MARIE: Do you think when John leaves I could ....

RUTH: Do you know, Jim and me went to the movies last week and sitting right next to us was this old man, an old man without a tooth in his head. He must have been seventy if he was a day. And do you know what he was doing? Do you have any idea?

MARIE: No.

RUTH: He had his coat over his lap, that's what!

MARIE: So?

RUTH: He was playing with himself! This disgusting old man sitting there right next to me in the movies was playing with himself. Jim called the manager, and do you know they couldn't throw him out because we couldn't prove it. So we had to move, Jim and me, while he stayed there playing with himself. Can you figure that out?

MARIE: Maybe he had nothing else ....

RUTH: He was crazy, that's what he was.

MARIE: (Pause) Ruth, do you think ....

RUTH: The old pervert. Can you imagine?

MARIE: Ruth, I was wondering if ....

RUTH: What if there were young children there?

MARIE: Would it be possible for me to ....

RUTH: To come and live with us until John comes back? You know I haven't the room. You know how Jim feels about you. My God, Marie. I couldn't feed you. And I don't mean that to be funny. The welfare would cut down on your check if they knew you were with me. It's impossible.

MARIE: They're going to put me in a room, alone. Ruth, they might take me to a mental hospital and tamper with my brain, and I have no one to stop them. They could put me away.

RUTH: Marie, Jim and I were talking the other night about you. Maybe a rest, just a rest and some sunshine and fresh air would do you the world ....

MARIE: Listen, they took Mrs. Swenson to Rockland and they shot her head full of electricity and now she walks around like a zombie. Please, Ruth! It would only be for six months.

RUTH: I can't. Don't make me refuse you. Don't ask me because I have to say no, no, no.

MARIE: Ruth, I'll lose weight. You won't even know I'm there. I'll go on a diet. I won't even eat at the table, I'll eat in my room. I'll stay in my room all day. Ruth, I can't live with all this silence around me. I need to hear voices in the next room.

RUTH: I'll visit you when I can. I'll bring you food, money, anything you want. But I can't, don't you understand, I can't. It's impossible. I don't have space for you even.

MARIE: You're my sister, my blood. Don't throw me on the mercy of other people, because they don't have any mercy to give.

RUTH: It's getting late. I have to go home.

MARIE: Home. It must be so nice to be able to say that. I have to go home . . . home.

RUTH: (*Putting on coat*) I'll come next week and clean the place up. I'm putting ten dollars on the table.

MARIE: Don't come back. I don't want to see you anymore.

RUTH: I'll come next week in the afternoon.

MARIE: Stay in your own home . . . stay home. Look in my eyes, Ruth, my sister.

RUTH: (*Unable to face her*) Next Thursday I'll be here in the afternoon. I'll give the place a good scrubbing.

(*She exits. Marie sits in chair, sips her gin. A knocking begins. She begins to chuckle to herself. Slowly this chuckle grows louder and louder until it becomes a torrent of hysterical laughter. She gets up still laughing, waddles over to the window and screams out*)

MARIE: John, John! He's here! He's at the door again. John! Come up here, he's at the door and I'm going to let him in. Do you hear me, John? I'm going to let him in if you don't come up.

(*She stops. The knocking ceases. She walks back to the chair, now softly laughing to herself. She sits. After a few moments John opens the door with a key*)

JOHN: You're crazy, you know that? People think you're crazy and they're right. There's nobody at the door. There's nobody in the hall. The building's empty.

MARIE: No, it isn't. He's out there somewhere waiting. He waited until your aunt left.

JOHN: I just saw Aunt Ruth on the street. Where is it?

MARIE: What?

JOHN: The telegram.

MARIE: She told you?

JOHN: Yeah, she told me. Where is it?

MARIE: I ate it. (*Laughs*)

JOHN: Where is it?

MARIE: I ate it. I eat everything, you know. Why, is it important?

JOHN: It's important! You know it's important.

MARIE: Is it more important than your mother?

JOHN: Yes, it is! Give it to me.

MARIE: It's on the table under the bowl. (*Pause*) Don't go, John.

JOHN: I'm going.

MARIE: I'll have no one. I'll be entirely alone. Ruth doesn't want me. Welfare wants me in a room.

JOHN: I'll be back in six months. I'll send you money.

MARIE: I don't want money. Everyone gives people money when they can't give them anything else.

JOHN: Ma, I'm not going to spend my life playing dominoes on the stoop and getting drunk at three o'clock in the afternoon, seven days a week. I'm tired of living off other people. I want to make my own way, pay my own way.

MARIE: Stay until the spring.

JOHN: Ma, I even packed a suitcase. That's how fast I'm ready to leave.

MARIE: You can't wait a while longer?

JOHN: I've been waiting.

MARIE: And I've been waiting all my life.

JOHN: And that's just what's not going to happen to me.

MARIE: Ingratitude. Do you know you're committing a mortal sin leaving me here alone now?

JOHN: You know, I used to think my father was the meanest bastard that ever lived, but now I can understand why he left. I don't understand how he could have stayed so long.

MARIE: You can't.

JOHN: (*Throwing shirts in gym bag*) He must have been a saint to go through this shit.

MARIE: Your father left me because he was a spineless man. He was a burnt-out piece of nothing. A scared little rabbit that just ran and ran.

JOHN: But he wasn't stupid, like you said. I'm just like him, so I'm following his example. Because I'm getting out.

MARIE: (*Pause*) Your father killed himself.

(*Pause*)

JOHN: What did you say?

MARIE: Your brave father cut his wrists in that bathtub in there and bled to death in ten minutes.

JOHN: You're insane.

MARIE: Am I? I found him, don't tell me. I found him in three feet of blood. So that's my going away present to you.

JOHN: You're lying! You're saying that so I'll stay. You're trying to scare me into staying.

MARIE: Go and see Aunt Ruth. Ask her if you don't believe me.

JOHN: Why didn't you tell me before?

MARIE: Because I didn't want you to know.

JOHN: So you tell me now.

MARIE: I'm afraid of being locked in somebody's closet and being forgotten about.

JOHN: You think because you told me that I'm going to stay? You're wrong. Before I wasn't sure why I was going, now I know. After living here for eighteen years with you, after living here in this filth, in this stink, in this rat's nest, I'd do the same thing. I'd cut my arm off up to here. Now that I know about my father I got a reason for going. (*He gets suitcase from bedroom*)

MARIE: Where are you going now?

JOHN: Out with my friends, and then I'm leaving for Chicago in the morning.

MARIE: (*Pause*) You have a spot on your shirt.

JOHN: I always have spots on my shirts, remember?

MARIE: Don't go with a girl tonight. Stay here and leave tomorrow.

JOHN: If I do, tomorrow will be next week, next month, never.

MARIE: Take the ten dollars on the table.

JOHN: I have money. I'll write.

MARIE: Yes, write. Goodbye, John.

JOHN: Yeah. Goodbye.

(*He exits. Marie sits. The room is almost in darkness now. She sips her gin. A quiet knocking begins. Marie listens, then she gets up, puts on the radio. Soft music begins to play. Then she moves toward the door. As she goes to the door she lets her hair down. She hesitates at the door, then she opens it as:*)

The Curtain Falls

Lorraine Hansberry

WHAT USE
ARE FLOWERS?

(A Fable)

Lorraine Hansberry

When Lorraine Hansberry's *A Raisin in the Sun* opened at the Ethel Barrymore Theatre, New York, on March 11, 1959, it not only was a personal triumph for its author but it also represented a landmark in American theatrical history. It was the initial play written by a Negro woman to be presented on Broadway and the first by a Negro dramatist ever to win the New York Drama Critics' Circle Award as the best American play of the season. *A Raisin in the Sun* (with a company headed by Sidney Poitier, Claudia McNeil, Ruby Dee and Diana Sands) ran for 530 performances, toured extensively and has since been published and produced in some thirty countries. Her film adaptation of the play, released in 1961, received a Cannes Film Festival Award and was nominated for the year's best screenplay by the New York Film Critics.

In 1965, during the run of her second Broadway play, *The Sign in Sidney Brustein's Window,* Miss Hansberry died of cancer. It was a severe blow to the theatrical community and as Howard Taubman wrote in *The New York Times:* "The loss of Lorraine Hansberry at the age of thirty-four is particularly poignant because her work hardly had begun and her potentiality for largeness of utterance in the theatre was great. . . . She brought a burning passion and a mature, sensitive viewpoint to a theatre where they are in short supply."

Since her death in 1965, her stature has continued to grow as more and more of her work is brought before the public. *To Be Young, Gifted and Black,* a dramatic portrait of the playwright culled from her writings, was a major success of the 1969 Off-Broadway season where it ran for 380 performances. It also has been recorded, filmed for national television, published in expanded book form, and has toured an unprecedented forty states and two hundred colleges.

In November, 1970, her drama, *Les Blancs,* with the text prepared for production by Robert Nemiroff (whom she married in 1953), opened at the Longacre Theatre, New York. A dramatically penetrating exploration of the making of a black revolutionary, it lasted for only forty performances yet many considered it to be Miss Hansberry's best and most significant play.

What Use Are Flowers?, in its present form, originally was published in 1972 in *Les Blancs: The Collected Last Plays of Lorraine Hansberry,* edited by Robert Nemiroff. In his critical background to the play, he includes a portion of a letter written by Miss Hansberry wherein she referred to a work *in draft* ". . . which treats of an old hermit who comes out of the forest after we have all gone and blown up the world, and comes upon a group of children. . . . The action of the play hangs upon his effort to impart to them his knowledge of the remnants of civilization which once . . . he had renounced. . . . He does not entirely succeed and we are left at the end, hopefully, with some appreciation of the fact of the cumulative processes which created modern man and his greatness and how we ought not go around blowing it up."

Characters:

AN ELDERLY AND SCHOLARLY HERMIT
A PARTY OF CHILDREN OF ABOUT NINE OR TEN YEARS OLD

Scene:

A vast rocky plain at the edge of a great forest.

Scene One

A plain somewhere in the world; darkness and wind. The Hermit appears from left—an old and bearded man in the residue of manufactured garb and animal skin—he walks with a stick and carries his life's possessions in a bundle. He surveys the area as best he can in the half-light, shuffles to an outcropping of rock at right and crawls up into a crevice and goes to sleep. As he sleeps, the light comes up slowly and the Children appear, on their knees, in stark silence. They are stalking a small creature. The most arresting thing about them, aside from their appearance, which is that of naked beasts with very long hair, is their utter silence—for not one of them is beyond the age of ten. The old man sleeps on. The light is that of dawn.

Presently, the Children pause, as instinctively still as their quarry. One of them rises with a rock in hand and lets it fly; then, as one, the Children rise and run screaming to the animal which has been successfully stoned and violently fall to fighting over it. They really fight one another; there is nothing to suggest the mere games of children. And, moreover, those who are strongest triumph.

Among the more savage of the group is a little girl who is wiry and tough and skillful in the fighting. She achieves her share as do one or two of the others, while the remaining children glower and whimper like unfed puppies watching them consume the raw meat; those who are most frail or slow are also, noticeably, the thinnest.

At the sound of their noise, the old man is roused and sits up rubbing his mouth and his beard and his eyes. He shifts his position to see out the cave. He does this while the Children are still actively fighting. He cannot altogether make out what they are fighting about. That is, he cannot see that they eat it.

HERMIT: (*Dryly but loudly*) Well, I see you haven't changed, to say the least. *Animals!* Down unto the fourth and fifth generation of you, that's what. (*Grumbling*) Well, what did I expect? What, indeed, did I expect?

(*The Children freeze in astonishment at the sound of his voice. He feels gingerly about for a foothold, shifting bundle and stick, and starts down from the rocks—which were easier ascended, even in the dark, than descended at his age.*

At the first move, one of the boys stoops, apprehensively, for a rock. The others are taut—ready for flight)

HERMIT: Why the devil don't you give an elderly gentleman assistance? I see that your manners haven't changed either. Well, no matter. The only thing you ever did with manners was hide your greater crimes. How very, very significant, how significant indeed, that the very first thing I should see upon my return is the sight of little hooligans abusing a creature of nature! With the blessings of your elders, I am sure, I am sure! (*He halts and gestures for assistance to the closest youngster*) You— I am talking to *you,* my little open-mouthed friend! (*The Children merely continue to stare. He shakes his stick*) Ah, you don't like that, do you! (*He gives a surprisingly sprightly jump, for his years, and clears the incline neatly—but then totters a second for balance*) There we are! What do you think of that! (*Breathing heavily from the exertion*)

And now if you undisciplined little monsters will be kind enough to give me directions to the city, I shall make myself absent from your admirable company. (*They stare*) You there—

with the eyeballs! Which way to the city? (*Holding the courtesy deliberately*) *Please.* I should like with your cooperation to reach some outpost of, if you will forgive the reference, "civilization" by nightfall. What is the nearest town? I no longer recall these points, apparently, and have got myself utterly lost. (*The Children stand fixed*) Do you hear? (*He takes a half-step towards one, who immediately draws back*) What you need, my little zombie, is a well-placed and repetitive touch of the cane! But I suppose that anything as admirable as that is still forbidden?

(*Looking around at all of them*) Well, close your mouths and go away, little uglies, if you won't be helpful. I am sure your doting parents are anxious for you—for some ungodly reason. Why are you all got up like that anyway? Is it Halloween? Dear Lord, don't tell me I've come back just in time for *that!* Well, I wonder then if you might interrupt your mute joke long enough to tell an old man just one thing. If only I might persuade you quite what it would mean to me. You see, I should very much like to know . . . (*Deep pause*) . . . what *time* it is. You think that's silly, don't you? Yes, I rather thought you would. That a chap might go off and hide himself in the woods for twenty years and then come out and ask, "What time is it?" (*He laughs*) But, you see, one of the reasons I left is because I could no longer stand the dominion of time in the lives of men, and the things that they do with it and to it and, indeed, that they let it do to them. And so, to escape time, I threw my watch away. I even made a ceremony of it. I was on a train over a bridge, and I held it out the door and dropped it. Quite like . . . (*He gestures, remembering*) . . . this.

But do you know the very first thing I absolutely had a compulsion to know once I got into the forest? I wanted to know what time it was. Clearly I had no appointments to keep—but I *longed* to know the hour of the day! There is, of course, no such thing as an hour; it is merely something that men have labeled so, but I longed to have that label at my command again. I never did achieve that. Ultimately I gave up seconds, minutes and hours, too. Ah, but I kept up with days! I made a rock calendar at once. It was a problem too. The wild animals would knock over the rocks. Finally, I gave up and made a game—a game, ha!—of keeping up with the days in my head. It got to be a matter of rejoicing that the seasons came when I knew they would.

(*Looking down*) Or, at least, that's how it was for the first fifteen years. Because, naturally, I lost track. I accumulated a backlog of slipped days which, apparently, ran into months because one year, quite suddenly, it began to snow when I expected the trees to bud. Somewhere I had mislaid a warm autumn for a chilly spring. I almost died that year; I had lost a season.

(*Boastfully, for his new-found audience*) Consequently, among other things, I expect that I must be the first adult you have ever met who did not know his age. I was fifty-eight when I went into the woods. And now I am either seventy-eight or perhaps more than eighty years old. That is why I have come out of the woods. I am afraid men invent time*pieces*, they do not invent time. We may give time its dimensions and meaning; we may make it worthless or important or absurd or crucial. But ultimately I am afraid it has a value of its own. It is time for me to die. And I have come out to see what men have been doing. And now that I am back, more than anything else just now, you see, I should very much like to know what time it is. (*The Children stare*)

Ahh . . . (*Stiffening and shaking his finger at them*) But you must not for one second take that to mean that I *regret* my hermitage or do in any wise whatsoever return repentant to the society of men. I return in contempt! (*More quietly*) And, if one must tell everything—*curiosity*. Not love! Not once, not once in all those years did I *long* for human company. Not once!

(*He flicks his fingers at them in sweeping gesture, settles himself on the ground and spreads a small cloth*) Get along, then; go ahead, shoo! I am going to have my breakfast and I prefer privacy.

(*He first looks to the setting-out of his food and then up again to see them still standing, apparently transfixed*) I am quite serious about it and will become stern with you any moment now! The diversion is *over!* Toddle along to your . . . (*Nastily*) . . . mummies and daddies. (*They do not move*) Do you *not* understand the language merely because it is literately spoken? I don't wonder—recalling the level of study. Shall I employ sign signals? (*Gesturing impromptu hand signals*) *Go a—way! Andale! Scram!* (*They do not move, and he is angry*)

All right. But you might as well know that you do not frighten me. I shall eat my breakfast and be content whether you stay or go. And when you recover your tongues, I will accept your directions. I must confess I do not remember this plain at all. I could have sworn that the forest continued for many miles more. But then my memory has to cover a long span of time. You little folk are the very first human souls that I have seen in twenty-odd years. Well, what do you think of that! (*He points to the woods, roaring proudly*) I've been in there, in the forest, for twenty-odd years! Deep, deep in the forest. I am a hermit! (*Showing off, stroking his beard*) What do you think of that? Just like in books!

(*To another child*) What is your name? You look like a pupil of mine. But, I suppose he would be a little older by now. I am Charles Lewis Lawson. Professor Charles Lewis Lawson. I was an English teacher.

(*He lifts out a handful of food from his bundle—begins to place it on his cloth. As swiftly the Children throw themselves upon him and the scraps of food. In the scramble he is knocked over. Those who get some wolf it down, and the old man gets himself aright in time to see one of them gulp down the last morsel. He reaches out tentatively to the child as if, in outrage, to recover it, but the child gnashes his teeth—like a cur. Others pick up his bundle and empty it and paw about in the articles in a cruelly savage search for more food. The old man turns from one to the other frantically*)

HERMIT: *Animals! Animals!* I'm an old man! Don't you

know anything! (*The Children fall back a short distance and now lounge about, still watching him*) Oh, all that I have missed, all that I have undoubtedly missed . . . (*Bitterly*) in the society of men!

(*He gathers up his things angrily*) Well, why don't you laugh? Go ahead. Go ahead. Go ahead! It is a great game to beat up an old man and take his food from him, is it not? (*In a curious rage about it*) I can see nothing at all has changed. Damn you! And damn your fathers! (*He sinks down and pouts rather like a child himself*) Why did I come out? Why, why, why?

(*The Children sit and watch him and do not move. Then, presently*) Well, are you all still with me? You must be looking for your grandfather. Or Santa Claus. Well, I am neither!

(*He gathers up his things and stamps off right; the Children sink down where they are and freeze as the lights come down—and then up again. The old man comes on from left, having gone in a circle on the plain. The Children are stretched out where he left them, asleep. They rouse*)

HERMIT: Oh, there you are. I was hoping I would find you again. Certainly haven't been able to find anyone else. Just this interminable plain. Now, look here: I must have directions to the city. You must end this little joke of yours and talk to me. I will admit it; I am impressed that you can hold your tongues so long. Well, I will have to stay with you until you tire of it. Or, until your parents come. (*He is mopping his brow and smiling at them. They look back at him and say nothing. He looks at each one separately*) Listen, I happen to know that you are not mute, because I heard you screaming before.

(*He neatly arranges a pile of dry twigs, dead leaves, and begins to twirl a flint. He works hard at it and, presently, as the first thin stream of smoke arises, the Children silently lean forward, fascinated*)

HERMIT: Pretty neat, eh? You get good at it if you stay in the forest long enough. I will tell you the truth though. There was not one time that I ever made a fire like this when I did not fancy myself an Indian scout on television. My word, television! I suppose the images walk right into the living room by now and have supper with you. (*Dryly*) Oh, all that I have undoubtedly missed! (*Fixing the nearest boy with an exaggerated glare*) Don't think that's funny, eh? What dry parents you must have! The lot of you. Speaking of your parents, where the devil are they? To tell you the truth, I was rather hoping that they might give me a lift. Ah, there we are. (*He gives a good hard rub at this point, and a small lick of flame rises. The largest of the boys jumps to his feet and shouts*)

BOY: *Varoom!* (*And simultaneously the Children hit the dirt, face down, and try to bury their heads under their arms. The old man looks up from the fire*)

HERMIT: "Bang, bang!" I gotcha! Rat-tat-tat-tat! (*He wields a "submachine gun." One of the littler ones raises his head*) You there, step here, since you are the least dead of the cowboys. I need a bellows and you will do nicely. (*The child does not move*) Now listen—come here. *Kommen sie hier! Venga!* . . . Well, I don't know Yiddish.

(*With total exasperation, he goes back to the fire, fixes a string of wild fowl he has caught on a skewer across the flames and then sits back comfortably to wait.*

The little bit of meat sends up its bouquet; the child sniffs and goes closer. The others lift their heads slowly. It is an unfamiliar smell. Then, like beasts of prey, they stealthily shift to stalking positions and start to close in on the old man—who mugs back at them, draws his "six-shooters" and stares them down as in a game)

HERMIT: Once upon a time there were seven little ugly, unwashed, uncombed and unmannered little childlren—

(*The Children throw themselves on his birds and tear them to pieces and devour them raw, precisely as they did his lunch the day before. The old man rises, horrified, his eyes wide, looking from child to child*)

HERMIT: Why, you're not playing! You *are* wild! (*He regards them for a long time and then reaches out abruptly and pulls one of them to him*) Are you lost children? What has happened to you?

(*He inspects the child's elbows and kneecaps, which are hard calluses*) Dear God! Calluses. You really don't understand a word I am saying, do you? (*Experimentally, but swiftly, expecting nothing*) "Mother." "Mutter." "Madre." "Mater." "Mama." "Bambino." (*He is looking closely at the child and smoothing the hair back from the face so that he can see the eyes for any sign of recognition. The others look on guardedly. The youngster is motionless in his hands*) No, words don't mean a thing to you, do they? Dear, dear God. What have I found? (*With desperate hope that he is wrong*) Here—(*He pulls out a pocket knife*)—lad, What's this? (*The boy looks but does not touch. The old man opens and flips it into the earth; then retrieves it and lays it flat on his palm. The boy clutches for it*) No, not blade first, lad! (*Closing and pocketing it, he sits back on his heels, stunned, looking around at them*)

You eat raw meat, don't know fire and are unfamiliar with the simplest implement of civilization. And you are prelingual. (*He stands up slowly, as if to consult the universe about his impending sense of what has happened*) What have they done? (*Slowly turning about; his voice rising in its own eccentric hysteria, crossing down center to the audience*) What have you finally done! (*In a rage, screaming*) What have you done!

Blackout

Scene Two

Many weeks later. Several rather serviceable lean-tos have been fashioned, and at far right a tiny garden is crudely fenced off. The Children, who have been combed the least bit, so that it is hardly discernible, sit cross-legged in a semicircle; the Master, in the stance of his old profession, stands in front of them.

HERMIT: Before we go any further at all, I must distribute names. I can do that, you see, because in this present situation I am God! And you must have names. Ah, you are wondering "Why?" Well, it is because it will keep you from having to remember who you *really* are as you get older. Let's see, quickly now, you are hereby: John, Thomas, Clarence, Robert, Horace, William. You may be Charlie, and you are henceforth Alexander. (*To Alexander*) But may I caution you at the outset to avoid all temptations toward any adjective to follow it. (*Indicating the little girl*) And you—you shall be Lily. (*Gruffly*) Now, down the list. (*He holds up items or gestures actions. First he picks up a piece of meat*)

CHILDREN: Food.

(*The Hermit holds up the knife*)

CHILDREN: Knife.

(*The Hermit holds up a crude earthenware pot*)

CHILDREN: Pot.

(*The Hermit gestures with his cheek on his hands, eyes closed*)

CHILDREN: Sleep.

(*The Hermit gestures*)

CHILDREN: Drink.

(*The Hermit gestures*)

CHILDREN: Lift.

(*The Hermit gestures*)

CHILDREN: Eat.

(*He has not had such a good time for twenty-odd years —though of course, if asked, he'd deny it.*

He speaks fluently to them regardless of their only understanding a handful of words. When he wishes them to do or understand something explicitly, he speaks slowly and with abundant gesture)

HERMIT: Very good. So much for today's academic lessons. Time now for the vocational section. And all I can say is that primitive though my knowledge of technical skills may be, you had better be bloody grateful that I have at least some! In my world, certain men prided themselves on *not* knowing the things I am attempting to teach you! So, I shall do the best I can, do you hear me? (*Under his breath*) And when you learn to understand what the deuce I am talking about most of the time, you will also understand that you have just had a profound apology for ignorance, disguised as a boast. I was indeed a true member of the tribe! (*Loudly*) Now let me see . . . "Ceramics." (*To himself*) If only we had a manual. Does one bake the clay before or after it's dry? There is a point at which the clay must be put into a kiln? Kiln? (*He clears his throat and looks up*) Yes, well, in any event—remember yesterday we gathered clay at the riverbank? (*Holding up a handful of clay*) Repeat it: "Clay."

CHILDREN: Clay!

HERMIT: Very good. Clay. And I did this to it—(*Holds up the clay pot*)

CHILDREN: Clay! (*He points again to the pot for a further answer*) Pot!

HERMIT: And we sat in the sun. "Sun." (*He points overhead*)

CHILDREN: Sun!

HERMIT: And now, see, it is hard. And now it is possible for one to carry not only one object—but several. Now this process is called . . . (*He makes as if he is fashioning the pot again*) "Work." Say it.

CHILDREN: Work!

HERMIT: And with "clay" and "work," you can make all you need of these. So that you can "use" it. "Use" it . . . "use." . . . (*The class is puzzled. He demonstrates by putting objects into the pot and taking them out*) Well, this, I will admit, is something of an abstract concept, but it is a vital one and you will have to master it quickly. "Use" . . . "use." . . .

(*The Children are silent; it is too abstract. And he goes through it again. Then, with great excitement as Charlie raises his hand*)

HERMIT: You *got* it, Charlie? Good boy! Come and show me what to "use" something means. (*The youngster gets up, picks up the pot and puts things in it*) Good . . . good . . . (*Charlie carries them back to where he sat and takes them out and looks at the teacher for his approval*) Capital! (*Pleased, Charlie puts them back in the pot and hands it back to the teacher*) Very good, Charlie! (*To the class*) Charlie has "used" the pot. (*He takes out his knife and whittles a twig*) I am "using" the knife. (*With a sense of urgency*) It is such a vital verb, you *must* master it. (*A beat*) Well, on with the weaving. (*He sits down, crosses his legs contentedly and picks up, as do the Children, the beginnings of the baskets they are making*) Cross one over, bring the other through, then. . . .

Dimout

Scene Three

As the lights come up this time: stone implements, baskets and hoes as well as drying meats are in evidence. The Master and the Children come on far right; they are rather more frolicsome than we would have supposed they could be. And, for the first time, Lily is the only one with long hair. The boys have been barbered and are dressed in foliage or animal skins now.

HERMIT: (*Pausing at the garden*) By heaven, those are most attractive radishes, Thomas. Very good! Come along now, time for class. (*The Children moan*) How quickly you learn! Come along, or you'll get a caning. (*They obey and take the *positions of the prior scene*) Well, now, you've made such—(*He considers them doubtfully*)—admirable progress that I think you are ready to graduate to an area of knowledge which, sadly enough, used to be known as "the humanities." And, in that connection, Charlie and I have prepared a surprise for you. A "surprise" is something that you do not know is coming and, in life, most "surprises" are quite unpleasant. But every now and then, there are those which are pleasant indeed, and they generally have to do with another abstraction which you do not know how to call by name but which you have already experienced—(*Touching one of them*)—by your nose, your eyes, and way, deep inside you. It is called: "beauty." Say it.

CHILDREN: (*Shouting, out of habit*) Beauty!

HERMIT: My word, you needn't shout it! Beauty is just as well acknowledged softly as loudly. Say it like this, so the word itself is beautiful. (*Sweetly, lifting his head back and gesturing*) "Beau-ty."

CHILDREN: (*In dead-earnest mimicry*) Beau-ty.

HERMIT: Again.

CHILDREN: *Beau-ty.*

HERMIT: Lovely. You see, your very voices have this abstraction in them. Now—(*He picks up the pot*)—here is our dear and useful friend the pot again.

CHILDREN: Pot!

HERMIT: Which, as we have learned, *works* for us, when we have worked to make it. Now, we have also learned that we can "use" it to carry all sorts of things: the berries we have picked; the water we wish to carry somewhere . . . but also—(*He lifts up a little bouquet of wildflowers*)—we may use it simply to hold that which we "enjoy" because—(*He puts the flowers into the pot*)—they have "beauty." Like these flowers, which are almost as beautiful as our little Lily, which is why we have named her after them. (*Lily promptly preens herself before the boys. William raises his hand*) William?

WILLIAM: (*Loudly*) Use?

HERMIT: What *use* are flowers?! (*A bit thrown*) Well, there were, in the old days, certain perfectly tasteless individuals who insisted on making wine out of them. But that was not a use—it was a violation! Ah, but the uses of flowers are infinite! One may smell them—(*He inhales deeply, then holds them out to the Children, who inhale deeply in imitation*) One may touch their petals and feel heaven—(*He touches them*) Or one may write quite charming verses about them—(*Abruptly, to head them off*)—now, do not ask me what verses are! When you have become proficient in language, I'm afraid no power on earth will be able to stop you from composing them! All right, now on to the surprise. I think that it will be perhaps the most satisfying thing I shall ever be able to teach you. (*He turns upstage, draws himself up, makes several false starts and finally, turning back, begins to sing—horribly*)

Alas, my lo-ove, you do me wro-ong—
> (*The Children giggle at the curious sound. He hesitates with embarrassment, but continues*)

To cast me out discourteously
When I have lo-oved you so lo-ong
Deli-ighting i-in your company.
> (*They giggle again, but he presses on and at last they hush and listen, caught in the phenomenon of the human voice lifted in song. He sings crudely but sweetly, gaining confidence*)

Greensleeves was my deli-ight
And Greensleeves was all my joy
Greensleeves was my song of so-ongs
And who but my La-ay-dy Greensleeves.
> (*He is momentarily overcome with the realization that such notes may never in fact be heard on this earth again. Then, recovering*)

Well, that—loosely speaking—is what is called a "melody." It belongs—well, properly sung, it belongs to a great body of pleasure which is called "music."

CHILDREN: Music.

HERMIT: (*He nods*) However, melodies do not necessarily need to be sung. Sometimes they can provide as much beauty when . . . ah, but that is Charlie's surprise. Charlie. (*He beckons to the boy, who hesitates. Reassuringly*) Come along, lad.

(*Charlie steps forward, as nervous as a performer has ever been and reveals a reed instrument which is a crude but competent flute. He lifts it to his lips and haltingly plays the first stanza of "Greensleeves." The Children's faces reflect the miracle. As Charlie begins the chorus, the Hermit stops him*)

HERMIT: That was lovely, Charlie. Lovely. Now—(*To the Children*)—*you* try it with us. (*He sings the melody to Charlie's accompaniment and conducts, expecting the Children to join in. They do not. Undaunted*) Come on, children, sing! Sing! (*He begins once more, louder and more urgently, as if by sheer force of will to sweep them along. There is no response and at last he stops. Helplessly*) Try . . . (*Silence. He turns away in defeat. Suddenly one takes up the song, then another, and another, and finally all—tentatively at first, then with growing conviction as the Master conducts, quite carried away, exultant*) Good . . . good! Yes, yes . . . keep to the tempo now! Good . . . good . . . (*Suddenly peering forward as Lily raises her hand*) Yes, Lily?

LILY: Use?

HERMIT: *Use? What use is music?* (*At a loss for words, he gropes*) Well, there are many uses . . . there are different kinds of uses . . . Yes, well—(*Decisively: an order*)—You just sing! (*As the voices rise to their fullest, he grins*) Tomorrow—Beethoven's *Ninth!*

Blackout

Scene Four

In the darkness, Charlie's primitive flute begins, very slowly and haltingly, the first measures of Beethoven's

*Ninth, the Choral; and presently, over it, we hear the
Hermit's voice.*

HERMIT: Yes, Charlie . . . there! I told you you could
do it! You're playing Beethoven, boy! Beethoven!

(*The notes become firmer, more controlled, as if we are
experiencing the learning process in microcosm, until
finally they are rendered almost perfectly in the temper of
the Hymn to Joy as we know it, the tempo addressed to
the spirit of man: martial, certain, aspirational*)

HERMIT: He couldn't *hear*, you know? But that didn't stop
him! We'll *do* it, Charlie! You will teach the others the melody
and I shall teach them the words! Well, that is—as soon as I
can recall them well enough to translate from the German—I
simply have no strength left for the declensions!

(*As the lights come up, Schiller's flash of ecstasy is
shouted out by the old man, and the Children's voices
burst forth. They are arranged in that stiff self-conscious
grouping which is the style and posture of all choruses—
except that Lily is beating time to Charlie's accompaniment on a great drum of clay, while the others add
flourishes of their own on improvised instruments. They
sing with pride and vigor—and what we should be forced
to thrillingly feel is childhood's assumption of the in-
evitability of the statement. And through it all the Master
stands facing upstage, waving his hands in accurate tempo
and lacking only flowing black robes*)

HERMIT: (*Shouting*) Joy, thou source of light immortal!

CHILDREN: Joy, thou source of light immortal!

HERMIT: Daughter of Elysium!

CHILDREN: Daughter of Elysium!

ALL: Touched with fire, to the portal
Of thy radiant shrine we come.
Thy pure magic frees all others
Held in Custom's rigid rings;

Men throughout the world are brothers
In the haven of thy wings . . .

HERMIT: Bravo, children. Bravo! (*He bows to them and they, formally, to him*) As the poet Emerson said to Walt Whitman upon the publication of *Leaves of Grass,* "I greet you at the start of a great career!"

(*The group disperses and various ones settle down to different onstage activities*)

HERMIT: Uh, Charlie. I should very much like to talk with you (*The Master ushers Charlie into his lean-to with oddly deliberate social mannerisms all of a sudden*) Have a seat, won't you? (*This lean-to is not, of course, what man or child can stand up in fully, and the "seats" are well-placed flat rocks*) Would you care for some water? (*The boy signifies "no" with his head and looks at the Master curiously. Hermit shoves a mug of water at him*) No, you must say "Yes," Charlie. (*Passing some grapes*) Because we are not pupil and Master just now. We are friends and (*Settling down on one rock after forcing Charlie to sit on another and to accept the water and grapes*) . . . what we are doing now . . . (*Taking a grape himself and smacking over it elaborately*) . . . is *socializing.* And, you see, since this is *my* home, it is my obligation to make you feel welcome and even to entertain you and give you refreshments. And, under the last codes that I recall, it was more graceful to accept than not. Though I will admit such rules frequently reversed themselves.

CHARLIE: How . . . you?

HERMIT: Socialize? Exactly like this. We sit and we look at one another and eventually begin to tell one another perfectly outlandish stories, you see. It was a kind of ritual. But I shall have to teach you quite what a joke is. The last one I recall—well—oh, yes, Why does a chicken cross the road? That is to say, Why does the wild guinea hen that we eat, you know, why does it run across the path? You are supposed to say, "I don't know, sir."

CHARLIE: Why?

HERMIT: Because if you don't say that, I shan't have an altogether logical reason to give you the answer, and it was the answers, I gather, which were purportedly the point of these quite extraordinary exercises of the human mind.

CHARLIE: (*Stiffly*) I-don't-know-sir.

HERMIT: Well, a chicken crosses the road to get to the other side. (*They stare at one another*) Now you do this, lad. (*Holding his stomach like jolly old St. Nick in order to instruct*) "Ho, ho, ho, ho!"

CHARLIE: (*Frowning mightily and imitating with exactitude*) Ho, ho, ho, ho!

HERMIT: Show your teeth rather more, I think. And throw back your head. Yes, very good. That will do. (*Looking down at his hands with sudden seriousness*) Look here, there's another reason for our little get-together this afternoon. And it has to do with something fairly serious. And this really is the proper setting, because what we are having here is a sort of cocktail party, you see, which is where most really important matters were generally decided. Under circumstances quite like this—I mean with people chatting amicably and drinking things. Be that as it may. I want to try to discuss something rather serious and rather difficult with you—and, well, the fact of the matter is that I don't really, to tell the absolute truth, know how to go about it. (*Blurting suddenly*) Not that I didn't know one hell of a lot about women myself, you see! But, with the young, we traditionally preferred to make an awkward process out of it. And I don't seem to know how to reverse the custom. (*The child simply stares at him*) What I am trying to say is: do you know why I did not cut *Lily's* hair? (*As quickly realizing the futility of that approach*) Oh, no, no! Listen, let us approach it this way: you are a leader, Charlie, and there are some things which . . . you poor fellow, I shall have to hope that you take responsibility for when I will have gone away.

CHARLIE: (*Jumping up*) Gone? Where?

HERMIT: (*Quietly*) That will have to be a different lesson one day soon. But, we still have time and for the moment this

other matter is more imperative—so that when I do go away
. . . What it has to do with is . . . (*Looking at the boy with
serious eyes*) . . . the survival of . . . (*His lips fall with the
weight of the impossibility of trying to suggest to a ten-year-old
that the perpetuation of the human race could possibly be his
responsibility.*

> *Throughout the prior scene the following has been oc-
> curring outside at right: of two boys making pottery, one
> has proven more an artist that the other, and thus the
> first has simply reached out and claimed one or two of
> the other's pots, and the other fellow has retaliated by
> yanking them back, for which he is socked—which now
> launches a grim, stark and savage fight with one bashing
> the other's head until it is red with blood and the other
> as passionately trying to choke all life out of the first. It
> is the fight of savages who mean to maim or destroy.*
>
> *As they tussle, they crash a lean-to here and some pots
> there. As it is not yet spectacle or sport in their society,
> the Children do not pay the fighters the least bit of at-
> tention, but merely move out of the way when they roll
> their way and go on with whatever they are doing.*
>
> *Hearing a crash finally, the Hermit looks out to see
> what is happening*)

HERMIT: (*Seeing and screaming at them*) Animals! (*He
runs to them and tries to tear them apart; they snarl and tear at him
viciously in their eagerness to get at one another again*) Animals, I
say! Will you never change! (*Now he is also being covered with
the blood of one of them as he is flung about trying to tear
them apart*) Even in your wretchedness—are you still at it!?
(*One of them flings him to the ground. Charlie is about to come
to his rescue but hesitates and stands back frozen*) Go ahead!
Destroy yourselves! You do not deserve to survive! You *do not
deserve to survive!* (*The fighting Children do not hear him but
continue tearing away at each other. The others simply stare
at the screaming old man with a quizzical expression on their
faces. Getting up almost in delirium, rolling and slipping and*

*falling in trying to get on his feet) Forget everything I have
taught you! (He rises and stamps on the pots, violently tears
baskets to pieces as the boys fight on) I renounce you again—
you and your passions and all your seed! May you perish forever from this earth!*

    *(He staggers with sudden pain and goes reeling off toward
the woods. The fight continues)*

Blackout

Scene Five

*A few hours later. Blue lights at rise. The Children sit in
a stiffly arranged group at right. With apprehension. The
old man is flat upon his back in his lean-to; one hand
is on his stomach, another trails to the floor.*

    *Each child hands Charlie a flower, and he crosses from
them to the lean-to of the Master. The old man says nothing. The child holds out the bouquet.*

CHARLIE: *(Tentatively, expecting rebuff)* Flowers.
HERMIT: If you got hungry enough you'd kill me and
eat me. Go away, Charlie. I've had enough.
CHARLIE: Music.
HERMIT: I do not want flowers, music or poetry.
CHARLIE: Beethoven.
HERMIT: No, not even Beethoven. You want to know
why, don't you? Well, because I hate you. You are human,
therefore you are repulsive! All of you. But *you* in particular!
(Charlie looks at him curiously but does not move) Now, *that*
is what is known as an insult and, in the face of them, people
generally go away.

CHARLIE: I don't like insults then.

HERMIT: Which only proves that you are an even more common type than I had supposed. Go away, Charlie, I have decided to die and I prefer to die alone, after all. Ah, you still don't know what *that* is, do you? Well, *you just stand there and watch!*

(*He turns his face gruffly away and Charlie, with the flowers, comes closer and peers down at him intently as if a lesson, like all others, is to be rendered pronto. The old man turns to see the earnest face above his own and shouts* "Get out of here!" *Primitive or not, Charlie is hurt by the tone and starts to back out as a hurt child must*)

HERMIT: (*Relenting*) Charlie . . . (*The boy halts; but the old man does not look directly at him*) When it does happen . . . (*Slowly, seriously*) . . . and it will be soon now—not tonight, but soon enough—I will get cold and stiff and still and it will seem strange to you that I ever moved at all. It will seem then, boy, that I was a miracle, but it will happen. Because I am old and sick and worn out . . . (*A hoarse rasp*) . . . and mortal. But what you have to know is this: when it happens you will all stand for a long time with your mouths hanging open with wonder. That's all right, boy, it's an awesome thing. It is in the nature of men to take life for granted; only the *absence* of life will seem to you the miracle, the greatest miracle—and by the time you understand that it should be the other way around—well, it will be too late; it won't matter then.

CHARLIE: (*Smiling*) Hen cross road.

HERMIT: (*Smiling the least bit in return*) No, it really isn't a joke. Some men, in my time, spent whole lifetimes writing books trying to prove that it was. But it isn't. The thing that you have to know is when mine is over, and I have grown stiff and quiet for a while, I shall begin to exude a horrid odor, and what you must all do is dig the deepest hole that you possibly can and put me in it. It doesn't matter which way and I don't have to be wrapped in anything. I shall be glad enough to merge, atom for atom, with the earth again. And that is all there is to it.

(*Charlie looks at him quizzically, mystified*) Ah, you are wondering, how will I get out? I won't! I will stay there for-ever. For always. For eternity. (*Shouting irritably*) Well, you've seen other things die! The birds, the fish we eat. They don't come back, do they? The wood we burn, it doesn't come back! Nothing comes back!

(*Looking at Charlie's puzzled eyes*) You are thinking that I am not a bird or a fish or a piece of wood. All right—I am not! (*Raising up on his elbow, screaming feverishly*) *Well, I cannot solve the question of immortality for you, Charlie!* (*Sinking back again, exhausted*) And you don't like that, do you? Thy name is man and thou art the greatest arrogance in the universe. Well . . . (*He shrugs. Gently*) . . . put a stone over my head when you have buried me and come and spend hours there pretending to have dialogues with me and you will feel better. It won't mean a thing to me, but you will feel better.

(*Then, more softly*) The truth of it is that you really are going to miss me, Charlie. All of you. You will discover an abstraction that we never got to because there wasn't time. Affection. And, for some of you, something worse than that even, something more curious, more mysterious, that I shouldn't have been able to explain if there had been time. Some of you— *you* for instance, because we have been closest—will feel it; it will make you feel as if you are being wrenched apart. It is called grief and it is born of love. That's what I was really trying to tell you about this morning, Charlie. Love. But, you see, it wasn't a very respectable sort of business in my time; as a matter of fact we tried any number of ways to get rid of it altogether.

CHARLIE: What use?

HERMIT: *Use,* boy? How to *use* love? Well, we never found that out either. Mostly it got in the way of important things. And, for all I know, they did get rid of it altogether.

(*Sitting up again with great determination*)

Now, look here, Charlie! Do you . . . do you like Lily? (*Charlie shrugs*) Well, you will. Agh! The problem is that you *all* will. You can't imagine how glad I am that I shall be out of here before all of that confusion erupts! But that's beside the point, the point is . . . . (*Once again lost in the Victorianism of his world*) Well, listen, let's put it this way, boy: you've got to take rather good care of Lily. What I mean is if there should be a time when . . . when there just isn't enough food for all of you . . . well, Charlie, you've got to see to it that Lily isn't the one who goes without. It mustn't ever be Lily as long as there are three of you. Yes, I know I taught you to share; but you can't have permanent rules about things. The only rules that count are those which will let the race . . . (*He halts once again; weighs this thought and its persistence and decides afresh*) . . . let the race continue.

> (*Charlie leans forward intently and, as if pushed by a compulsion to get through to the boy, the older man strains forward in turn. In its matching intensity, the child's pose takes on a startling resemblance to the old man's*)

HERMIT: I'm avoiding a good part of the thing about Lily, Charlie. Mainly because I can't help myself. I promised myself that I would tell you only the truth. Only the truth is so damned. . . . Well, let's have a go at it this way: (*Slowly*) Lily is different, you see. That is to say that someday perhaps, when one of you is feeling . . . well, as I am feeling now—that is to say, sick—Lily is the one who will make it tolerable by bringing you an extraordinary cup of tea and looking at you in a way that will be different from the way the others . . . *hang it, this is impossible!* (*He turns away in a fury at his own inability to deal honestly with the moment. Charlie stands and waits attentively*)

The truth is, Charlie, you are right: the thing I saw in your eyes before when I was explaining death. I am nothing more and nothing less than a bundle of mortality, an old package of passions and prejudices, of frightful fears and evasions and reasonings and a conscience. And deep in my heart I long for immortality as much as you do already without even understanding it. We all did—and cursed one another for it! And renounced one another for it! That is why I went into the woods, you see.

I was outraged with mankind because it was as imperfect, as garrulous, as cruel as I.

(*Turning and looking at him*) But tell me something, Charlie, I've puzzled out a lot about you. I know that you were prelingual when I found you; you must have been perhaps five or less when . . . it happened—as you seem to be about nine or ten now. Can't really tell; with your diet you might be much older. But let us suppose you are ten. The thing is, it seems strange to me that you've not seen human death before. I assumed at first that there had been more of you, some who died around you. But you don't know human death. Why were there so few of you? (*Raising up and enunciating carefully as when he really means to be understood*) How did you get here?

(*Charlie begins a narrative in flowing articulate gesture*) Yes, Charlie . . . (*Studying a gesture which sweeps from one place to another*) Why, you were brought here! Yes, go on . . . (*As a stone rolls, so did that vehicle*) . . . in a thing that moved! Yes, yes! (*Great blades of grass grew here on that day; high like this*) Yes, there were many trees then! I understand, boy, go on! (*The outline of the human figure*) You were brought here by one like you—(*No. Charlie points to the Hermit*) Like me! (*Charlie nods, then shakes his head. The Hermit peers at him. Charlie points to him again*) Like me? (*Charlie nods and shakes his head. The Hermit is confused. The boy picks up a flower: the lily*). Ah, by one like Lily, only big! A woman. Yes, yes, go on! (*Charlie smiles and goes to him and reenacts the only kiss of his memory*) She kissed each of you . . . (*The sweeping gesture from one place to another*) . . . and went away. And then . . . and then? (*A circle of the arms collapses*). "The sun fell down." Yes, I see, I see. Of course. A woman brought you here to the perimeter of danger and then went back. A nursery school teacher or counselor or—some great woman had tried to guarantee the human race and then went back for more! She *chose* to go back . . . . (*Throwing his head back in anguish*) Dear God! What a strange tribe they were! Lunatics and heroes all.

CHARLIE: *Heroes?*

HERMIT: A hero was a fool. No—come here, Charlie. (*He draws the boy to him*) How ashamed we were of our heroes always. That one, like Lily, who brought you here, she was like the song I taught you. Do not ever be ashamed of what you feel when you think of her.

(*Lying back in obvious weakness*) Listen, Charlie, I've not tried to weigh you down with a lot of moral teachings; for one thing there hasn't been time. And so much of what I would have tried to tell you about all of that would have been absurd and obstructive, and you will get into your own habits in time about that. But look here, fellow, about that woman—well, for reasons that we never did agree on, the vast majority of human-kind over the centuries became committed to the notion that . . . that this particular unpremeditated, experiment of the cosmos which was the human race—well, that it *ought* to go on. It was a defiant notion, and only something as fine, as arrogant as man could have dreamed it up. Only man could have dreamed of triumph over this reckless universe. But the truth is, we didn't quite know *how*. In the beginning, you see, we had such a little to work with and we never quite believed our poets when they told us that, in the main, we were doing the best we could. We demanded more of ourselves than that; for above all else, boy, man was valiant. Really— (*An admission*) quite splendid, you know. Ah, the things he perceived! You will be like them: heroes all of you, merely to *get on* as long as you do.

(*Thomas enters with a thing: a crude wheel with little clay scoops attached to its spokes*)

HERMIT: Hello, Thomas . . . Now, what is that, boy? (*Thomas brings it and puts it on the old man's stomach*) Well, it's fetching, child, but what is it? Look, Charlie, Thomas has made something. Now the question is, what has Thomas made?

(*He turns the thing about, utterly confounded. Thomas races out and then back again and, mutely, pours water from a pot into the topmost scoop so that its weight forces the wheel to turn and scoop up more water*)

HERMIT: Yes . . . yes! (*Drawing Thomas to him*) I understand, boy. You have found the wheel as simply as this! Creation, what ignites this flame! (*Smoothing Thomas's hair about his face with adulation*) I should have christened thee "Leonardo," Thomas!

(*In a rage of jealousy Charlie seizes the invention and hurls it out of the lean-to. Thomas's instinctive move to seize him in return is arrested by the realization that Charlie is stronger. The Hermit shakes his head in distress*)

HERMIT: Ah, Charlie, Charlie! You can't understand, can you, that it is something for all of you? Thomas saw a problem and invented something to solve it. It's all right to be jealous, in fact it's a fine thing; it means that you have placed value on something, and that is fine. But you must *use* your jealousy, Charlie. You must help Thomas to build another wheel, a bigger wheel, and then you won't have to waste all that time carrying water and can do something else, sit around and sing if you like, or make up new tunes on your flute—in the time that you used to spend carrying water before Thomas invented the wheel. Of all things you must learn, this is the most difficult and that from which you most will profit. (*Charlie's face continues ugly with resentment. Thomas retreats cautiously backwards and turns, when a safe few feet away, to dart towards his invention*)

But the truth is, I don't think you will learn it. The truth is, children, that I don't think you will survive at all. I have been indulging myself, no more. Engaging in a timeless vanity of man. Pretending with you that it would be possible. Pretending that *you* wild little things could conceivably raise great Egypt and China again, claim the equations of Copernicus and Newton—ha! the perceptions of Shakespeare and Einstein! Pretending that I could hand to you the residue—badly learned and hardly retained—of five thousand years of glory . . . (*Turning gruffly away*) . . . on which I turned my back with all the petulance of our kind! (*Turning back and shouting*) Why, you don't even know what steam will do yet! We didn't even get to steam!

(*Crying out to Thomas*) Steam, Thomas! A force that would make your wheel turn with revolutions undreamed of in your primitive soul! Mere simple heated water! You don't know it. (*Outside, the children, drawn by the excitement, come one after the other to observe Thomas and his wheel*)

That foolish, foolish woman! That silly sentimental female! Why did she leave you here to torment me in my last absurd hours! It's all finished with you, the lot of you! Our little adventure among the stars is over! *Finis!* The brief and stupid episode will end now! The universe will have peace now! (*He falls back, spent. Charlie stands and holds out the lily. The old man lifts his head*) Use . . . What *use?* Charlie, the uses of flowers were infinite.

(*He lies still. Charlie gently places the flower by his face and after a moment crosses out to join the children who, unaware that the old man has left them, are now clustered intently about the wreck of the wheel which Thomas, squatting in the dirt, is patiently reconstructing*)

Curtain

Michael Weller

TIRA TELLS EVERYTHING THERE IS TO KNOW ABOUT HERSELF

Michael Weller

Michael Weller sprang to prominence in February, 1972, when his play *Moonchildren* opened at the Royale Theatre, New York. It was an occasion that evoked considerable praise for both play and author. Clive Barnes of *The New York Times* called it "the best new American play of the past three or four seasons . . . a phenomenal, virtuoso display of wit and verbal imagination," while Henry Hewes reported in the *Saturday Review* that it "established Weller as a discerning and talented playwright."

Set in a student commune, the play began its circuitous route to Broadway in 1970 when it opened (under the title, *Cancer*) at the Royal Court Theatre in London. In 1971, the play underwent a change of title and as *Moonchildren* was performed at the Arena Stage, Washington, D.C. Prompted by its reception there, the presentation was brought to New York and although it stirred controversy as well as praise its engagement was brief. Nonetheless, *Moonchildren* was chosen as one of the ten best plays of the year and Mr. Weller won a Drama Desk citation as one of the season's most promising playwrights.

The author was born in New York in 1942 and was graduated from Brandeis University in 1965. He has had four short plays produced at the Open Space Theatre, London, one of these being *Tira Tells Everything There Is To Know About Herself,* which appears in an anthology for the first time in *The Best Short Plays 1973.*

In his production notes for the acting edition of the play, Mr. Weller has written:

"All the male roles are played by a single actor.

The style of each scene is exaggerated. As indicated, each of the men is a grotesque. Each should have one very marked mannerism.

In her monologues, Tira is herself. In her encounters she gradually acquires qualities complimentary to those of her suitors. She plays roles. But her roles aren't rigid, aren't fixed. For brief instants where the line or the moment feels that way she lapses into Tira.

The piece is, in part, a stylistic exercise. When the tone, pace and style of each scene evolves, play into the the eye of it."

Mr. Weller, who now lives in London, recently completed a new play, *The Greatest Little Show on Earth,* dealing with the assassination of President Kennedy and which was commissioned by the Royal Court Theatre.

Characters:

TIRA
EDWARD
POOF
LUCIO
BRUTE
TIB

Scene:

*Bare stage. One long seat in the centre. Tira sits, knitting.
She drops a stitch. Counts. Corrects the error. Then she
notices the audience.*

TIRA: Oh. Hello. Tira. My name. That's my name. Tira.
Capital *tee*, small *eye*, small *are*, small *ae*. That's that bit done.
I'm going to tell you something. Well, in fact I'm going to tell
you everything there is to know about myself. (*She smiles to her-
self.*) Ho-hum. I'm waiting for Edward. Edward's my lover.
(*She sighs*) He's so bloody boring. I'm not complaining. In fact,
I love him very much. A good deal more than I'd love not
having him. If you see what I mean. (*Pause*) You do. (*Pause*)
Good. I call him Pickles. He hates it, which is probably—by and
large and taking the long view—a good thing. I think.
   (*Edward is on. He is a blimpish grotesque*)
TED: Tira, my love, have I kept you waiting long?
TIRA: No, darling, I only just arrived ...
TED: Good.
TIRA: Twenty-one years ago.
TED: (*Oblivious*) ... Well, here I am.
TIRA: Yes. (*They embrace. They kiss*) Are we safe?
TED: Yes. Quite safe. She doesn't suspect a thing. Not a
thing, poor creature.
TIRA: Good.
TED: Ah, Tira. Tira, my dove, my dear one, my little

colt, whenever we meet like this I'm always so profoundly moved.

TIRA: Oh, then you must be tired. Do sit.

TED: Sit. Yes. Yes. Oh, Tira.

TIRA: Oh, Edward.

(*They embrace. They kiss. They sit. Edward looks skywards*)

TED: Nasty weather, eh?

TIRA: Mmmnnnn.

TED: Yes, she's sitting home, poor wretched thing that she is.

TIRA: Good for her.

TED: Tell me, my Guinevere, how've you been?

TIRA: No change.

TED: What an odd thing to say.

TIRA: I'm exactly as I was the last time we met. And the time before. And the time before that. No mysterious encounters. No aches. No visions. No pregnancies, no abortions, no amputations. (*Edward is uneasy. Then he chuckles*)

TED: You devil.

TIRA: (*Flat*) Pickles. (*Edward jumps*) Did I say something?

TED: No. No. It's nothing.

TIRA: Please sit. You must be ever so. . . .

TED: (*Sitting*) Yes, it was hell at the office today.

TIRA: Poor Edward. They abuse you.

TED: You have no idea.

TIRA: But I do, darling. Truly, I understand.

TED: No, no, you see today was no ordinary day. Everything blew up in my face. Had an argument with Prebble . . .

TIRA: The fool.

TED: Said I was inaccurate.

TIRA: Inaccurate indeed.

TED: The bloody fool. He resents my game of squash.

TIRA: That's what it comes down to.

TED: Bad cess to him.

TIRA: Yes.

BOTH: Quite.

TED: Do you mind if I pick my nose?

TIRA: Please do.

TED: D'you know, when I was a lad in school—I've never told you this one before—there was a pimply young chappie sat directly in front of me in geography, and one day, during a lunch break, I sneaked in and did a piddle in his inkwell.

TIRA: You didn't!

TED: Yes, yes, as a matter of fact I did.

TIRA: You must have been quite a lad.

TED: Oh, I have hidden dimensions here and there.

TIRA: You rascal.

TED: It bubbles up *de temps en temps* as they say.

TIRA: Do you mind if we walk?

TED: Not at all. Why not? After all, why not? (*They walk*) Ah, the night.

TIRA: Pardon?

TED: It's ravishing. Absolutely ravishing.

TIRA: It is?

TED: Glaringly so.

TIRA: How do you mean, Edward?

TED: It simply is, Tira. It's one of those things either one recognizes or one doesn't. The darkness, for instance. Take the darkness. It's very dark indeed, like, perhaps like a . . . a . . . a very dark object, for example a black object—licorice or fresh Tarmac . . . metaphorically speaking. And then there are the stars. Very beautiful. The moon is full, reflecting the rays of the sun on to the earth below and illuminating those portions of the landscape most exposed in an upward aspect, especially rooftops.

TIRA: *Yes,* Edward, I think I see how the night is ravishing.

TED: It's odd. You know, I keep thinking of her, alone in front of the telly.

TIRA: Guess what, Pickles. (*Edward jumps*)

TED: (*Burning rage*) What?

TIRA: You bore me silly.

TED: What? I . . . I . . . .

TIRA: . . . bore me.

TED: You can't possibly mean that.

TIRA: No, I don't suppose I do.

TED: Then why on earth did you say it?

TIRA: Passing time, I suppose.

TED: Of all the things to say. My God, for one horrible moment, for one detestable instant I thought . . . heaven forbid. I know I'm not riveting twenty-four hours a day. It's not possible. Life isn't like that. The mind . . .

TIRA: . . . grows weary, yes, I know. Do you know what I like best about you?

TED: (*Calmer*) My fond caresses?

TIRA: Your Samurai war dance.

TED: My what?

TIRA: Your dance. Your Japanese war dance.

TED: You're not yourself this evening, Tira.

TIRA: Don't be afraid of me. Admit it. Every night it's in your dreams. You, standing alone on a windswept plain with your long black hair tied in a knob at the top, splitting rice stalks down the middle with your razor-edged sword.

TED: (*Stunned*) Yes. Yes. Oh, my God, how did you know?

TIRA: Dance for me, Edward.

TED: What, right here? Right now?

TIRA: Yes. Yes.

TED: But. . . .

TIRA: No one's looking. We're alone. Just you and me.

TED: You won't laugh?

TIRA: I promise. I swear on everything that's sacred between us.

(*Edward dances. Awkward but with growing intensity. Tira laughs*)

TED: (*Stopping*) You promised. You swore.

TIRA: Oh, Edward, I do love you.

(*Edward resists her blandishments*)

TED: Stay away. You laughed at my dance.

TIRA: But I loved it, Edward. Don't you understand? I love your dance. I love you *for* your dance.

TED: That dance means the world to me. That dance is life itself.

TIRA: I'm sorry, Pickles. Truly I am. (*Edward has jumped*) Oh, no, I didn't mean that. Edward, my darling. My love. I'm sorry. I'm very sorry. (*Edward is calmer*)

TED: And to think, I had a present for you.

TIRA: A present?

TED: Yes.

TIRA: For me?

TED: Yes.

TIRA: But I don't need a present.

TED: You see, nothing I do is right.

TIRA: I'm sorry. What is it?

TED: You'll have to guess.

TIRA: I don't feel in the mood for games, Edward.

TED: My games. Oh, no, you don't want to play my games, but *your* games, well, that's different, isn't it?

TIRA: A fire engine.

TED: What?

TIRA: You've bought me a shiny new fire engine with bells.

TED: Tira, my love, please be serious. Ask for clues.

TIRA: Does what you've bought me go ding-ding-ding and put out fires?

(*Edward rises*)

TED: Very well. It's obvious. I'm no longer wanted.

TIRA: No, no, please, don't go. I didn't mean it. I'll concentrate. See. I'm serious. (*Pause*) How in the world am I supposed to guess?

TED: Just think of something you've told me you always wanted.

TIRA: But you're what I always wanted—sort of.

TED: Concentrate.

TIRA: (*Concentrating*) What? Have? I? Always? Wanted? (*A pause*)

TED: Have you guessed yet? First thing that comes into your head. You can have several guesses if you'd like. There needn't be a limit. Go on, try, have a guess. Tira. Tira? Time's up, Tira, open your eyes. Look, I'll show you. I say, are you there? Look. Look here. (*He reaches into his pocket. He looks startled. Tira's eyes are still closed and she's concentrating*) That's odd. I'm sure I brought it from the office. Damn. Must have left it at home. Ah, well, never mind, some other time, my dove. Oh, no. Good heavens, no. I left it on the telly. She's sure to find it. She's so unstable she's liable to . . . stay right here, Tira, don't move. I'll be back. One hour. No more. Tira.

(*Tira is still in her trance. Edward rushes off. Tira blinks*)

TIRA: (*Thickly*) I don't know what I always . . . Edward? Gone? He left? Yes, that's right, you saw, didn't you? Oh well, easy come, easy go. (*She weeps very briefly, then controls it*) I'm sorry. Sorry. I won't do that again. It's just that I was thinking. I know exactly what I don't want. But I don't know exactly what I do want. I'd like the future to be different. Better. I don't want what went before. "Tomorrow is the first day of the rest of our lives." Where does that come from? *Woman's Weekly,* probably. Yes, page eleven. Right-hand column, about halfway down. Those things matter a great deal. No, I suppose they don't. You know, sometimes I think I'm a bit indecisive. But sometimes I think I'm quite. . . .

(*Poof is on. He's a faggot grotesque. Tira sees him*)

POOF: Yoo-hoo.

TIRA: What do you want?

POOF: Do you mind if I flit over and perch for a bit? I'm called Poof.

TIRA: I'd never have guessed.

POOF: Mnn, bitchy, bitchy. Who and/or what was that scrumptuous great turkey I just saw rolling off?

TIRA: None of your business.

POOF: Well, that's me in my place.

TIRA: Are you going to sit down and talk to me?

POOF: Oh, ta, don't mind if I do. (*Sits*) You seem rather nice, in a depressing kind of way.

TIRA: Thank you.

POOF: I mean, you know, for a woman.

TIRA: I suppose I remind you of your mother?

POOF: Isn't that just a little antique, ducky? Nothing on this desperate earth reminds me of my mother, thank Alfred. Feed a gorilla whole, unshelled peanuts for a week, suspend him upside down by his toes and thrash his belly with a lead pipe and the mucky-doo that came oozing out of his nostrils would only just barely remind me of my mother, and then only sometimes. No, you've got Freud to thank for me, daughter, thank Freud. Didn't see any of us around before him, did you?

TIRA: I wasn't looking then.

POOF: God was queer, did you know? Mnn, Alfred told me. He knows about those things. He's a religious queen. Choirboys and such. Will your friend be coming back or am I sniffing up the wrong lamppost?

TIRA: I don't think he'll come back.

POOF: What a shame.

TIRA: Yes, isn't it?

POOF: Did he ever kiss you? I don't mean to be pornographic, but did he ever . . . you know. . . .

TIRA: In his way, yes.

POOF: Yeeech. Not that you aren't attractive, but . . . (*Shudder*) What did you say your name was?

TIRA: Tira.

POOF: *Tres* un-i-kew. What does it mean?

TIRA: I don't know. Just Tira, I suppose.

POOF: Oh, but it has to *mean* something. Names always mean something. Take mine. Poof. Self-evident. Or Po Ling Ch'en, which means:

Mountain stream.

Trees bend.

Frog jump. Gronk.

That's a haiku. Just Tira?

TIRA: I'm afraid so.

POOF: Now if you had said "Alfred," I could have told you quite a story. Yeeech, it's obscene, you and him sucking on each other's digestive system.

TIRA: Filthy.

POOF: Frightening, yes. You don't seem to mind.

TIRA: Mind what?

POOF: Well, daughter, in case you hadn't noticed, I'm a few feet off the ground. Raving.

TIRA: That's your business.

POOF: Tsk, tsk, tsk, tough, tough.

TIRA: (*Laughing*) No, of course I don't mind.

POOF: You're nice, Tira.

TIRA: For a woman.

POOF: Of course. Well, here we are, just sitting, chatting away, Tira and Twinkletoes. Woo-hoo, if my friends could see me now, well, I mean, they'd hoot me off the railway arches. Can I tell you a secret?

TIRA: Tell me a secret.

POOF: Well, sometimes, late at night, and it only happens when I'm alone, you understand, I'm suddenly overcome by an absolutely oceanic surge of masculinity. Isn't that a hoot? Me, I mean, I feel like stomping down the street in me mountain climbing woollies and me leather chaps and raping the first bitch I see. If, you know, she were a boy. What are you laughing at?

TIRA: You. I think you're funny.

POOF: Sometimes. Sometimes I'm quite sad. Pathetic, in fact. Do you feel any better?

TIRA: Yes. (*Pause*) Yes, in fact I do. Much. Thank you.

POOF: Do you think I'm at all masculine?

TIRA: I don't know. What am I supposed to say?

POOF: I was given all the standard apparatus. I mean, really, all I'm doing is ignoring the instructions that came with it . . . them. I could fancy being a bit more butch. I think. Be good for a giggle anyway. Are my eyelashes crooked?

TIRA: Perfect.

POOF: Thank Alfred. Small mercies. Tell me something, Tira. If right now you were sitting with a full-scale, three-dimensional, Technicolor hetero, what would he do?

TIRA: Depends on the hetero.

POOF: Don't be difficult, ducky, I'm trying to come on. What do they do? What on earth do they say?

TIRA: "Tira, I love you, and I don't use the words lightly. You are . . ." Then they tell me all sorts of silly things I am that neither of us believes. (*Pause*) It passes time, I suppose. "And I've never desired anyone as I desire you. Come, I know a lovely little spot where we can . . . just the two of us . . . etc., etc. . . . come to bed, you were magnificent, Tira, you've changed, my darling, somehow you're not as exciting as I remember you, I must be doing dreadful things to you, I'll never forget you as long as I live, what's-your-name."

POOF: I don't believe it. I mean, don't you ever giggle? If Alfred ever said anything like that to me I'd pee myself, absolutely.

TIRA: Why? What does Alfred say?

POOF: Alfredo is crude.

TIRA: What does he say? Go on, tell me.

POOF: "Put it on the table, Bubbles, and we'll carve it up for supper."

TIRA: Well, it's direct.

POOF: Tira, you are remorselessly beautiful, for a woman. Well, I mean, that's what they say, isn't it? You said so yourself. Yours is the burning beauty of a polished emerald in moonlight. Oh, Alfred help me, do they really say that?

TIRA: Close your eyes and put out your hands.

POOF: Game?

TIRA: Um-hmn.

POOF: Oh, goodie, I adore games. (*Poof, eyes closed, hands out. Tira rips off his false eyelashes*) What are you doing? You giddy bitch, you nasty old cow, give them back. (*Tira steps back*)

TIRA: Never.

POOF: I'm naked. Me poor little eyelids. What are you looking at?

TIRA: You. You'd make a rotten man.

POOF: Pissy missus. Hag. Witch. I could take off me street slap. Put on me West Side Story walk. I'll have you know I've been mistaken for Clint Eastwood on numerous occasions.

TIRA: You could've fooled me.

POOF: I happen to do an extremely effective imitation of the fabulous Clint.

TIRA: Well, go on.

POOF: Oh, yes, lovely, lovely, I do me strut in spurs and you'll be on the floor with a female hernia.

TIRA: I'll try not to laugh.

POOF: Spit in the wind and slap your knee?

TIRA: No promises.

POOF: And you'll give me back me eyelashes?

TIRA: If I'm impressed.

POOF: Nnn, you're hard as nails, Tira.

TIRA: (*Sing-song*) We're waiting.

POOF: Don't crowd me. This takes concentration. Oh, hell, here goes nothing. (*He does the walk very well. As the fabulous Clint*) This town's as dead as stale bathwater.

TIRA: (*Drawl*) Where yuh from, stranger?

POOF: (*Queen*) Hey, that's good, that's very good.

TIRA: (*Tira*) Come on, don't stop. (*Drawl*) Where yuh from? (*Tira*) I asked you.

POOF: Oh. (*Clint*) Ah, some place where gals like you are a dime a dozen.

TIRA: Why, gents round these parts pay faahve bucks just to touch my ostrich feathers.

POOF: (*Raving*) Ostrich feathers?

TIRA: (*Tira*) Come on, serious.

POOF: (*Poof*) Very well. (*Serious. Pause. Corpses*) *Ostriches* in the Wild West? All right. Serious. (*Baffled*) What am I supposed to say now?

TIRA: You say "show me why."

POOF: (*Clint*) Show me why. (*Tira slinks into his arms*)
Hey, mind me juj. Look, this just has to be cheating.

TIRA: It's the game. Kiss. (*Poof pecks gingerly. Drawl*)
Ah ain't maide of toothpicks, hombre, ah won't break.

POOF: (*Poof*) I give in. You win. I'd make a rotten man.

TIRA: Go ahead. Kiss me. Hard. (*She pulls him. They
kiss. He reels away wiping his mouth. Drawl*) Hay-ow was they-
at?

POOF: Yech. All wet and smelly. (*Tira smiles, almost a
purr. Poof looks at his bulging crotch*) Oh, Alfred, it's hard.
You're ruining me! Actually, it sounds twisted, but I didn't altogether dislike it. I mean, it was pretty sickening but I can't say I
didn't get a trickle of satisfaction. I'm not burning with regret or
anything. I mean, I'm glad it's over. What am I saying? Forgive
me, Alfred. I feel like I've stepped into a whirlwind of hetero-
sexual debauchery.

TIRA: Now put your hand here. (*Breast*)

POOF: Aren't we getting a bit personal, dearie?

TIRA: I don't mind. I'd like you to.

POOF: Look, I'm only just starting to bend back. Too fast
and I'll snap. Why don't we sing songs for a while? I know, I'll
tell you all about Alfred. Wouldn't you like to hear about Alfred?

TIRA: You can't stop now, Poof. (*Tira pulls Poof down on
her. Poof is horrified. He screams*)

POOF: *No!* Leave me alone. Why'd you have to go and
ruin everything. Grabbing me brittle little forearm like that.
Could have snapped it right off. Why should I want to squeeze
your flabby old dugs, anyway!

TIRA: Calm down, Poof.

POOF: Calm down yourself. Oh . . . now I'm going to
puke!

TIRA: But I thought you. . . .

POOF: You have no idea, bitch-eyes, none. You're like all
the rest. One kiss and woof, mons veneris hurtling at you from
all directions.

TIRA: (*Quiet; sad*) No, Poof.

POOF: Oh, now we're feeling sorry for ourself, are we? Well, no thank you, mother-of-the-bogs. It may work with every other Tom, Dick and Ivan, but this little queenie-oo is wise to that spin. Don't do me any favors, sweetheart. (*Poof starts off*)

TIRA: Please stay. Please.

POOF: Oh, go suck your gums, Tira!

(*Poof leaves in a huff. Tira collects herself. Sits. Tries knitting. No good. She stifles one huge sob when it's half-way out*)

TIRA: Change the subject. I have a mole on the inside of my left thigh. Fascinating, that. I'm twenty-one. I live here. I didn't always. I used to live somewhere else in a kind of house with two older people. A man and a woman. My parents. I moved here precisely one year ago today on my twentieth birthday. (*Pause*) Yes. (*Smile*) That's right. (*Pause*) God, what a pack of lies. The thing is, I keep trying to think of something interesting to tell you about myself and . . . there's nothing, really. So I make up a good deal of it. All of it, in fact. It's like that riddle, "If a man from Chelmsford told you that all men from Chelmsford are liars and I'm from Chelmsford," how could you know if he was telling the truth? I probably got that all wrong. I know; I'll show you a trick. Magic. My grandfather taught me. No, actually I read it somewhere. *Woman's Weekly?* Watch. See my hands. Empty, right? Both empty. (*Tira makes some passes with her hands then opens them with a flourish. They are empty. She sits*) Question: Did the trick Tira just showed us fail, or was it meant to go like that? If it failed, please describe what was supposed to appear in her hands. If not, summarize briefly what she meant to communicate. Oh, I'm a veritable paradox, I am. (*Enter Lucio, an Italian lover-boy grotesque. He drives a sports car in mime, making the engine noise*) Here we go again.

(*Lucio spots Tira, jumps out of his car and approaches*)

LUCIO: No, don't tell me, let me guess. Claudia? No, Claudia had red hair, fire-red like a mad goddess. Janine, is it Janine?

TIRA: Try Tira.

LUCIO: No, no, don't tell me, no hints. No clues. San Remo? On the glorious crystal sands of San Remo? No? Istanbul, before the blinding white towers of the . . . no, Malta? Hong Kong?

TIRA: Wimpy Bar, Dagenham?

LUCIO: Count to twenty-five.

TIRA: Why should I?

LUCIO: No female of the species resists past twenty-five. (*Wink at audience*) Gretchen tried in Amsterdam, but a hot lick behind the ear and Gretchen is yours for life. Still she waits for me. Perhaps I shall visit her one day. My car. You like? She was made for me by Auguste Broglio-Montepetruccio in his Sisalpine metalworks. You come for a drive? Caro? Hübschen? Doucette. Babushka. Yes, I am talking, believe it or not, to you. Come, ma belle, ma cherie.

TIRA: Do you drive fast?

LUCIO: Like a hummingbird.

TIRA: I get carsick at high speeds. I toss up.

LUCIO: Like Stephanie, but she became accustomed. . . .

TIRA: I'm not Stephanie. (*Tira knits with concentration*)

LUCIO: No, surely, you are like no other woman on earth.

TIRA: I am exactly like every other woman on earth.

LUCIO: Yes, you are, how shall we say . . . intense.

TIRA: Hold this, please. It won't bite. (*Lucio takes the proffered ball of wool. He laughs*)

LUCIO: Enchanting. A dying art, yes? Maria loved me in mauve wool. I was fantastical in mauve for months with mauve Maria, mauve from head to foot in mauve wool beneath the sensual sunlight of the Cairo afternoons.

TIRA: Very well, go on. Tell me about Maria.

LUCIO: Ah, jealousy. No, my sweet, Maria is a thing of the past. She was once, and now she is gone. You only wish to know if she was the woman that you most evidently seem to be. I know the heart of a woman.

TIRA: Then tell me about me.

LUCIO: Ah, you. . . .

TIRA: Touch me.

LUCIO: You are like the raven at midnight.

TIRA: Touch me.

LUCIO: The raven that trembles and quakes its midnight feathers at the knell of the church bells. Sometimes I write poetry, you see.

TIRA: Right. (*Shutting her eyes*) Tell me the color of my eyes.

LUCIO: Ah, yes, but what color are mine?

TIRA: Brown. Now mine?

LUCIO: Ah, your eyes. Yes. Perhaps brown, like mine, no?

TIRA: Hazel.

LUCIO: Brown like the cocoa bean in the Columbian twilight.

TIRA: Hazel.

LUCIO: What?

TIRA: My eyes are hazel.

LUCIO: Yes, hazel, the hazel of Imperial Chinese jade.

TIRA: Just plain old hazel.

LUCIO: Yes, life is so like this. The bodies shimmer forever in the cinema house of memory, but the faces are ever out of focus. I am not happy. No! I am a man not of common discontents, but of immense, profound sorrows.

TIRA: Well, get you.

LUCIO: You strike me as, how you say, very commonplace.

TIRA: Can't take it, huh?

LUCIO: You laugh, yes. Outside, the face is grave, but inside you are full of mirth at my suffering, yes? The pain inside my soul amuses you.

TIRA: Oh, go on, take me.

LUCIO: I want to tell you that I had sex for the first time when I was seven years of age. She was thirty-four. Two of her sons were older than me. Is this the experience of a happy man?

TIRA: Take me away from here.

LUCIO: But, of course. And where shall we go?

TIRA: You choose, I don't care. China, Iceland, Java.

LUCIO: Ravenna. Yes, to Ravenna. Ah, the Ravenna of sweet Maria!

TIRA: Oh, for God's sake, *do* something. (*Lucio touches her cheek with panache*)

LUCIO: There. Shall I tell you a secret?

TIRA: Yes, anything, anything at all.

LUCIO: I am a wonder in the bed.

TIRA: And modest with it.

LUCIO: The world is altogether too modest. I am blessed with a sensual nature. Can I help this? Show me a woman like the woman I see before me now . . . what did you say your name was?

TIRA: Alfred.

LUCIO: Yes, show me a woman like yourself, Alfred, and I burn inside to show you the secret of passion, wild passion, dizzying ecstasy beyond words, beyond thought, beyond conception. Ah, Alfred, your cheek is . . . you laugh openly? You find my passion amusing? I am droll, yes?

TIRA: No, no, please go on.

LUCIO: Trudy found me amusing. Ah, but such a temper!

TIRA: I can't resist. (*Tira starts undressing*) I mean, the number of women you must have had. I suppose I ought to be paying you for the privilege.

LUCIO: Excuse me, please. . . .

TIRA: Don't want to look a fool, do I? It's a swinging decade and all that. Go with the times. (*Tira stands half-naked before Lucio*) Don't tell me, you know the body but you can't place the face, right?

LUCIO: This is a game, yes?

TIRA: If it is, I'm winning. Take me. (*Tira starts to bump and grind seductively. She doesn't notice Lucio getting back into his sports car until he starts the engine and roars off. The noise of the engine catches her attention*) Lucio! Come back. Please. (*Pause*) I must be going mad. (*She is slightly hysterical, but she keeps it under control as she dresses. To audience, while dressing*) I'll bet you didn't know how that would turn out. I wanted that phony bastard. (*High drama*) I would have sacrificed my virginity for him—if I had any around to sacrifice. The first time I ever undressed in front of a man, I worried about my feet. I just kept praying he wouldn't look at my feet. (*Lucio drives on again and races across the stage*) Lucio, I'm pregnant. I'm going to have your bambino. (*Lucio drives off*) A friend of mine told me that works sometimes. She's had five abortions. She did marry, finally. Settled near where we grew up together. It's not the city, where I come from. It's not the countryside either. In fact, it's only just barely suburb, but it tries hard. I'm the last of three daughters. An accident. I'll grow tall. I'll marry. I'll move to something like a suburb and have three daughters. The last will be an accident. It could be pretty depressing if one didn't bear in mind that we all enjoy free will. It also helps to read those heartening letters in *Woman's Weekly*. "Dear Mary, I was born without a vagina and my husband is a sex fiend. Can you recommend an effective position?" I'm told I have a resilient personality. That's nice to know. (*While she has been talking, Brute has entered and sat himself on the block. He is big and filthy. He takes a mime sandwich out of a lunchpail, bites into it, spits out a mouthful and opens the sandwich, frowning at the contents. He takes the contents out, throws it on the ground and takes another bite. He decides he liked it better with the contents. He gathers the contents from the stage, wipes them off and replaces them in the sandwich. He takes another bite. At this point, Tira spots him. She goes down on all fours. To audience.*) Right. Wish me luck. (*Tira crawls to Brute, who has been vaguely listening to her monologue*) Hi.

BRUTE: You talk a load of shit, you know that?

TIRA: Yes, yes, I know.

(*Brute laughs. Tira laughs. Brute hands her the sandwich. She bites it and returns it. Brute pushes her away with his foot. Tira sprawls*) I'll bet you say that to all the girls.

BRUTE: Scram!

(*Tira returns on all fours. Brute starts to push her away with his foot, but stops when he sees that she enjoys it*)

TIRA: Go on. Again.

BRUTE: No deal.

TIRA: Please.

BRUTE: Uh-uh.

TIRA: Why not?

BRUTE: She wants it. Screwed up inside her head.

(*Brute laughs. Tira hits him. He kicks her. She sprawls. She returns*)

TIRA: Again.

BRUTE: No use hitting. I got your number. It don't work twice. Pervert. Everyone in the world is a goddamn pervert! (*Tira hits him again. He doesn't respond. She tries again. Still no reaction. Brute continues eating*) You know what I say to that? I say (*Exaggerated*), "It feels like there's a mosquito somewheres around here." (*Brute laughs. She hits him again*)

TIRA: Hit me. Hit me, damn you, hit me! (*Tira collapses in anger*)

BRUTE: You got a terrible smell.

TIRA: (*Smiling again*) Yes, yes, I know.

BRUTE: You ever try washing?

TIRA: It's no use. My stench is organic. Sticks to me like flypaper.

BRUTE: Sweat, huh?

TIRA: Yes, everywhere.

BRUTE: You proud? You proud of stinking like a. . . .

TIRA: I've tried everything. Talcs, scented soap, bath cubes, vaginal sprays, underarm deodorant, eau de Cologne . . .

(*Brute stomps on her hand as he speaks*)

BRUTE: Shaad ap. I don't wanna hear.

(*Tira withdraws her hand in pain, then replaces it*)

TIRA: Again.

BRUTE: Twisted kid. (*Tira breathes in Brute's face and laughs*) Shit, your breath is like a sewer.

TIRA: I know.

BRUTE: So, brush.

TIRA: It's no use. I've tried everything. Dental powd . . .

BRUTE: Shaad ap. (*Brute starts to stomp on her hand, but catches himself*) Very clever.

TIRA: Coward.

BRUTE: Sticks and stones, kid, sticks and stones.

(*Tira pulls up her dress and shows her leg to Brute*)

TIRA: Hairy, isn't it? It grows and grows and grows. All over my body. Want to see?

BRUTE: You gotta be so fucking crude?

TIRA: Yes.

BRUTE: (*Laughing*) You're ugly as hell, aren't you, girl?

TIRA: I'm an accident, you see. Can't help myself.

BRUTE: You're O.K. by me. You're cute.

TIRA: I am?

BRUTE: Shaad ap. I'm eating.

TIRA: I'm glad you think I'm cute.

BRUTE: What's so great about that?

TIRA: I don't know. Just is. I think you're cute.

(*Brute punches her. She sprawls, laughing. Brute curses himself*)

BRUTE: Goddamn you devious bitch.

TIRA: Hey, you're pretty ugly yourself, you know that? (*Tira pulls his hair*) Look at that. All stiff and wiry. Like a Brillo pad.

BRUTE: What do you know about Brillo?

TIRA: Plenty. Nothing. (*Grabbing his abdomen*) Fat. Fatty. Fatty-fatso. Blubber guts. Smelly, too. You smell. People who live in glass houses. . . .

BRUTE: (*Eating*) Go away, kid, you bother me.

TIRA: No. (*Brute spits a mouthful of the sandwich in her face. Tira picks off a piece and examines it*) Ham and cheese roll. (*She eats it*) With mustard.

(*Brute laughs. She sits on his lap, faces close. She pecks at his chewing mouth. He kisses her roughly. They roll on to the stage, in an embrace. Brute holds his sandwich out, trying to rescue it from ruin*)

BRUTE: Hey, my ham 'nd cheese. (*Tira shrieks with laughter*)

TIRA: With mustard! (*Brute, broody, sits back on the block and resumes his eating*) Oh me, oh my, what a lover! Such style! Such technique! Hey, blubber-guts, what else can you show me? Besides chewing, I mean.

BRUTE: I'm eating.

TIRA: You're a slob. (*Brute gulps and belches*) And a poet. Smashing. Terrific. What do you know that rhymes with belch, slob? Blubber-guts. (*Brute belches again*) Bravo. That's right. Uninspired, but spot on, spot on.

BRUTE: Hey, I'm getting mighty sick of you.

TIRA: They all do. Tell me something poetic, slob. Beautiful. (*She laughs*) Oh God. Well, he ain't much, but he's all mine.

BRUTE: I'm trying to eat.

TIRA: I know that.

BRUTE: Lay off, huh?

TIRA: No. I'm enjoying this.

BRUTE: Look, it ain't gonna work again.

TIRA: I'm Tira.

BRUTE: I'm eating. (*Brute roars with laughter. Tira slaps the sandwich from his hand*)

TIRA: (*Nasty*) I want poetry, slob.

BRUTE: You hit me in the sandwich! You got no right. Pick it up.

TIRA: Talk to me of daffodils.

BRUTE: Pick up my goddamn sandwich.

TIRA: Go on, hit me.

BRUTE: Jesus, you're nuts, kid.

TIRA: Take me.

(*Brute takes up the sandwich and grinds it in Tira's face. He then sits and polishes an apple from his lunchpail. Tira cleans her face*)

TIRA: Hey, I didn't like that. I didn't enjoy it. You know what I think, fatso? I think that deep down inside you there is a delicate soul longing to burst forth. (*Tira becomes a flower in growth*) Hey, look. Look at me.

BRUTE: What's that all about?

TIRA: Tell me what I am.

BRUTE: Hey, you better not be a witch. If you're doing like a witch, I wanna know, 'cause I don't go in for that.

TIRA: I'm being something. Tell me what I'm being. (*Pause*) I'm a flower growing. See? An Iris. I'm an Iris.

BRUTE: What?

TIRA: I'm being an Iris growing. Don't you think I look like an Iris? It's a flower. An Iris is a flower.

BRUTE: You're a flower, huh? (*Brute roars with laughter*)

TIRA: (*Angry*) O.K., fatty-fatso, let's see what you can do. (*Brute stands, strikes a pose and belches*) Bravo!

BRUTE: That was nice. I liked that. How'd you like being a flower? (*Brute laughs*)

TIRA: Oh clever. Clever-clever. Clever-Charlie. Clever-head. Smarty pants. (*Tira tickles him*)

BRUTE: Cut it out.

TIRA: I like it.

BRUTE: Stop doing that. It aggravates me. (*Brute throws Tira aside. She sprawls, laughing*) Goddamn it. Goddamn you. (*Brute cries*) Shit, tickling. Son of a bitch, I'm crying in front of a smelly pervert!

(*Brute starts packing his lunchpail. Tira stops and turns away from Brute. She looks at the audience as if she's afraid to turn and see what Brute is doing*)

TIRA: He isn't going away, is he? No, he's sneaking up behind me. He's sneaking up and he's going to put his hands over my eyes and say, "Guess who?" No, he's going. I didn't mean to make him go. I swear I didn't. (*Pause*) He's pissed off, isn't he? Pity, that. Those kind make the best husbands, according to *Woman's Weekly*. I mean, you always know where you are with them, don't you? (*Brute has gone. Tira examines the empty block*) Took his lunch. Just as well. I don't fancy mustard with ham and cheese. Goddamn it, what's wrong with me? They all go away. I just want to know, what's *wrong* with me? (*Pause*) Look, I'm sorry about all this. There's only one more bit to go. It's short. I wrote home once. I said, "Dear Mum. Dear Dad. Love Tira." It was a busy week, you see. Lots of news. Christ, have you ever seen such bloody self-pity? (*Enter Tib. He is lean and stringy. Shy. Broody. He sits on the block with his head between his legs*) Yes, that's right. There was this boy on the bus one day. He was just sitting there. Our eyes met. He didn't say a thing, but his eyes told the whole story. They said he'd been dreaming of a girl like me all his life and . . . and . . . (*Pause*) I warned you I read *Woman's Weekly.* (*Pause*) I'm not moving because if I do, he might go away. I might try talking to him, but I can't think of a thing to say, except, perhaps, please just let me stay with you and if I do say something, ignore it because everything I say is stupid and ignorant, like me, but I'd like you to like me and . . . and . . . (*Pause*) Oh, hell, I'll take a step. (*Tira takes one step towards Tib*) So far so good. He didn't move. I seem to be handling this with uncommon tact, don't you think? Try another. (*She takes another step*) Perhaps he doesn't know I'm here. It was the other end of the bus. I forgot to tell you. I only saw him get on. There were a lot of other people sitting between us. (*Pause*) Ahem. (*Pause*) Ahem. (*Tib looks up*) He's looking up. (*Tib looks back down*) The point is, he did look up. He did. He must have seen me. Yes, he saw me and he didn't go away. P.S. Dear Mum and Dad. He didn't go away. Ahem. May I? Hey? You? Ahem. May I? (*Tib looks up*) Please? (*Tib looks down*) He seems a bit shy. Perhaps he's a mute. I'm not complaining. A mute will do. Would do. If. Then again, I wouldn't complain if it turned out he could talk. Hey, I'm coming over, O.K.? Hey, is that all right? Here I come. Sneak-sneak. Hey? (*She tiptoes over*) May I sit next to you? I'm sitting. Yoo-hoo. Look at me. Sit-sit. (*She sits*) Here I am. Hey, can you talk? (*Tib rises*) Please don't go. Please stay. You're nice. I like you. Not too much. I mean, not yet. I'm trying not to be overbearing. I hope you appreciate that. (*Tib sits. To audience*) He likes me. (*To Tib*) Can you talk?

TIB: Yes.

TIRA: Thank God for that. My name's Tira. What's yours? Am I going too fast? Please talk to me. If you say something, I'll lick you behind the ears. Not sexually. I'm not sexually dominant. You don't fancy sexually dominant women, I can tell. You don't, do you? Do you? I mean, if you do, I am sexually dominant. But

I don't think you do. I'm doing most of the talking. This is looking like a very one-sided relationship. I'll give you a "thank-you-
for-talking-to-me" type lick. But wet. Move your hand. (*Tib
shakes his head "no"*) You wouldn't like a nice, moist, friendly
lick behind the ear? (*Tib starts to rise again*) No, stay. I'll be
quiet. Won't say a word. (*Tib sits. Long pause. Tira hums a bit,
eyeing Tib*) Gets pretty boring, doesn't it?

TIB: (*Long pause*) Please.

TIRA: (*Quickly*) Yes? What?

TIB: Lick.

TIRA: You want me to lick you?

TIB: Please.

TIRA: Sexually, or otherwise? (*Pause*) Not saying. Right.
Guess. (*Pause*) Otherwise. (*Tira starts to lick. She stops*) Look,
do something for me. Anything. Just something I can repay you
for. I can't give you an otherwise lick behind the ear if it isn't to
thank you for something you've done for me. Does that make
sense? Try moving your hand. (*Tib moves his hand to her face
and touches it*) Yes, very good. Like that. Now I can thank you.
(*Tira licks him behind the ear. He doesn't smile*) Was that nice?
Did you like that? (*Tib nods*) I like you. Very much. Please.
What's your name?

TIB: Tib.

TIRA: Weird name. Lovely, you know, but weird. It's
exotic.

TIB: So is Tira.

TIRA: You remembered. Yes. Two weird names. Just like
in the magazines. Are you frightened of me? No, you don't have
to answer that. I'm pushing.

TIB: (*Slowly*) Am I....

TIRA: What? Handsome? (*Tib nods*) Handsome, yes.
Talkative, no. Can't you think of a single thing to say?

TIB: What?

TIRA: I don't know. Anything that comes to mind.
Ramble.

TIB: I can't.

TIRA: Poor Tib. Poor Tib. Can't even ramble. (*Tib rises*)

No, I wasn't making fun, honestly. Please don't listen to what I say. Ignore me. Just be with me but ignore me. I know. I'll give you something, then you can thank me for it. Thanking is legitimate talk. I'll give you a strand of my hair. (*She pulls out a hair*) Damn. Here. (*Tib refuses it*) What's wrong with my hair? I hurt myself pulling it out. I'm making sacrifices.

TIB: It's dead. Hair is dead. Like fingernails and teeth.

TIRA: How about a cuticle?

TIB: That's dead.

TIRA: You're a vicious little fellow on the quiet. (*Tib starts to leave*) Blood! How about some blood? That has cells in it. Cells are alive. I can prick my finger.

TIB: All right. (*Sits*)

TIRA: Do you have a penknife?

TIB: No.

TIRA: Anything sharp? I can't prick myself without something sharp.

TIB: Use your teeth. Bite.

TIRA: That's masochism. (*Pause*) Yes, well, it's only blood, after all. Lucky thing my blood clots quickly. Wouldn't settle for a cuticle. Naturally not.

(*Tira bites herself, drawing blood. Tib watches*)

TIB: Bite hard with the incisors and the skin will separate enough to sever a small blood vessel and you'll get a nice, clean wound.

TIRA: That hurt, damn it.

TIB: I'm sorry.

TIRA: I'll bet you are. All right, my blood. Now what?

(*Tib licks the finger clean*)

TIB: Now we're like brother and sister.

TIRA: Oh, no, I've heard about that. You're supposed to mingle blood. Yours and mine. You'll have to cut yourself first, and you'd better do it quickly because I'm starting to clot and I'm buggered if I'm going to do it again.

TIB: I would, Tira, but I saw how much pain it caused you. The world is already too full of pain.

TIRA: A moralist, no less.

TIB: You may kiss me. You'll get some blood back mixed with my saliva.

TIRA: You're certainly talking a lot all of a sudden.

TIB: You don't have to kiss me.

TIRA: Oh hell, here I go. (*They kiss*)

TIB: How was that?

TIRA: It was all right.

TIB: I mean, how did I kiss?

TIRA: What am I supposed to say? It was fine. Just fine.

TIB: You know something?

TIRA: I know my finger hurts.

TIB: You kiss very nicely, too.

TIRA: Thank you, Tib. You're very sweet.

TIB: Almost as well as me.

TIRA: What?

TIB: It's a question of experience. You're still very young. But still, for your age, you kiss quite nicely.

TIRA: Hey, I thought you were all modest and shy?

TIB: I am, Tira, but I kiss fantastically well.

TIRA: Well, I mean, it was a fair kiss, certainly.

TIB: No, it was a kiss like no other you've ever tasted.

TIRA: It was all right. So-so. I enjoyed it. Nothing special, technically speaking.

TIB: Tira, I know Edward and Poof and Lucio and Brute and I know they don't kiss as I kiss. They're common. I know them.

TIRA: Look, if you're going to be like that, it was a bloody awful kiss. Awful. Any one of the others could have kissed you off the street. I made you kiss like that. It was probably the best kiss you ever kissed, come to that, and even so it wasn't all that hot, nothing to write home about. You couldn't tie your shoes without me! (*Tib rises to go*) No, no, I didn't mean it. I warned you not to listen to me. Yes, yes, of course it was the best kiss ever. Tib, I love you; please stay with me. I'll leave you alone. I'll ask nothing of you. I'll give and give and ask nothing in return. I'll cook and clean and scrub and wait for you every night and never ask where you've been or whom you've seen, I swear. Do what you will, I'm yours.

TIB: Can I beat you?

TIRA: Yes.

TIB: And lie about you to friends?

TIRA: Yes, yes.

TIB: And bring the others back home?

TIRA: Yes, oh yes.

TIB: And you'll cook for them and offer them your bed and bring up the children I have by them?

TIRA: My God, all this on that little bit of blood?

TIB: Will you?

TIRA: Yes.

TIB: Debase yourself before my eyes?

TIRA: Yes, yes, anything and everything, yes, now and for evermore.

TIB: No one with an ounce of self-respect would go near you. (*Tib spins on his heels and walks off*)

TIRA: Tib! (*Tira moans and sobs throughout this speech*) Yes, I know I know I know. I said I wouldn't. I'm trying very hard to stop. It's not easy. Keeps burbling up. Disgusting thing, tears. Mucks up the complexion. Causes pimples. (*She stops crying*) There. I think we've got it under control, at least on the outside. (*Pause. Thinks*) That's about all there is to it. I mean, if you see me on the street, say hello. "Hello, Tira, I know all about you." You don't, of course. It's my fault. Left school at fifteen. Never learned to express myself properly. There's just one more thing. I'm about to commit suicide. Hang on for a minute and you'll see it. I've thought it over. I mean, why should you have to listen to all this drivel about me if I just up and walk away? At least if I commit suicide you'll read about it in the papers and you'll be able to say: oh, terrible thing, such a pity, she had a hard time. (*She giggles to herself*) The trouble is . . . sorry, this is quite funny, you see. I'm going to commit suicide by holding my breath. Have you ever heard of that kind of attempt succeeding? I haven't. I'm sure it won't work. Poor people, having to watch all this. At least I get to do it. O.K. Ready? Tira, having told everything there is to know about herself, which is nothing, now commits suicide. (*Tira braces herself and holds her breath. A drum roll starts offstage. The man enters and stands behind Tira miming a drum and pretending to make the noise with his mouth*) Oh, yes, drums. Very dramatic. (*She holds her breath again. For an entire fifteen seconds she crumbles to the floor in slow motion while the man continues to play more and more frantically behind. With a final burst of the drum Tira dies. The man sprinkles flower petals or confetti over Tira and exits. Pause. Tira opens her eyes, feels herself and sits. To audience.*) Woops. Well, anyway, that's one thing about me. I'm consistent.

(*Tira freezes in the middle of an awkward gesture timed to capture her as if in a snapshot, at the moment she utters her last word*)

Blackout

Kendrew Lascelles

TIGERS

Kendrew Lascelles

Kendrew Lascelles was co-author and one of the leading players in the celebrated South African musical entertainment, *Wait a Minim!* which was seen in many parts of the world. The revue originated in 1962 at a small Johannesburg theatre, then for two years toured South Africa and Rhodesia in three editions before being presented at the Fortune Theatre in London. After an engagement there of two years, it opened in 1966 at the John Golden Theatre, New York, and played 456 performances. A subsequent tour took the company across the United States and later to Australia and New Zealand.

It was during his association with *Wait a Minim!* that Mr. Lascelles began to devote more and more time to writing. Since then, he has turned out a number of revue sketches, television scripts and plays; among the latter, *The Trophy Hunters,* set in the South African bush country, and which was published in *The Best Short Plays 1970.*

As for the earlier period of his life, the author has supplied the following biographical data: "Born in Gatley, Chester, England, on September 20, 1935. Immigrated to South Africa in 1938, though not from personal choice. Sporadic and incomplete education, having left school prematurely to take up ballet. Studied and performed for eight years, eventually becoming principal *danseur* for the first professional South African ballet company. Following three years of this, gradually turned to straight theatre through the channels of musicals and from there to comedy, including cabaret and films."

Tigers, published for the first time anywhere in this collection, originally was performed on national television during the winter of 1972. Mr. Lascelles portrayed Adam in the production and his performance, just as with his writing, created a subtle and impressive balance between the comic and the serious, illusion and disillusionment.

Characters:
ADAM
MRS.

Scene:
A drab flat. The essential furnishings are: a chest of drawers, a wardrobe, a double bed, a chair or two, a table. There is one entrance door.

The time is the present.

Mrs. is dressed in a bathrobe, stockings and high heel shoes. She is in the midst of packing a suitcase which is open on the bed. She removes a number of dresses from the wardrobe and lays them out on the bed to be packed.

Mrs. stops. Listens, moves to the door, opens it, listens, closes the door, returns the dresses to the wardrobe, closes the suitcase and places it out of sight under the bed.

Mrs. moves to the mirror and applies makeup to her face.

Adam enters with a folded whip. He wears riding boots, riding britches, a heavy sportscoat, a turtleneck pullover and a cap.

ADAM: Hello.
MRS.: Hello.
(Adam removes his sportscoat and cap and hangs them up on a peg behind the door. Silence)
ADAM: You're home early, then?
MRS.: That's just what I was going to say. (Pause)
ADAM: I didn't expect to find you home so early.
MRS.: No, I don't suppose you did. (Pause)
ADAM: Didn't you go, then?
MRS.: Yes, I went, but I left.
ADAM: Oh! Well, it's a bit cold today. It's been getting quite chilly.
MRS.: What are *you* doing back so early?

ADAM: Dunno. I just came back. (*Pause*) What made you leave?

MRS.:   Something happened. Something came over me. Quite suddenly. So I left.

ADAM: What was it?

MRS.:   Thoughts, mostly. Thoughts about things and the way everything is, and then this feeling came over me so I left.

ADAM: Oh.

MRS.:   I'm not going to go back there again, either.

ADAM: Oh?

MRS.:   No, I'm not. And I mean it.

ADAM: Oh! Well, that's good. That's a good decision. I'm proud of you. Well, if you really want to know the truth . . . I don't know how you stuck it out as long as you have done.

MRS.:   Well, it's been better than loneliness, hasn't it?

ADAM: What?

MRS.:   I said it's been better than loneliness.

ADAM: What loneliness?

MRS.:   Up here.

ADAM: What do you mean up here? You haven't been lonely.

MRS.:   Haven't I?

ADAM: I haven't left you alone.

MRS.:   That's not the sort of loneliness I'm talking about.

ADAM: Well, I'd like to know what sort you are talking about, then.

MRS.:   The sort I've had when you are here. (*Silence*) There, that's it exactly.

ADAM: That's what exactly?

MRS.:   What I mean. That silence. That's exactly what I mean. That's what it's been like most of the time.

ADAM: Well, we haven't had much of a chance to say anything.

MRS.:   No, we haven't, have we?

ADAM: No. Not with you down there day after day, week after week.

MRS.: That's why I've been down there day after day, love. That's why. I mean if I'm going to be lonely, if there's going to be loneliness and silence between us, I'd rather have a whole lot of loneliness and silence down there than up here with you. I mean, if I'm not going to say anything or if you're not going to say anything, I'd rather sit there next to his headstone than up here day after day. (*Pause*)

ADAM: How long have you been back, then?

MRS.: About an hour.

ADAM: Oh.

MRS.: Why? Why do you ask?

ADAM: I was just wondering about something, but if you've been back for an hour it doesn't matter.

MRS.: What is it?

ADAM: Nothing.

MRS.: Oh, come on.

ADAM: It's nothing really. Just a man.

MRS.: What man?

ADAM: Just a man sitting in a car downstairs outside the front door, but I don't suppose he would have been sitting there an hour ago so it's not important.

MRS.: He was.

ADAM: Oh. Was he?

MRS.: Yes, he was.

ADAM: Oh! So you saw him, then?

MRS.: Yes, now that you mention it, I did, yes.

ADAM: Do you know him?

MRS.: Why do you ask?

ADAM: I don't know. I just asked if you knew him.

MRS.: What makes you think I know him?

ADAM: I didn't say I thought you knew him. I just asked if you did.

MRS.: Why?

ADAM: Well, it's just that there was something familiar about him.

MRS.: Oh! Was there?

ADAM: Yes.

MRS.: Familiar in what way?

ADAM: I don't know. I didn't look very hard. Just a glance, but there was just something familiar about him. Perhaps it was just his hair.

MRS.: His hair?

ADAM: Yes.

MRS.: What about it?

ADAM: Well, you must have seen it if you saw him.

MRS.: I saw him all right.

ADAM: Well, he's a redhead.

MRS.: Yes. That's right.

ADAM: Well, he looked familiar to me.

MRS.: What? Because of his hair?

ADAM: Well, there's something about them. Something about redheads.

MRS.: What?

ADAM: I don't know properly. Perhaps it's just that one redhead reminds you of another or something. Perhaps it's just that seeing one redhead suddenly reminds you of all the redheads you ever met or something.

MRS.: Perhaps.

ADAM: Yes, perhaps it's that.

MRS.: Yes. Perhaps. (*Pause*)

ADAM: You haven't worn those for ages. Those shoes and stockings.

MRS.: No, I haven't, have I?

ADAM: No. Why the sudden change?

MRS.: I've decided I'm not going to wear anything black anymore.

ADAM: Well, that's another good decision. Have you just decided that?

MRS.: Yes.

ADAM: You decided quite a lot today, didn't you, Mrs.?

MRS.: Yes. Quite a lot, love. It was as if I saw everything quite clearly for the first time.

ADAM: What actually happened?

MRS.: I've told you.

ADAM: You haven't.

MRS.: I've told you all I want to tell you. (*Pause*)

ADAM: The funny thing is . . . I was thinking about things myself.

MRS.: What things?

ADAM: Oh, thing things.

MRS.: What thing things?

ADAM: Well, I was thinking about that night we went slushing along. Slushing along in those rain puddles that night. You know, that night we went slushing along through those rain puddles together and that drunk policeman came up.

MRS.: That was ages ago.

ADAM: Yes, I know, but I was thinking about it anyway. Just thinking about that and how it used to be. That's what I was thinking. How it used to be. I was thinking about that, and how it was when we still had Timmy with us as well. How it was when we used to go out together, like that time we took him to the playground. I did enjoy that. Just sitting there watching those children on the swings and things. We had some lovely times together. Didn't we? Mrs.?

MRS.: Yes. I suppose so.

ADAM: Like those nights for instance. Those nights we had together after you got that way. Pregnant. That's what I was thinking about. How you looked that night just slushing along through those puddles and how you looked with all those raindrops on your face.

MRS.: Well, that's all over and done with, isn't it? Water under the bridge.

ADAM: Well, I was just thinking about it, that's all.

MRS.: What are you smiling over?

ADAM: That policeman.

MRS.: He wasn't so funny.

ADAM: He had his eye on you.

MRS.: He didn't.

ADAM: He did, you know.

MRS.: I was all pregnant.

ADAM: He still had his eye on you.

MRS.: Well, I didn't notice.

ADAM: I did. There. That's nice.

MRS.: What?

ADAM: That smile.

MRS.: What smile?

ADAM: You were smiling.

MRS.: I was not.

ADAM: You were, you know.

MRS.: Well, perhaps I was. But I didn't feel it. (*Pause*)

ADAM: It's a good thing I went back that night, after the matinee. It's a good thing I went back like I did because she attacked me. (*Pause*) Ate attacked me that night. (*Pause*) I thought she was going to. That's why I went back straight away, you see. Because I knew she was going to do what she did. I knew she'd do it while she still had that taste in her. There and then while she still had it in her. That's why I went straight back and it turned out to be a good thing I did. (*Pause*) Do you want to hear about it? (*Pause*) I was going to tell you about it before, but things weren't sort of right, really. Not to talk about it at any rate. (*Pause*) Do you want to hear about it? Mrs.!

MRS.: Not really, no.

ADAM: Well, she attacked me whether you're interested or not. She did just what I expected her to do and fell right into my trap. (*Pause*)

MRS.: What trap?

ADAM: I set a trap for her. In the silence. You know, that silence after I make the announcement about the big bit?

MRS.: Yes.

ADAM: Well, I turned my back on her.

MRS.: That was a bit stupid, wasn't it?

ADAM: No. I told you. It was part of my trap. That was the trap, you see. Turning my back on her. In that silence. I did it then in the silence so I could concentrate better. Made the announcement and waited for the silence to settle the way it does, and then, just like I was being careless or something, I turned my back on her, and she came slinking down, slinking down the way she slinks, off her podium.

MRS.: And you knew that with your back turned?

ADAM: Yes.

MRS.: How?

ADAM: I sort of heard her.

MRS.: On the sawdust?

ADAM: Yes. I can sort of hear things like that. I heard her slinking down and then she started off for the back of my neck, like I thought she would.

MRS.: And what did you do? Turn and catch her at it?

ADAM: No. Not right away. I didn't turn right away. I wanted to give her a split second or two to get into a full sprint. To give her enough rope to hang herself with. I wanted her to think she'd already got me in her jaws like, so I kept my back to her a split second or so.

MRS.: You took a bit of a chance.

ADAM: Yes, but I turned and cracked her and stopped her stone dead.

MRS.: Sounds like sheer luck.

ADAM: No.

MRS.: Sheer luck.

ADAM: I said no and I mean no. There was no luck about it. I turned and cracked her like I used to turn and crack flies in half.

MRS.: Flies?

ADAM: Yes. Flies.

MRS.: You cracked flies?

ADAM: Didn't I ever tell you about that?

MRS.: You've told me some stories in your life.

ADAM: Didn't I ever tell you how my father taught me to cut flies?

MRS.: No.

ADAM: Didn't I? I thought I told you how he did that. Out in the fields behind the caravans.

MRS.: You never told me anything like that.

ADAM: Well, he did. He used to go out with his whip in

the fields behind the caravans and kill flies. He just used to stand there in the sunshine and wait for them to come zipping along the way they do. Have you ever seen that? Ever seen a fast fly go zipping along over the top of the grass with its wings flashing all silver in the sunshine? Ever seen that, Mrs.?

MRS.:   Yes. I've seen that.

ADAM: Well, my father used to cut them in half. He'd flick that whip of his out and cut a fast fly right in half from anywhere to ten up to fifteen, even twenty feet—one crack, right in half. He taught me how. He taught me how to do that from the age of eight. We went out every day, starting when I was eight years old. By the time I was eighteen, I hadn't missed a fast fly in six years. I can still do it to this day. I never miss. And I'm not likely to either. (*Pause*) I suppose you find that hard to believe. Well, I'll tell you something, Mrs., I could cut a hair off your head from here. I could, you know. I could cut a hair off your head from here to there and you wouldn't even feel it. I could, you know. (*Pause*)

MRS.:   Sit down, Adam.

ADAM: Are you frightened? (*Pause*)

MRS.:   Sit down! (*Pause*)

ADAM: Do you know what he used to say? My father? He used to say you had to have the know-how of using a whip. He said it wasn't just cracking, it was all in the *know-how* of what to crack and when. That's exactly what I did to Ate. I used all the know-how I knew. Let her have enough rope to hang herself, then turned and cracked her right across her eyes, not the air above her head as I'd always done in the past, not just the thin air as I always do with them, not with her, then. I actually cracked her across both eyeballs—Cracked her for the first time in her life. Do you know something? She didn't expect that. And she didn't know what hit her. . . . I haven't had very much trouble from her since, as a matter of fact. Not that she's stopped, not that she'll *ever* stop wanting my head in her jaws, but she's a little more careful with me now. Just that little bit more careful. (*Pause*)

MRS.:   I wish you could be a woman for one pregnancy. I

wish deep down in my heart, Adam, that you and all the bloody men in this world could be a woman for one pregnancy. I wish you'd given birth to Timmy. I wish you had a womb and I wish he'd been inside you for nine months and I wish you could feel what it's like to have a baby coming out of you into this world. I wish you could feel that to know the pain I had, not the pain of giving birth, love, but the pain of seeing that life, that little life that was inside you, destroyed.

ADAM: I saw him.

MRS.: Not with my eyes! (*Pause*) Not with a mother's eyes. You saw him with *your* eyes. I'm talking about me and what I felt. I'm talking about my pain and my feelings and how I felt that night. I wanted you here—here with me that night. I wanted you here holding my hand or something. Just holding my hand or drying my tears or even sitting there with your bloody whip mumbling to yourself, but I wanted you here so much and you weren't. And do you want to know what's worse? Do you want to know what really hurts? The fact that you chose to go back to your stinking tigers!

ADAM: I had to.

MRS.: You chose to.

ADAM: Well, all right, I chose because I had no other choice. Because if I hadn't gone back and worked them there and then that night, if I hadn't gone and worked Ate and caught her out like I did, I would never have been able to work those cats again.

MRS.: I don't care about that.

ADAM: Yes, I know you don't. (*Pause*) It was just the same for me as it was for you in a way.

MRS.: It could never have been the same.

ADAM: You don't know that. Just as I don't know what it's like to have a womb and a baby inside me, you don't know what it's like to be locked in with a dozen man-eaters. Just as much as you felt what you were feeling that night, I felt what *I* was feeling and we don't know what each other was feeling. Just as much as I don't know what you were feeling and I'd only know if I had a womb for one pregnancy, you'd only know what I was feeling if you knew a little more about tigers.

MRS.: I don't want to know anything about the filthy things!

ADAM: That's the trouble, Mrs.

(*Pause. Adam takes keys from pocket, unlocks bottom drawer of chest of drawers and removes tin of saddle soap and cloth*)

MRS.: I've been wondering about that.

ADAM: About what?

MRS.: About that. You locking that drawer. Since when have we had secrets like locking drawers and not telling about attacks?

ADAM: That's what I'd like to know. Since when have we had secrets?

MRS.: What are you getting at?

ADAM: Whatever I'm getting at I'm not going to bother to get at anymore, Mrs. If you want to tell me, you will. If you don't, you've got a secret. That's your choice. (*Pause. He commences to saddle soap the whip*) I've been keeping it locked for your sake. I didn't want you to see it.

MRS.: What?

ADAM: My jacket.

MRS.: What jacket?

ADAM: The one I used to wear.

MRS.: You mean the one you were wearing when she got him?

ADAM: Yes.

MRS.: That one?

ADAM: Yes.

MRS.: You said you'd never touch that jacket again.

ADAM: I know.

MRS.: You said you were going to get rid of it.

ADAM: Yes.

MRS.: You said you were going to throw it away, that you never wanted it near you again.

ADAM: Yes, I know I did, but I haven't done with it yet.

MRS.: Done what with it?

ADAM: Those buttons and braids. I've got to cut them off.

MRS.: Cut them off? What for?

ADAM: To have the tailor put them onto my new jacket.

MRS.: Onto the new one? What for?

ADAM: Because that's family stuff. Those buttons and braids have been in my family for generations. My grandfather wore them. And his father before him, as far as I know. My father wore them before he handed them down to me. My father gave me those. He gave me those to keep and wear and he gave them with pride. I can't throw them away. I can't just throw them away. I'll throw the jacket away but not those because they're, well, sort of heritage, that's exactly what they are. Heritage, like.

MRS.: I don't want that jacket in this house!

ADAM: Well, I had to bring it back to cut them off.

MRS.: I don't want it near me.

ADAM: Well, that's why I put it in the drawer and that's why I've kept it locked. (*Pause*)

MRS.: I suppose it's all stained, isn't it?

ADAM: I had it dry cleaned.

MRS.: Oh! (*Pause*) Did it all come out?

ADAM: No. It's still stained but, well, it doesn't look like anything. It just doesn't look like what it is. (*Pause*)

MRS.: Bring it out.

ADAM: I thought you didn't want to see it.

MRS.: Bring it out.

(*Pause. Adam goes to drawer and produces the lion tamer's jacket*)

MRS.: Let's see ... It doesn't, does it?

ADAM: What?

MRS.: Look like it.

ADAM: No.

MRS.: It looks more like a brown paint stain, doesn't it?

ADAM: Yes. I suppose it does. Yes. (*Pause*)

MRS.: Put it on.

ADAM: Why?

MRS.: I don't know why. I just want you to put it on, that's all. Put it on. (*Adam puts the jacket on*) Do it up . . . no, button it all the way up, the way you do when you work. (*Pause*) Look. It's ripped.

ADAM: Yes.

MRS.: I never knew it was ripped.

ADAM: It wasn't before.

MRS.: How did it get ripped?

ADAM: Ate.

MRS.: Did she do that?

ADAM: Yes.

MRS.: Did she? When?

ADAM: When she got him between us.

MRS.: When she clawed at you like that?

ADAM: Yes.

MRS.: When Timmy ran 'round?

ADAM: Yes.

MRS.: You mean she actually got you?

ADAM: Just the jacket.

MRS.: I didn't know she'd actually touched you.

ADAM: I was lucky, that's all—a little deeper and there's no telling what might have happened. I saw a man disemboweled by a tiger's claws once.

MRS.: Don't! (*Pause*)

ADAM: What are you doing?

MRS.: I want to touch it.

ADAM: What for?

MRS.: I don't know, love. I just want to touch it, that's all. Can I?

ADAM: I don't see what for. It doesn't feel like anything. It's got no feel to it. It's all been dry cleaned out.

MRS.: I want to touch it anyway.

ADAM: It's only an old stain. Dry cleaned right out.

MRS.: Wait. Stand still, love. (*Mrs. approaches, touches the blood stain*) It doesn't feel like anything.

ADAM: No. I told you that.

MRS.: It doesn't feel like anything at all. Wait. Stand still.

ADAM: I don't like this.

MRS.: Stand still, love. It doesn't feel like anything. (*Pause*)

ADAM: Now look. You're going to cry.

MRS.: No. No, I'm not. I wasn't going to cry. I was just thinking. What a lovely kid he was.

ADAM: That's funny you should say that. That's just what I was thinking.

MRS.: Were you, love?

ADAM: Yes. I was thinking the very same thing. What a lovely kid he was.

MRS.: Wasn't he, love? Wasn't he a lovely kid?

ADAM: Yes. A really lovely kid. A loving and lovely kid. He loved you so much, Mrs. I've never seen a kid love anyone or show so much love as he showed you.

MRS.: He did, didn't he?

ADAM: Yes. He did.

MRS.: And you.

ADAM: Yes.

MRS.: He was so proud of you, you know. Proud as Punch. You should have seen him when he saw you. You should have seen the way he sat up when you came striding into that cage. You should have seen the way he sat up watching you.

ADAM: I wish I had.

MRS.: And when you put that one through the hoop. . . .

ADAM: Shiva?

MRS.: Whatever its name is, you should have seen him. You should have seen how he bumped that woman next to him. With his elbow. Yes. He bumped the woman next to him with his elbow like this, sort of, well, like he was being very confidential.

ADAM: He didn't.

MRS.: He did, too. He bumped like this and said, "That's my daddy."

ADAM: He didn't.

MRS.: He did, you know. He was so proud of you. (*Pause*)

ADAM: What a lovely kid he was.

MRS.: He was so happy sitting there watching you. He loved watching you. He loved watching everything you did. That's why we sat there.

ADAM: Where?

MRS.: Well, where we were sitting in the front row. We sat there so he could see you better.

ADAM: Nothing wrong with that.

MRS.: I wish I hadn't though. I wish we'd sat up in the stands.

ADAM: It had nothing to do with where you were sitting.

MRS.: Well, it might not have happened if we'd been sitting up in the stands.

ADAM: Now you're not to think that. It had nothing at all to do with where you were sitting. It was just a horrible accident and that's all.

MRS.: But I can't help thinking that sometimes. I can't help thinking that it might not have happened if I'd sat him up in the stands instead of right there on top of the cage.

ADAM: I said it had nothing to do with that. It was just a horrible accident and that's all.

MRS.: We might have been safer in the stands.

ADAM: A horrible accident.

MRS.: But he did so love to watch you. (*Pause*) You didn't see his face, did you?

ADAM: I never look out of the cage when I'm working.

MRS.: No, not then. I mean when it happened.

ADAM: I don't think you should think about it now.

MRS.: You didn't see his face then, did you?

ADAM: You'll only upset yourself.

MRS.: You couldn't see his face, could you?

ADAM.: Listen, Mrs. . . .

MRS.: I mean, from where you were standing. You couldn't see his face, could you?

ADAM: Mrs.

MRS.: When she got him. I'm talking about when she got him. You were standing behind him when she actually got him, weren't you?

ADAM: Well, she came at me and. . . .

MRS.: Yes, but you were behind him. . . .

ADAM: Well, she did that run 'round and doubled back like that and I couldn't get there.

MRS.: Yes. I saw what she did, but what I'm saying is that you weren't in a position to see his face, were you?

ADAM: No. I didn't see his face. No.

MRS.: I wish you had, love.

ADAM: Well, I didn't, so it's no good going on about it, is it, Mrs.?

MRS.: Try and imagine it in your mind.

ADAM: Don't go on about it.

MRS.: Please, Adam. Please try.

ADAM: But what's the point?

MRS.: I want to. I want to make you imagine Timmy. I want you to try and imagine you're Timmy.

ADAM: Why?

MRS.: Because I want you to, that's why. Me! I want you to. Me, me, me! I want you to. Imagine you're him and think back how things seemed to be when you were four years old. How things around you looked then, how much bigger everything seemed—objects, colors, people, things, noises and smells— think those things as though you're his age and put yourself in his place, standing there the way he stood, seeing me the way he must've seen me struggling to get away from those ushers, and feel and hear everything going on around you the way he must've. Put yourself there. Feel it. Feel the silence and look at Ate suddenly in front of you, not as you see her but as he must've. Twice as big as she is to you. Imagine her padding up on you twice or three times as big as she is. That's how it was for him. Imagine how it was for him! Imagine the smell of her. Imagine the size of her teeth. Now she stops, everything's silent, no one's moving and she stands almost on top of you and now she snarls that quiet little snarl she snarled. Tell me, how do you feel? Frightened?

ADAM: S'pose so. Yes.

MRS.: He wasn't. He wasn't frightened. I know. I know he wasn't because I could see his face. He wasn't at all frightened. Not then. In the end he was, but not then. He wasn't then and I know why. Because of you. He wasn't frightened because you were right there behind him.

ADAM: Listen, Mrs. . . .

MRS.: I know that. I know what was in his head. I could almost see how his little mind was working. I could almost see his thoughts through his eyes and his face, and he wasn't frightened because you were right there. Do you know what I think he was thinking? That it was a sort of trick. As if the whole thing was like one of those difficult tricks you do. Like when you have all those tigers mill about on top of you—you know, when you lie flat on the sawdust and you get them to mill about and walk all over you?

ADAM: Yes.

MRS.: Well, it was just as if he was thinking it was another trick like that. Just another trick and that everything would be all right as soon as you said the magic word. All you had to do was say one magic word and she'd go away. Like you do when they're all milling about on top of you. Like you just say that one word, "hup," like that, and they all trot off back to their podiums. Well, that's how he looked to me. Not frightened, just as though he was waiting for you to say that word. That's why he didn't run. That's why he didn't do anything until that scream.

ADAM: He did not scream, Mrs.

MRS.: He did. Right at the end he did.

ADAM: He did not.

MRS.: Right there at the end, right as she struck out at him, his little face twisted up in fear and he opened his mouth and screamed.

ADAM: Well, I'll tell you that you might have seen his face twisting up and his mouth opening but my son did not scream, Mrs.!

MRS.: Well, I heard him scream, I heard him scream right then, right at that instant she ripped his little throat out.

ADAM: He did not scream. There was no scream.

MRS.: Well, I heard him scream! I can still hear it. I hear it in my sleep. I hear it in my dreams.

ADAM: All right, Mrs. It's all over now.

MRS.: I dream it. I dreamed about that scream the other night. I dreamed it quite clearly. I heard that scream as clear as anything. I was having this dream . . . I was having this dream about Wynkin, Blynkin and Nod. Wynkin, Blynkin and Nod. Sailing off in a wooden shoe. I was dreaming about it, about sailing up among the stars, just like they have them in those stories about space and stuff. I was dreaming I was out there, right out in the stars and I saw everything the way it was— all those things, you know those big whirls of stars . . . you know them, what do they call them?

ADAM: It's galaxies, isn't it?

MRS.: Yes, I think so. I saw big whirls of things like that, and millions of stars, and I dreamed I even knew what it all was. All space and eternity and everything, and through it all there was this screaming. It just went on, echoing and echoing through space. It was so clear. I heard it so clearly. I heard it and I saw it. I actually saw the color of it, like light's supposed to have all those colors. Well, I saw the color of that scream. In my dream. (*Pause*)

ADAM: It was quick. He didn't suffer. It was quick.

MRS.: Yes.

ADAM: Death was instantaneous.

MRS.: Yes. Instantaneous.

ADAM: My father died in the ring.

MRS.: Yes. You started to tell me one night.

ADAM: I was holding him when he died.

MRS.: Yes, you told me that. You told me what he said.

His last words. "It's right, it's right, we could never live apart."

ADAM: That's it. That's what he said.

MRS.: Yes. I remember you told me that.

ADAM: Did I tell you why he said it?

MRS.: He was talking about your mother, wasn't he?

ADAM: Yes. That's right.

MRS.: She died the same day.

ADAM: The same time, yes.

MRS.: Your mother died that day and he died in the cage that night.

ADAM: No. That's not it.

MRS.: You didn't finish telling me.

ADAM: She didn't die that day and him that night. That's not what it was.

MRS.: What was it, then?

ADAM: They both died at the same time. Just about the same time.

MRS.: I didn't know.

ADAM: I was with her when she died. I was in the caravan holding her hand. She was in a coma. I was just sitting there holding her hand waiting for the doctor to come.

MRS.: Where was your father, then?

ADAM: In the tent, working. He was in the tent working his cats and I was in the caravan with my mother, you see, just holding her hand. That's all I could do, just hold her hand. There was nothing else I could do for her. I was just sitting there holding her hand watching her in the lamplight and listening to the crowd. I could hear the crowd in the tent. The caravan was very near to the tent, you see, and I could hear everything. I could hear the crack of the whip and the crowd ohing and ahing, the way they used to do during my father's act. I could hear all that, and that's what I was doing . . . just holding her hand and listening and waiting for the doctor. Then she gave this sort of spasm. It was like a spasm—she sort of caught her breath and shivered like, and then she was dead. It was as quick as anything. Just like that. I actually felt her pulse stop. I did.

I swear I felt her pulse just stop. And that's when it happened. The attack. That's when that lion of his got him. Right at that moment, you see. Just as her pulse stopped there was this horrible cry from the crowd, and I ran like hell.

MRS.: So you didn't actually see the lion get him?

ADAM: No. I never saw that. I just left my mother there and ran like hell when I heard that horrible cry and there he was. Lying on his face in the sawdust. Covered in blood.

MRS.: That's when you held him, then?

ADAM: Yes. I went in and took him in my arms. I rolled him over in my arms and held him and that's when he said it. He looked right in my eyes and said, "It's right, it's right, we could never live apart."

MRS.: I didn't know it was like that. You never finished telling me before.

ADAM: Well, that's how it was and that's what was so uncanny about it. I didn't say anything, you see. I didn't even tell him she was dead. I didn't say, "Mum's dead," or anything. I just rolled him over and he said it first. He said, "It's right, it's right, we could never live apart." Just like that.

MRS.: But how did he know if you didn't tell him?

ADAM: I don't know. That's what's uncanny. To this day I don't know, but he knew, Mrs. He knew. He just knew she'd left his life.

MRS.: But it doesn't make sense.

ADAM: No. It doesn't, does it?

MRS. No.

ADAM: Sort of like me in a way, isn't it?

MRS.: Like you, how like you?

ADAM: Like knowing what was going on behind my back. When Ate came down behind my back.

MRS.: You said you heard her.

ADAM: Yes. I know I did. But I didn't actually hear with my ears. But I knew she was up to something behind my back. And I caught her at it, didn't I? (*Pause*) I can feel things, you see. Like he did. (*Pause*)

MRS.: What things?

ADAM: Oh, just goings on.

MRS.: You mean with your tigers?

ADAM: Yes. With all my tigers.

MRS.: Is that how you do it, then?

ADAM: What?

MRS.: Stay alive. Is that how you do it?

ADAM: Yes. That's half of it.

MRS.: What's the other half, then?

ADAM: Being one jump ahead.

MRS.: Oh. And how do you do that?

ADAM: By thinking like a tiger. Like you made me imagine I was Timmy, I make myself imagine I'm a tiger. I know what it's like to be a tiger.

MRS.: What? What's it like?

ADAM: Watchful. Very watchful, just like they are in the foliage. The jungle foliage. That's how they are in the jungle foliage. Very watchful. Like when they're hunting, like when they're after something in a jungle village, they don't just go blundering in. Not tigers. They get up in a good position, usually on a hill above the village and then they lie there in the foliage watching. They lie there watching from sunrise to sunset, day after day, sometimes they even watch for weeks on end. They're very watchful . . . And they learn. They learn by watching. They watch until they know every single movement of every single living thing in that village, be it man, woman, child, dog, cat, goat, pig or anything you like. A tiger watches every movement, not just the movements of what he's hunting, but the movements of everything around it so that when he goes in for the kill, he'll have as little trouble as possible. That's why they never know a tiger's made a kill in a jungle village until long after he's been in, done it and gone.

MRS.: Oh!

ADAM: Yes. He strikes in silence, you see. A tiger strikes in silence and you never know what's happened until after it's happened. You only know it's happened when you find something missing, like they find something missing in a village. Well, that's why I keep watchful, you see, because to be one jump ahead of a tiger you have to think like one. That's why I am like I am. That's why I go like I go in the cage. You know, when I'm working, how I keep on the move. Kali up there, Ate, Mughal over here, Rajah there, Shiva here, Devi over there, then Khan. . . .

MRS.: Oh! Adam!

ADAM: What? What is it?

MRS.: No. Nothing.

ADAM: What?

MRS.: No, it was just when you turned the . . . just as you were turning about like that.

ADAM: What?

MRS.: Well, it's nothing really. Just that they were shining. Those braids and things, they were shining.

ADAM: Were they?

MRS.: Yes. Just as you turned then like you do in the cage. There was a quick little shine. That's all.

ADAM: Like that?

MRS.: No.

ADAM: Here. Have a look . . . there. Like that?

MRS.: No. No, it's not doing it now.

ADAM: Oh, well, it's the light then—there's not enough light in here actually. I must have turned in a bit of light or something. It shines like hell in the lights, I can tell you.

MRS.: Yes. I remember.

ADAM: Don't think about that anymore.

MRS.: I wasn't thinking about that. I was thinking about the very first time I saw you, actually. That's what I was thinking then.

ADAM: What were you thinking about it?

MRS.: Just that. That shining business. Just how you came shining into that ring, all those buttons and braids sparkling away. Sparkling like a fiery sort of thing. Strutting about the way you strut about—about and in and out among those tigers. All that rum-pah-pah from the music and you with that whip of yours cracking up and down, this way and that; and your eyes flashing from one place to the next, and your head held the way you walk so, so straight and everything when you're in the cage. I don't think I'll ever forget what I felt about you then. Like what you were. What you looked like. The feeling I had from what you looked like.

ADAM: What did I look like?

MRS.: Well, I've never sort of thought about it in words before, but you looked sort of, well .... Sort of ... indestructible. That's it. That's exactly how you looked. Indestructible.

ADAM: Did I really? (*Pause*)

MRS.: I wasn't even afraid of your tigers. The first time I saw you and those cats I didn't feel anything about the act. I didn't feel it was very dramatic or anything like that. I didn't. I didn't think there was anything dramatic about it, and I know why. Because I wasn't frightened of your tigers, that's why.

ADAM: Weren't you?

MRS.: No.

ADAM: Why?

MRS.: Because they weren't the frightening things. Not next to you. They weren't the frightening things. *You were.* You were frightening. That's why I wasn't ever afraid of them. I never used to be afraid of them. I never used to be.

(*Mrs. moves to the wardrobe, removes a light colored dress and petticoat, lays them on the bed. She removes her bathrobe and is wearing light colored panties and a bra*)

ADAM: I think we should have another child. As a matter of fact, I think we should have lots more children. That's the whole thing about you, you know. What you are, not just the person you are, but what you are as a woman. To look at. (*Mrs. takes up the petticoat*) No. Wait. I want to look at you.

MRS.: Adam.

ADAM: I said wait. .... Everything about you. Everything. Your legs. Your arms. Your hands.

MRS.: Adam.

ADAM: Your stomach. Your breasts. Your lips. Your eyes, Mrs. . . . you're so beautiful. You're so very beautiful. You're more beautiful now than you were before. (*Short pause*)

MRS.: Before when?

ADAM: Just, before. You know, before. When you were still on the trapeze. That's why you did so well. Because of your looks. You could go back to it. You could go back to the trapeze tomorrow.

MRS.: Yes. I know.

ADAM: You'd have to practice.

MRS.: Not very much, love.

ADAM: A lot.

MRS.: No. Not very much.

ADAM: A lot. I said a lot and I mean a lot.

MRS.: How would you know?

ADAM: Because you weren't a very good aerialist.

MRS.: I was.

ADAM: No, you weren't. I've seen quite a few aerialists in my time and you weren't very good. It's your looks that got you your engagements. Your looks not your ability. You weren't so good.

MRS.: I was, you know.

ADAM: Not as good as that partner of yours. That red-headed chap. What was his name? (*Pause*)

MRS.: I don't know. I've forgotten.

(*Pause Mrs. puts the petticoat on. Adam removes the lion tamer's jacket*)

ADAM: Going to the pictures, then? I'll walk you if you like. I'll walk you if you're going to the local. Are you going to the local, then?

MRS.: I don't know what I'm going to do yet.

ADAM: Well, I'll walk you.

MRS.: No. Don't wait for me. (*Adam puts on sportscoat*) Adam. Don't go tonight. Stay here with me. Just tonight. Phone and tell them you're sick.

ADAM: No. I can't do that and you know it.

MRS.: Just one night.

ADAM: No. I said no, and I mean no. But I'll tell you what. We'll go out afterwards. We'll go out and have a bit of dinner somewhere. Somewhere nice. We'll have a nice bottle of wine and some dinner somewhere nice. Shall we? (*Pause*) Come with me and wait and watch the act.

MRS.: No.

ADAM: Well, I'll come back and pick you up, then. Where will you be? Here? Or at the local?

MRS.: I don't know yet.

ADAM: Well, I'll come back and wait for you here, then. (*Pause*) Well, if you don't go out, do me a favor. Cut those braids and buttons off for me, will you?

(*Adam puts on his cap, picks up the whip and moves to the door. He stops at the door*)

MRS.: What is it?

ADAM: I was just thinking about my dad again, what he said once—about life being like a tiger. That's what he said, you know. He said that life was like a tiger and that you could let it jump in on you and maul you or you could do something with it.

MRS.: What?

ADAM: Tame it. You could let it maul you or you could tame it. (*Adam opens the door, stops*)

MRS.: What're you smiling at?

ADAM: What he said about taming it—that it'd take a lot of taming but it'd be worth it in the end.

MRS.: Did he happen to tell you why?

ADAM: Yes, because, he said, "It's the biggest bloody tiger of the lot," that's why. (*Pause*) Hey, Mrs., I love you.

(*Adam exits, closes the door. Mrs. picks up the jacket and buries her face in it as she begins to cry*)

Curtain

Charles Gordone

GORDONE IS A MUTHAH

Charles Gordone

Charles Gordone, recipient of a 1970 Pulitzer Prize for his first produced play, *No Place To Be Somebody,* distinguished himself as both an actor and director before he turned to playwriting. Born on October 12, 1925, the author grew up in Elkhart, Indiana. He attended Los Angeles City College and U.C.L.A. and after receiving his B.A. in drama came to New York and soon was engaged for a role in Moss Hart's *The Climate of Eden.* Other parts followed including an appearance with Eartha Kitt in *Mrs. Patterson.*

In 1961, he was in the original Off-Broadway production of Jean Genet's *The Blacks* and subsequently played in it at the Berlin and Venice Festivals and in Washington, D.C. Another impressive performance was in Luther James' all-black production of John Steinbeck's *Of Mice and Men* (for which he won an award as Best Actor of the Year Off-Broadway) and in 1967 he portrayed the title role in *The Trials of Brother Jero* by Wole Soyinka.

Equally accomplished as a director, in 1959 he staged the Judson Poets' Theatre's first production, *Faust,* and since then has directed many other plays, including the original showcase presentation of *No Place To Be Somebody.*

Following its showcase performances, *No Place To Be Somebody* opened on May 4, 1969, at the New York Shakespeare Festival's Public Theatre (under the auspices of Joseph Papp) and it drew many laudatory reviews and press comments including *The New York Times'* pronouncement that "Charles Gordone is the most astonishing new American playwright to come along since Edward Albee." The play ran for a total of 576 performances and won, in addition to the Pulitzer Prize, a Drama Desk Award.

Gordone Is A Muthah, published here for the first time, originally was presented at the Carnegie Recital Hall, New York, with the author as a member of the cast. A series of sketches and poems (six are included in this collection) related to the "black experience," they were conceived, as Mr. Gordone has indicated in his prefatory note, for dramatic performance.

Charles Gordone was founder and co-chairman, with Godfrey Cambridge, of the Committee for the Employment of Negro Performers, and he was the associate producer of the movie *Nothing But a Man*. Most recently, he completed the screenplay of *No Place To Be Somebody* which is scheduled for filming this year.

Author's Note

These poems and the monologue-story were written to be performed. After all, I am an actor first and a writer second.

Be that as it may, they come out of the bowels of my past, some of the present and some, hopefully, a projection into the future as regards "the souls of Black Folk."

They are what I call the nitty-gritty folk elements in my life.

1. Ah Wanna Tell Ya 'Bout Me

Ah wanna tell ya.
Kin ah tell ya?
Lemme tell ya
A-bout me.

So keep yo' han'books handy,
Turn yo' page along with me.
Since we's all in God's eyes equal,
Turn to page four-hundred-three.

Now it may not be a pretty story
But don't let that make you worry,
An' I ain't the least bit sorry
'Cause there's sum pictures here to see.

Ah wanna tell ya.
Kin ah tell ya?
Ahm gon' tell ya anyway.
In this world of tribulation
This is sum of what I gotta say.

2. *A Child's Garden of Lessons—Dedicated to Black Castrated Fathers*

She went to a dance
For a touch of romance.
Quite harmless, a body would say.
Fell in love with a clown,
A big teasin' brown,
And she got in the family way!

It was a lesson she had not learned, not learned—
A lesson she had not learned!

But he pledged her his heart
With a death do us part,
Before God and all those concerned.
And they married one day
And he whisked her away—
From my Mother, respect he did earn.

It was a lesson she had not learned, not learned—
A lesson she had not learned!

But how could she know that castration, frustration
Burned holes in this brown, posturing fop!
He had pledged her his heart
With a death do us part,
In his mind he feared God was a cop!

It was a lesson she was to learn, to learn—
A lesson she was to learn!

And how could he know some want-ads in papers,
Some brooms, dust pans and mops
Had drained and defeated her,
Had raped and had cheated her
Of the blossom of her youth?

It was a lesson he had not learned, not learned—
A lesson he had not learned!

Well, he found him a hame (job)
Chauf'ring some rich white dame.
Her husband was away a lot—
And one day in the parlor
She flicked a speck from his collar.
That was his moment of truth!

And he laid her down,
This black, frustrated clown—
And he showed her his African soul!
She wept and she moaned
And he grunted and groaned
As the limousine went out of control!

It was a lesson they'd never learn, learn, learn!
A lesson they'd never learn!

And they found them there
At the foot of the stair—
All gory and tangled and naked!
The husband admitted it,
The Judge he acquitted it,
And the rich man found another dame somewhere!

It was a lesson we were about to learn, to learn—
A lesson we were about to learn!

Mama packed us up and took us back
Where she said she used to belong!
Oh, the look in her eye!
Oh, the heave of her breast!
And her cry of what had gone wrong!
Hadn't he pledged her his heart
With a death do us part
Before God and all those concerned?
Hadn't he made the pact?
Were we not the fact?
And now he would never return!

It was a lesson we had to learn, to learn—
A lesson we had to learn!

So Mama went back to her ads in the paper,
Back to her brooms and her mops!
And she married a janitor,
A practical progenitor—
For a time we were just like his own!
But then he got evil,
Primitive, medieval!
People said he was crazy as hops!
He'd beat us!
He'd bang us!
He'd torture, harangue us!
"Be thankful!" my Mother would say.
But we knew that he hated us,
The way he degraded us—
A black monster, we were forced to obey!

Now this railroad track
Is my way back
To the city of my disgrace!
I have found me a hame
And a rich white dame
And I drive her all over the place!
But I'll be smart—
Never pledge my heart
Before God and all those concerned!
For men of my breed
Must live without need—
Must live with catch as catch can!
For the price we pay
In every way
Is the price that we're less than a man!

It is a lesson that I have learned, learned, learned!
It is a lesson I had to learn!

3. A Black Woman's Brood

Wake up chillun an comb yo kinky hayuh
'Cause the welfare lady is sittin' out theah!
She's fat an funky an fulla sense,
Broke up mah day—all them clothes ah gotta rense;
Be polite an nice—say all the right things;
Hol' still Caline—lemme get at them kinks!
Wake up chillun an comb yo kinky hayuh
'Cause the welfare lady is sittin' out theah!
Tell huh yo daddy lef' us all by ouahseves
An we ain't got nuthin' sittin up on ouah she'ves
Mayry eats roaches and chews on plastah;
Joonyuh's a junky—and dont you dayuh sass huh!
Wake up chillun an comb yo kinky hayuh
'Cause the welfare lady is sittin' out theah!
In the wintah no heat—in the summah no coolah,
Mos'a the time we ain't got no wawtah.
The tawlit's stopped up—the sink wont let go;
The lanlawd—ain seen him, don' cum roun no mo!
Wake up chillun an comb yo kinky hayuh
'Cause the welfare lady is sittin' out theah!
Clara is smawt—evbody says so,
Say huh varmint is bad fuh huh—an that make huh slow!
Lawd ebm if ah wus to git that welfare check
Sho wouldn't mount ta much—not ebm a speck!
But the Lawd'l provide—so the Bible say
But ah always git ta doubtin'—when ahm in the fambly way!
Wake up chillun an comb yo kinky hayuh
'Cause the welfare lady is sittin' out theah!
Petah b'longs ta Paul—an Jennie is Jacob's,
Caline is Naythun's an Mayry is Caleb's,
Joonyuh's papa went crazy—tow mah ahm frum the socket,
Billy's daddy seem ta have holes in his pocket!
The fathah of Clara wus a edcatid man,
Always tried ta do the bes' he can!

He luv me ahm sho—but his buden got hahdah,
Ah wus no longah putty—no usin' no powdah!
So you all be nice—say all the right things.
Theyuh you are Caline—ahm thoo with them kinks!
Wake up chillun an comb yo nappy head
'Cause that welfare lady gonna membah whut you said!

4. A Prayer for the Sixties

Lawd, do you 'member whut happen to us durin' the Civil
Rights Movement? An' whut happen with our Po' Peoples' in
    March?

We thanks ya, Lawd, jus' the same that we no longer minds
    bein' called niggers.
An' thoo yo' he'p, we kin finally say,
"Ah's black an' ah's proud!"
Along with yo' lovin' servant, Brother James Brown.

We is provin' that we's proud, Lawd.
We's lettin' our hair go nachul.
An' we's wearin' Dashikis too.

We thanks ya, Lawd, fuh Reb'm Adam
Cee.
He got a big mouf, Lawd.
But what he do, he do all to the glory of Thee.

An' we thanks ya fuh Muhammad Ali.
He got a big mouf too, Lawd.
But he was a man, Lawd,
Who stuck to his gloves.

We prays fuh them brothers who been callin' fuh
Sum "Black Power," Lawd.
'Cause sum of 'em got a terrible hurtin' put on 'em
An' had to split over to a place called Fiddla-Cuba.
An' sum of 'em stayed home an' got kilt!

An' Lawd, put a special blessin' on all them
Thousands of orphans who grew they hair long
'Cause they couldn't grow it kinky.
But they speak the language pretty good, Lawd.
An' tha's cool.

One thing we don't understan', Lawd.
Why you keep lettin' them po'leece do all them dirty, rotten
    things they been doin' to us?
While you let them other bad people who been puttin' 'em
    up to it go scot-free?

We thanks ya fuh lettin' us have all them
Student demonstrations of one kind or another.
Lawd, we prays fuh sum a'them brothers an' sisters,
Both white an' black who groove on pot, pills an' LSD.
They is jus' tryin' to git nex' to you, Baby!

We also thanks ya fuh sendin' all them Gurus that
Went back to Injah.
We thanks ya too fuh givin' us sum groovy music
To go 'long with all them neon lights ya give us.
Bless The Beatles an' Jimi Hendrix.
Bless the Rollin' Stones.

An' bless Broadway Joe Namath.
He's still out there groovin' as usual.
Thank ya fuh changin' his heart so's he wouldn't quit an' blow
    everything fuh the Jets.

An' please, Lawd! Lay yo' sweet evah-lovin' foot
On to Jimmie Brown the actor's ass
So he don't blow his cool so much.

We gotta 'member in our prayers, Lawd,
The great Mickey Mantle.
An' of course, Mistah "Say Hey," himself. Brother Willie Mays.

An' Lawd, put yo' lovin' arm-pits into Sidney Poitier's nose!
We's waitin' on him to grow a beard but we knows
West Indians don't go fuh that sheeee.

Lawd, we thanks ya fuh chicks.
Specially them that wears mini-a-kneee-skirts.
By the way, we wants to thank ya fuh inventin' them
Bell-bottom pants.
We also thanks ya fuh these old pioneer clothes
An' fuh them Injun an' cowboy outfits
We been seein' fuh so long in the movies.
We's wearin' 'em now, to 'member our dear ancestors by.

Now, Lawd, we particularly wanna 'member in our prayers
Prez Jay F. Kay.
He was a very han'some, cool cat who made a lotta groovy
    moves.
    'Member Miss Jackie too, Lawd.
Fuhgive her, 'cause she know not whut she do!

An' we thanks ya fuh the good li'l time we had with
Li'l Bobby Kay. He was another outta sight cat who
Was caught by the spirit an' cut down by the ghost.
An' of course we all got to 'member the gret Reb'm
Doctah King who loved evahbody.

An' our dear blessed brother, Malcolm X who blew
A lotta people's minds.

We is now puttin' in a gassy word fuh brother Teddy Kay, too,
    Lawd. But we know you is gonna cross that bridge when
    you come to it.

Bless them Astro-Nuts who grooved with a spoon on the moon,
    fuh the sak'a peace on earth and good will to mens.

Don't wanna fuhgit "Fas' Draw," El Bee Jay neither, Lawd.
    'Cause he wuz the fust real cowboy to become Prez.
Provin' that even cowboys kin become President.

An' above all, Lawd. Please, please bless the
Prez we's got now. Mistah Mill-house Nix.
He ain't much, Lawd.

But he's all we's got!
Thank ya, Lawd, an' Ay-man!

P.S. Bless all them swingin' dudes who been kilt over there in
Vee-eat-Numb.
Ay-man again.

5. *Mule*

Ol' Granpap knowed li'l Wullie wanted a mule! Knowed
he wanted a mule mo' than anythang! The fambly an' neah
'bout all the cullud folks roun' these heah pahts knowd
Wullie wanted a mule—sho didn't want no hawse, jus wanted
a mule—wanted a mule bad! Ahm Wullie's sustah, an' ah can't
tell ya how bad mah li'l brutha wanted a mule!

Jus' bout the time li'l Jerry—li'l Jerry's a jackass—jus' bout
the time he studded ol' Bessie, ol' Granpap taken sick in bed
with his cunsumshun. Granpap's cawfin' an' spittin' got wuss.
Doc Gibson an' the women fum the chu'ch seem ta me like wus
cumin roun' much mo' ofun, an' they wus whusprin' mighty
much in the kitchun an' all out on the poach. Mama an' Gramaw
be tryin' ta keep they teahs down—an' sumtime they cain't he'p
it—an' we be heahin' 'em cryin' sumpm awful in the house when
we be goin' 'bout ouah choahs!

Wun mawnin' Mama sent Wullie on Jerry ta go git Doc
Gibson ril quick—an' putty soon Doc cum rollin' up in his bran'
new Modul Tee Fo'd long 'fo Wullie an' Jerry git back. An' Doc
Gibson cum inta the house an' zamun ol' Granpap. Putty soon
he cum out an' tell the fambly ol' Granpap's bout done fuh an'
won't be long 'fo he gon' have ta meet his makah. Then Mama
she sen' Wullie an' Jerry down the hill ta git Reb'm Davis—an'
'fo the dus' cleah, Reb'm Davis cum inta the house!

Reb'm Davis, he take a long look at Granpap, an' he say
ol' Granpap wus a good man all his life. An' 'en sum'a the
womens say Lustah—(that wus Granpap's name)—they say

Lustah wus a good providah fuh his fambly—eb'm in hahd time he wus—say he wus a good man tho he nevah prayed nuh went ta chu'ch eb'm down! An' he cussed an' drank an' chewed snuff! But he wus a good man they say! An' Reb'm Davis say he gon' preach ol' Granpap a good funral an' that staht all us womens ta cryin' all ovah agin!

Aftah Wullie git back, he went out ta the bawn 'cause ol' Bess wus bout ta foal an' tho huh colt. 'Fo Bessie taken down, Wullie be's hangin' roun' Granpap's bedroom gittin' in the way'a all the womens an' botherin' 'em bout ol' Granpap —til they gotta put him out'a the house, he worr'in' 'em so much!

Wullie—he luv ol' Granpap sumpm awful, an' evahbody knowed Wullie Dee wus allus Granpap's fav'rit—they wus allus togathah when they wus out in the fiel's cuttin' hay uh choppin' cotton uh doin' the pickin'. An' when ol' Granpap git drunk evah Sat'day, Wullie be right theah fuh to take cayuh him—when he couldn't stan' nuh sit no mo'—he be so drunk! An' as luttul as Wullie wus, he allus manage ta git Granpap off ta bed, take his shoes off an' roll him in. Guess they wusn't nuthin' li'l Wullie Dee wouldn't do fuh ol' Granpap!

Soon's Bessie tho huh colt, Wullie cum'a runnin' inta the house ta tell ol' Granpap 'bout it. Mama let him go in, an' when he see how ol' Granpap is breathin' hahd an' how bad he looked, Wullie fuhgit all bout the colt an' he commence ta cry! Ol' Granpap so'tuh raise up an' he tell Wullie ta hush up all that hollin'. Wullie he try his bes' but the teahs keep on a cumin' anyways. Granpap ax Wullie how ol' Bess is doin', an' Wullie tell him she done jus now tho huh colt an' they is both doin' jus fin'! An' 'en Granpap say Wullie kin keep the colt fuh his ownse'f, an' he say he know Wullie will take good cayuh of him too! An' fo' the res'a the fambly kin git in ta tell ol' Granpap goodbye, ol' Granpap he ups an' dies!

Doc Gibson put two nuckuls on ol' Granpap's eyes ta close 'em, an' 'en all us womens staht ta hollin' sumpm turbul, an' Reb'm Davis commences ta shoutin' preachin' wurds an' jus makin' evahthang wuss than they is! Wullie he don't cry no mo. He take wun mo look at ol' Granpap an' 'en he git up an' go out ta the bawn wheah Bessie an' huh colt is.

They buried ol' Granpap out undah the willahs long side Gre't Gramaw an' Gre't Granpappy an' Pappy who died'a the same cunsumshun like him an' now Big Brutha an' the res'a the boys is runnin' the fahm now. Gramaw—she jus sit aroun' hittin' flies with the swattah. Sumtime she be's out on the poach rockin' an' hummin' uh singin' wun them slav'ry time songs ya cain't heah the wurds fum. An' Mama—she go on 'bout huh wuk way she did aftah Pappy die!

An' Wullie—ya cain't git him ta do no choahs no mo. He ain't hahdly tu'ned a lick since ol' Granpap die. Wun time Mama had ta beat him ta git him ta feed the hawgs eb'm down! Jus be's with his mule all the time. He done name his mule "Mule!" Tha's all—jus "Mule." Mos'a the time he done gone off with that mule—Lawd knows wheah they go—an' don't git back 'til neah 'bout suppah time. Mama used ta sen' him off ta bed 'thout no suppah, but that didn't do no good. Eithah me uh Gramaw'd jus sneak up an' bring him sumpm t'eat!

Tell ya—Mule wus jus 'bout the fines' lookin' mule in the whole state'a Ten'see. Seem ta me like he must'a stood 'bout twen'y han', an' he wus all black an' slick an' putty! Wullie wus all time brushin' him an' combin' him down. If the white folks would'a let Wullie put Mule in the contes' at the Coun'y Fayuh, he would'a a wawked off with the blue ribbun prize—ah'll pray fuh lyin'! A whole lotta fahmahs roun' heah wanted ta buy Mule but they would'a had ta leench him ta git Mule!

Mule'd do jus 'bout anythang Wullie wanted—had him trained just like a dawg, Wullie did. Sumtime he be stretched out on that big mule's back jus like it wus a feathah tick bed—an' he be soun' asleep too! White mens in town'd tease Wullie all time 'bout who wus the blackes', him uh the mule! Wullie'd jus grin an' say, "Ah don' know, boss. Reckon you'll haf ta ax mah mule bout that!"

The boys got ta tawkin' wun day, an' Aaron said Wullie's

mule wusn't earnin' his keep. Said any animal as big an' strong as Mule—wus a sin an' a shame fuh him ta be eatin' up as much hay an' grain as t'uthah stock! An' he 'lowed he wus gonna hitch ol' Mule ta a plow!

Wun mawnin' Mama made Wullie take huh inta town fuh ta git sum supplies. Aftah Wullie hitch up the team ta the wagon an' call fuh Mama ta come on an' he see 'em go off down the road—Aaron decide that wus the mawnin' ta put ol' Mule ta the plow. All the boys follahd him an' Mule out ta the fiel' 'cause they wus sho Mule an' Aaron wus gon give 'em a good show, an' they didn't wanna miss it! They wus all laffin' an' jokin' 'bout Mule nevah seein' a lick of wuk a day in his life! We could tell by Mule's eahs—way they wus layed back—he knew sumpm funny wus goin' on—an' it wus culia to us too 'cause Mule couldn't let nobody lay a han' on him but Wullie! But Aaron kep' on a'coaxin' him along. Mule wus showin' his teeth an' we wus all waitin' fuh him ta make a move but he went along with Aaron 'bout as peacebul as you please!

Well suh, when ol' Aaron hitch him up an' thode the reins down on him, ol' Mule commence ta pull that plow jus like he wus made fuh plowin'! Had ol' Aaron jus'a runnin' an' fallin' down 'tween the furruhs tryin' ta keep up with him! Plowed up that fiel' like they wusn't nuthin' he didn't know 'bout plowin' he did! And they wusn't hahdly a bead'a sweat layin' on him when they got thoo neithah! An' the boys, they jus' fall out laffin' 'cause nobody spected Mule ta do nuthin' like that a'tall! An' when Aaron unhitch Mule an' staht ta take him back ta the bawn, ol' Mule ups an' bites a big chunk out'a Aaron's ahm! Aaron he let out a yell ya could hear all the way ta Nashvul an' run git him a limb fuh ta beat Mule with, but the uthah boys say they don't think he bettah do nuthin like that, an' big bruthah hol' him back an' take the limb away fum him! An' they all say the joke's on Aaron—an' he ought'a take it like a spoaht. They 'lowed ol' Mule had 'bout as much sense as Aaron uh maybe mo an' suhved him right fuh tryin' ta make a fool out'a a smawt mule like Mule!

After Wullie got back from town, he ax Aaron whut happen to his ahm. Aaron say he wus flushin' jackrabbits 'n' one ov'em jump up and bite him on his ahm, 'n' Wullie say das funny cause I ain' hardly nevuh seen no jackrabbits in this section uf the country. Nobody nevuh tol' Wullie whut happen.

It hap'm wun Friday aft'noon. Mama sent Wullie inta town fuh sum bakin' soda—sh'run out. They say Wullie wus ridin' down Cahlahl Street. The white mens as us'al wus hangin' 'roun outside'a Ben's Bahbah Shop. It bein' Friday—guess sum of 'em had been drinkin' they likker, an' they hollah fuh him ta hol' up so's they could have sum fun with Wullie an' his mule. Wullie wouldn't stop so wun'a the mens runs out an' grab Mule by the haltah! Wullie tell the man he can't stop cause Mama done sen' him in town on a erran'! But the white man he tell Wullie he don't give a dam an' ta git down off that mule so's he could do a tu'n on him! Guess Wullie wus a luttul slow 'cause the white man knock him off'a Mule down onta the dus'! An' 'en he climb up on top'a Mule. Well, when the white man did that, ol' Mule hunches up his back an' those him off fuh a good piece! Them uthah white mens outside the bahbah shop they jus laff they heads off 'bout that an' that make this white man mad! He grab a big whip frum offun a wagon an' he commence layin' that whip on Mule! Ol' Mule whurl an' kick that ol' white man dead in his stummik! Knock the breath clean out'a him! Them uthah mens they run up ta Mule ta try ta git him settuld down, but he be's kickin' out at evah thang in sight! An' they's gotta keep runnin' back ta git out'a they way'a them huffs! The white man Mule done kicked—he huht, he huht bad an' he be's holdin' his side, but he manage ta git up an' he go at Mule sumpm awful this time! Mule he rayuh up an' put bofe feet in that white man's ches' an' knock him down an' commence ta stompin' an' trompin' on him like he wus nuthin' but a bed bug! Sum womens cum out'a the house 'cross the street an' they screams sumpm turbul an' them mens outside the bahbah shop is yellin' too! Wullie—he jus' stan'in' theah wringin' his han's an' watchin' the whole thang—an' bein' a chile he don't rightly know whut he should do! Ben, the bahbah, he run inside an' d'reckly he cum out with a riful in his han's. The white man on the groun' is neah 'bout dead fum the trompin' an' he ain't nuthin' but a ugly, bluddy mess! Ol' Ben —he raise his riful an' put a bullit right 'tween Mule's eyes, an' Mule fall like a dead piece'a timber! Wullie scream at Ben the bahbah an' pull out his pocket knife whut Big Bruthah give him on his birthday an' run at Ben sumpum feerce! Well, when ol' Ben see Wullie doin' that, he raise his riful agin' an' blow the top off'a mah li'l brutha's head!

We buried li'l Wullie out undah the willahs 'long side Gre't Gramaw an' Gre't Granpap, Pappy an' ol' Granpap— don't know wheah they buried ol' Mule! If ya ax me, ol' Granpap shouldn't a'waited fo he died ta give li'l Wullie a mule!

6. *They's Mo' to Bein' Black Than Meets the Eye*

They's mo' to bein' black than meets the eye!
Bein' black is like the way ya walk an' talk;
It's a way'a lookin' at life!

Bein' black is like sayin', "Wha's hap'nin' baby?"
An' bein' understood!
Bein' black has a way'a makin' ya call somebody
A mutha fuckah an' really meanin' it!
An' namin' evahbody bruthah
Even if ya don't!

Bein' black is eatin' chit'lin's an' wahtahmelon
An' to hell with anybody if they don't like it!
Bein' black has a way'a makin' ya wear bright colors
An' knowin' what a fine hat or a good pair'a shoes
Look like!
Bein' black has a way'a makin' ya fingah pop!
Invent a new dance!

Sing the blues!
Drink good Scotch!
Smoke a big seegar while pushin' a black Cadillac
With white sidewall tires!
It's conkin' yo' head!
Wearin' a black rag to keep the wave!
Carryin' a razor!
Smokin' boo an' listenin' to gut-bucket jazz!
Yes! They's mo' to bein' black than meets the eye!

An' then—an' then it has a way'a makin' ya git
Down loud an' wrong—uh huh—or makin' love without
No hangups—uh huh—or gittin' sanctified an' holy
An' grabbin' a han'full'a the sistah nex' ta ya when
She starts speakin' in tongues!
Bein' black is havin' yo' palm read!
Hittin' the numbahs!
Workin' long an' hard an' gettin' the short end'a the
Stick an' no glory!
It's knowin' they ain't no dif'rence 'tween white trash
An' white quality! Uh huh!
Bein' black is huggin' a fat mama an' havin' her smell
Like ham-fat, hot biscuits an' black-eyed peas!
Yes! They's mo' to bein' black than meets the eye!

Bein' black has a way'a makin' ya mad mos'a the
Time!
Hurt all the time!
An' havin' so many hangups the problem'a soo-side
Don't even enter yo' mind!
Its buyin' whut you don't want!
Beggin' whut you don't need!
An' stealin' whut is yours by *rights!*
Yes! They's mo' to bein' black than meets the eye!

It's all the stuff that nobody wants but cain't live
Without!

Its the body that keeps us standin'!
The soul that keeps us goin'!
An' the spirit that'll take us thoo!
Yes! They's mo' to bein' black than meets the eye!

A-a-a-ay Ma-a-an!

Norman Smythe

THE RAGPICKERS

Norman Smythe

Norman Smythe makes his initial appearance in *The Best Short Plays* annuals with his poignant study of loneliness, *The Ragpickers*. The play, published here for the first time, originally was produced on radio and television in Dublin, then converted to the stage by Mr. Smythe. It had its first performance in its new form at the Ambiance Lunch Hour Theatre Club in London in March, 1972, where it drew much praise from the British press. *The Stage* described it as "hypnotic" and concluded that it "must be one of the best short plays to be seen at midday anywhere." Michael Billington of the *Guardian* concurred: "The play admirably combines compassion for the individual with the indictment of the social system . . . I've seen few plays better suited to the lunch hour than this."

Mr. Smythe was born in New York City, the son of Irish immigrants who had settled in Hell's Kitchen. He was sent back to Ireland at the age of three and remained there until he was sixteen. He then rejoined his mother in New York and during the pre-war depression worked at a variety of jobs. Eventually he became a seaman and one of the founder members of the National Maritime Union.

After serving with the U.S. Army in World War II, he returned to New York where he became a sales engineer. It was during this period that he also published short stories and feature articles and wrote for radio and television.

In 1962, after a spell with a consulting engineering firm in London, he went back to Ireland and devoted himself to full-time journalism. He then joined Radio Telefís Éireann where he presently is a script editor in the drama department.

In addition to *The Ragpickers*, Mr. Smythe has had a number of plays produced on stage and television including *The Station*, presented at the Dublin Theatre Festival in 1967, and *The Prison*, which won a special award at the Golden Prague Festival in 1970 and has since been translated into several languages.

TOM

JOE

FERGUS

Scene:

*A room in the basement of a factory. In the center of the
room, four long tables or working benches are set at right
angles to each other so that they form a hollow square. In
one corner, the end of a steel chute is seen. At the opposite
end of the room there is an open lift, operated by a rope
and pulley like a dumbwaiter. There is a push-button bell
by the lift to give the signal to hoist. Central heating pipes
run through the room as do many ventilation shafts. The
walls are covered with junction boxes from which cables
run to the factory above. There is an old table and two
chairs set against the wall. Nearby is another table with a
gas ring on it. Beside it is a sink with one tap. The room
has one entrance—through a four-paneled door. Screwed
in this door is a coathook upon which Tom's shabby raincoat is hung.*

*Tom is at one of the benches sorting rags into two
separate piles. On his right side, on the floor, there is a sack
half full of rags. At his feet are two more sacks, almost
full, into which he puts his sorted rags. Tom concentrates
on his sorting. All his movements are deliberate and quick
through long practice. He has developed a certain routine
from which he never deviates. He sings the first four lines
of "April In Portugal" and hums as he works.*

*When he has finished sorting through the pile of rags
on the bench he carefully stuffs the sorted rags into the
two sacks on his left. Then there is the sound of a sack
landing down the chute. He notes this but goes to the sack
on his right and carefully takes out three handfuls of rags
and dumps them on the bench in a neat pile. Then he
walks over to the chute, picks up the new sack on his*

back, carries it over to his bench and places it next to the sack he is working on. He then resumes sorting. Tom is medium built, in his late forties and poorly dressed.

There is a knock on the door. Tom stops singing and cocks an ear, then walks to the door. Joe is standing there. He is a small, slightly built man, wearing glasses, and is in his middle thirties. He wears a raincoat too big for him and a flat cap.

TOM: I heard you the first time. I was busy.

JOE: Sorry. I didn't know. The Labor sent me. I'm to start here. (*Pause*) I was to ask for a feller called Tom.

TOM: That's me.

JOE: I'm to start here today they said.

TOM: Come on in, then.

(*Joe enters. Tom closes door and walks back to bench*)

TOM: Take your coat off, so, you can't work in it. (*Joe removes his coat and looks vaguely around*)

JOE: Where will I put it?

TOM: (*Looking around*) There's only the one coat hook here and that's mine. Hang it over there. (*Indicating junction box*)

(*Joe hangs it on a corner of the box and returns*)

TOM: Ever do this work before?

JOE: No.

TOM: What did you do, then?

JOE: Sweeping.

TOM: Sweeping. What kind of sweeping?

JOE: On the roads. I was with the corporation.

TOM: What happened? Good steady money. Coming in regular.

JOE: The damp. The rain, you see. The clinic says I should get inside, out of the damp like. It's my chest. It gets at me something fierce.

TOM: There's sweeping up there. (*Jerking thumb in di-*

rection of ceiling) You'd think you'd want to stick to your own trade.

JOE: The Labor sent me here to sort rags.

TOM: Not that sweeping is really a trade, you know.

JOE: It's steady enough working for the corporation. If it wasn't for my chest. . . .

TOM: Sweeping isn't sorting. There's more to it than just pushing a broom. Not everyone has the knack.

JOE: The feller at the Labor said I'd learn it all right. Pick it up, you know.

TOM: Pick it up! On your own? You have to have someone teach you. Did the feller at the Labor say anything about that now?

JOE: He said I'd pick it up all right. No bother. (*Pause*) I needed the job, you see.

TOM: These fellers at the counter think they know everything. And what do they do? Make you sign on three times a week, stamp your card and fill in forms. They know bugger all about this job. I can tell you that for nothing.

JOE: (*Pause*) If you could show me like. (*There is the sound of another sack landing down the chute*)

TOM: Jasus! Now what are they up to? I've only the one pair of hands! You'd think they'd show some bloody consideration. (*Pause. Looks at Joe*) You're wearing glasses.

JOE: But I've always worn them, you know. Ever since I was a kid. I can see all right with them.

TOM: It isn't sight you need for this job, let me tell you. It's *feel*. You tell by the feel of the rags, you see. Not by looking. Now you stand over there and watch me. Just watch me and don't say nothing. You can ask questions afterwards. You follow?

JOE: Yeah.

TOM: But first come over here. (*They walk 'round the table until they can see the chute*) Now you go and get that sack and bring it here. (*Joe walks over to the sack and starts to drag it to the workbench*)

TOM: No! Hump it on your shoulder! (*Joe lifts it awkwardly on his shoulder*) No! Get under it, man. Did you never carry a sack of coal?

(*Joe drops the sack, then bends down and picks it up again like a sack of coal. He staggers over to the bench, with Tom watching him critically*)

TOM: I hope you'll be able for this job. That's the easy part. It's *sorting* where the real skill comes in. (*Joe drops the sack beside the other*) Now come on and watch me. We're after wasting time. And remember, no questions till I'm good and ready. All right?

JOE: I'll remember.

TOM: What's your name?

JOE: Joe.

TOM: Joe, eh? All right, Joe. Now I'll finish sorting this pile I got on the bench. (*Demonstrates*) Here goes wool and here goes cotton. (*He rapidly sorts through the pile*) Now I put the wool in here and the cotton in here. (*Stuffing rags into open sacks on his left*) Now, you push down as hard as you can, see. Tight. Got it?

JOE: Yeah. Yeah.

TOM: You want to try your hand at it now? Or do you want to watch me again?

JOE: How do you tell the wool from the cotton?

TOM: By the feel. (*Gives Joe a rag*) What's that now?

JOE: Would it be wool?

TOM: Right first time. Lucky guess. Wool is thicker than cotton. Not always, but most of the time. You can tell by the feel. Cotton's more slippy-like. (*Gives him two more rags*) Now then, what's them? (*Joe takes the rags, feels them. Starts to speak. Hesitates*) Come on, we haven't got all day. Speak up, man, what are they?

JOE: I think they're cotton.

TOM: Think! You've got to be certain sure. That's the job. That's what they're paying you for. Well, what are they?

JOE: I'd say they're cotton.

TOM: (*Checking*) Cotton they are. All right, I'm going to let you have a go at sorting but I'm going to watch. Now get cracking. (*Takes a handful of rags and dumps them on Joe's bench*) Now, get on with it.

(*Joe starts to sort slowly. Tom watches critically. After Joe has sorted half a dozen, Tom snatches a rag*)

TOM: What's that? What would you say that is?

JOE: (*Feeling*) Wool?

TOM: Are you sure?

JOE: I think so. I mean I'm sure.

TOM: You'd better be sure. This isn't sweeping, you know. Any old eejit with a broom can sweep. Well, is it wool or is it not?

JOE: It is, Tom.

TOM: Then why the bloody hell did you put it on the cotton pile?

JOE: It was a mistake. I wasn't thinking.

TOM: Wasn't thinking! You wasn't thinking. But that's the job. I'm not paid to do your thinking for you. They don't like mistakes here. They raise holy hell if they find wool in the wrong sack. All right now, put it in the right pile and get on with it.

(*Joe resumes sorting slowly. Tom checking occasionally. Joe holds out a rag*)

JOE: What's this? I'm not quite sure.

TOM: What do you think it is?

JOE: I don't know. That's why I asked.

TOM: Well, give a guess. What would you say it is?

JOE: It feels like wool. But it's thin and slippy-like.

TOM: It is wool. But I wouldn't call it slippy. Yes, it's wool all right. (*Joe resumes sorting*) All right. I've got my own work to do. Will you be okay on your own for a while?

JOE: I think so.

TOM: You're very slow. Ah well, keep at it. And for God's sake ask me if you're not sure. Do you hear?

JOE: Yeah. Yeah.

(*Tom returns to his own bench and deftly sorts his rags. They work in silence for a while. Tom stuffs his rags into the appropriate sacks*)

TOM: Come over here till I show you something. (*Joe walks over*) Now these sacks are full, see. They have to be sealed up. (*Takes a large needle and twine and sews mouths of sacks*) Now this one is cotton and this one's wool. We know that but how will they know, eh?

JOE: I don't know, Tom.

TOM: Well, watch. I'll mark one of them. (*Takes a can of whitewash and marks a cross on one of the sacks*) That's wool. You don't have to mark them both. They know the one with this cross here is wool. Follow?

JOE: Yeah, Tom.

TOM: Now for the last stage of the operation. Grab ahold of that sack, will you? (*Tom grabs one sack, lifts it on his shoulder and walks over to the lift. Joe follows with the other sack. They load them on the lift*) Now we give them the old signal. (*Presses button. We hear the bell ring and soon the lift goes up*) There you are now. Job right!

JOE: That's handy all right.

TOM: It's all organized, Joe. All thought out. (*Sound of sack dropping down the chute*) Holy Mary! They're going mad today. Go on, Joe. Don't just stand there. Go and get the sack. (*Joe goes and brings back the sack*) You'll have to shift for yourself. We're falling behind. I suppose when you first came in here—when you first walked through that door—you thought it was a soft job, eh? Be honest now. You thought there was nothing to it?

JOE: They said I'd pick it up all right. I mean, I never done it before.

TOM: You don't have to tell me that. It's as plain as the bloody nose on your face. But there's more to it than you thought. Go on. Admit it, Joe.

JOE: It'll take a lot of getting used to all right.

TOM: Different to sweeping?

JOE: Like chalk and cheese.

TOM: All right, so. Now, I've got to get back to the job. I've shown you all I can, have I not?

JOE: You have, Tom.

TOM: Well, get on with it and cut out the blather.

(*Tom takes his place at his bench. They both continue to sort. Joe still works slowly but a little quicker than before. When he has finished his pile he calls to Tom*)

JOE: I've finished this lot. Would you ever check it?

(*Tom checks it*)

TOM: That's all right. No mistakes so far. But you've been taking long enough about it.

JOE: Better sure than sorry, Tom.

TOM: Now go over there. (*Points*) There in the corner. You'll find some empty sacks. Bring two over here. (*Joe does so*) Now open them up like this. (*Shows how the mouths of the sacks are left open*) All right. Now we're ready to start filling these. Now you put more rags on the bench yourself. Not too many. Say, three handfuls.

(*Joe arranges a new pile of rags on his bench and they resume work. Joe is now working a little quicker*)

TOM: You always do sweeping?

JOE: I worked up at the brewery once. St. James's Gate.

TOM: Did you now? That'd be a good billet, I'd say. What were you doing, sampling the pints?

JOE: In the bottling department.

TOM: What happened to you?

JOE: The work was a bit heavy-like.

TOM: You got laid off?

JOE: I got laid off.

TOM: What else you done?

JOE: I worked in Murphy's pub in Ringsend.

TOM: Barman?

JOE: Not in the union. Just helping out. Collecting the glasses, washing them, you know. Weekends.

TOM: You'd need more than that to keep you going.

JOE: I used to deliver for a grocery on Grafton Street during the week but they went out of business.

TOM: On a bike?

JOE: Yeah. On a bike with a big carrier in front. I liked that. Look, I finished, Tom.

TOM: (*Checks pile*) Right. All in proper order. Now you can put them in the sacks yourself. Don't make a mistake now. This one's the wool.

(*Joe stuffs rags in sacks*)

TOM: (*Checking pocket watch*) It's just about dinner time. I'll put the kettle on. (*He lights the gas ring. Fills the kettle from the one tap at the brown sink. Puts it on the flame. They both resume work*)

JOE: You been here a long time, Tom?

TOM: Long enough. I'm on steady. Paid by the week. I'm not casual, you know.

JOE: Oh, I figured that all right. It's a nice enough job. Bit hard on the old pins standing all day. Too bad there isn't a couple of stools.

TOM: You want it too soft altogether. Sitting wouldn't be right. You've got to stay alert. You need your wits about you for this job.

JOE: I'll manage all right. I've had too more than a few jobs in my time, you know.

TOM: This is a standing up job, Joe.

JOE: And I never had no trouble learning the work. I just packed up the jobs when I felt like it. Not because I couldn't do it.

TOM: Fair enough. I was just telling you the rules. That's what I'm here for.

JOE: I didn't think there'd be any harm in sitting on a stool every once in a while. I never meant all the time.

TOM: Let me put it to you this way, if the gaffers upstairs (*Pointing up*) thought the job called for stools, they would have put them in here, right?

JOE: I suppose so. Still and all. . . .

TOM: It's all organized, Joe. All thought out. You'll get used to it.

JOE: (*Pause*) Where's that steam coming from?

TOM: There's a boiler over there making steam for the works up there. (*Pointing*) Some of it leaks out—like when the pressure's up.

JOE: I don't think it'll be too good for my chest. (*Coughs*)

TOM: Go way out of that, man. It's the dry air that grabs you in the throat.

JOE: It's the chest you see, the damp....

TOM: Damp, is it? This place is as dry as a bone. You don't know when you're well off. Many's a feller I've heard complaining about being crucified with the cold in some of those old factories. But not here, eh, Joe?

JOE: If you think it's all right.

TOM: Amn't I telling you that there's no harm in that bit of steam at all but just the opposite? It'll do you all the good in the world—especially if you're prone to a bit of weakness in the old box. (*Tapping chest*)

JOE: Well, if you say so, Tom. (*The factory whistle blows*)

TOM: There you are! Dinner time and the kettle should be ready.

(*The kettle starts to sing. They both stop work. Tom goes to his coat and takes out a paper bag of sandwiches and a carton of milk*)

TOM: You bring something to eat, Joe?

JOE: I've a couple of sandwiches.

(*He gets them from his raincoat and they both sit down at the table. Tom sets out two cups and saucers and makes the tea*)

TOM: How long did you say you were here for?

JOE: A couple of weeks, maybe three.

TOM: Well, you can use my tea this week. Next week you can chip in if you like.

JOE: I'll pay you for the tea and the milk this week, soon as I get paid.

TOM: Be better if you bought it next week. How much sugar?

JOE: Four spoonfuls. I like it sweet-like.

TOM: Right you are. What kind of sandwiches do you have?

JOE: Jam. Strawberry jam.

TOM: I've got one cheese and one corned beef. You can have half the corned beef if you like.

JOE: I wouldn't rob you, Tom.

TOM: Go on, man. Take it. (*Offers a sandwich*)

JOE: And I'll give you half of one of mine. Do you care for jam?

TOM: It's all right. Makes a change. (*They both eat. Tom quickly and noisily. Joe slowly and quietly*) Live at home, Joe?

JOE: Not now. Since the mammy died I stayed with the sister. But she got married last year.

TOM: You're on your own, so?

JOE: I've a room in a house off Talbot Street.

TOM: That's very handy for you. Do you get out much?

JOE: Where?

TOM: Out. Into town. To the flicks. The pubs.

JOE: I'm not much at drinking. A pint or so weekends.

TOM: No family?

JOE: Only the sister. And she's married now and living in Carlow.

TOM: Well, you have somewhere to visit. A trip down the country.

JOE: Yeah. I'll have to go down someday.

TOM: It'd be nice. Make a change.

JOE: Yeah. (*Pause*) What about you, Tom, are you married?

TOM: I was. I lost the missus—going on ten years ago now.

JOE: Any kids?

TOM: No. We never had any. Used to keep pigeons though. We rented our own house. Very nice.

JOE: Still got it?

TOM: It was too big, you know, just for me. I live with the brother and his wife now.

JOE: You've got company, so.

TOM: It's not like you think. The place full of kids. Now the eldest is getting on and wants his own room. Begob, I wish he had it too. Him and his old guitar. I'll have to move out.

JOE: Guitar?

TOM: Always at it, screeching and moaning, and him only fourteen.

JOE: It's nice all the same. When you can play proper, that is.

TOM: You wouldn't say that if you could hear him at it. Always on about the hills of Tennessee and him never been further than the hill of Howth.

JOE: I always fancied playing the guitar meself.

TOM: You never!

JOE: I did so, or the melodeon. It'd be nice all right, all the people standing 'round listening, joining in the chorus, like.

TOM: Fair enough if you've the talent for it. I like a bit of music meself. Always did. But this feller now, he has no ear for music at all. And a voice on him like an old donkey with asthma.

JOE: You'll miss the company, all the same.

TOM: I won't. Be my own boss. Get a nice room somewhere, handy to town. Cook what I want and eat when I want. I've got a good steady job. Shouldn't be too hard to find a decent room somewhere.

JOE: I'd say you're fond of the odd pint now and then.

TOM: Why do you say that?

JOE: I saw the way you looked when I said I used to work at the brewery. Like it would have suited you.

TOM: I like the occasional pint all right. Play the odd game of darts. More for the company, you know, than the booze. But I keep pretty much to myself.

JOE: But you've company at home.

TOM: It's not like that, I tell you. Always having to move when the sister-in-law wants to get on with the housework. Can't get settled. Kids running in and out all the time. Doors always banging. Can't settle down to read the paper, never mind watching telly.

JOE: Telly. You've got a telly? That's grand. You'll miss that.

TOM: And what's to stop me renting one on my own? By the week. I've got steady money coming in. There'd be no bother about that.

JOE: No. There'd be no bother about that. Just sign your name. It's well for you, Tom, in a good steady job like this. Permanent.

TOM: That's what it is. Permanent. I don't know if there's a pension in it. I never asked. But I've saved a few quid, you know, for the rainy day.

JOE: You're pretty well fixed. I wish. . . .

TOM: Now, Joe, don't feel bad. Maybe they'll keep you on longer than the fortnight. Maybe they'll get really busy and need an extra man. Steady.

JOE: They said two weeks, maybe three at the most.

TOM: But what the hell do them fellers know? They know nothing. We're busy enough now and maybe we'll stay busy. Who knows. Look on the bright side.

JOE: I always did, Tom. My mammy said I was always the cheerful one.

TOM: Well, there you are then. And if you're not kept on here, maybe you'll get a steady job somewhere else—an inside job away from the damp.

JOE: I'll look on the bright side, Tom.

TOM: That's the idea. (*Pause*) Ever go to the zoo, Joe?

JOE: The zoo?

TOM: Yeah, you know, Phoenix Park.

JOE: I used to go with my mammy and Bridie, the sister.

TOM: I go just about every Sunday. I like looking at the flamingos. Then I have a bite to eat in the café.

JOE: That'd make a nice day out.

TOM: It does. And you'd spend more on having a few jars in the local. It doesn't cost all that much.

JOE: When I get paid. . . .

TOM: Yeah?

JOE: As soon as I get a few bob I'd like to go.

TOM: You mean it?

JOE: I would. Honest to God. I'd like to see the lions and the monkeys. And the flamingos of course. Is them the birds that bury themselves in the mud up to their necks?

TOM: Them's ostriches. You can see them as well. Queer looking beasts they are, too. No, flamingos is pink. They've long legs and long necks, all right, but when they move about it's like they're doing a slow dance. Ostriches are a different kettle of fish altogether. They're clumsy and ugly. You should see those flamingos, Joe, when the sun's shining. All pink and graceful-like among the green grass. It's a sight worth seeing, I can tell you.

JOE: What would they eat?

TOM: I don't know. Bits of things in the grass or in the water. Worms maybe. I don't know. But if you could see them lifting up their legs when they walk and their neck stretched out. (*Pause*) Do you mean it, Joe?

JOE: What?

TOM: About going?

JOE: I do surely. As soon as I get the readies. I'll go this weekend. This Sunday. Maybe I could meet you, and you could show me around. I mean, you must know the place pretty well.

TOM: None better. I know all the keepers by sight. To nod to, you know. I've got pretty pally with the keeper in the reptile house. His name is Peter. We often have a regular old chat about snakes. Very interesting, too.

JOE: That's very decent of you, Tom.

TOM: What?

JOE: Letting me go along with you.

TOM: Not at all. I'll be glad of the company. Some more tea?

JOE: If there's any left.

TOM: Plenty for both of us. (*Pours*) Right. That's settled, so. This Sunday. We can make the arrangements later. (*The whistle blows. Tom gulps down his tea*) Go on. You finish your cuppa. I'll get on with the job. You take your time.

(*He rinses his cup and goes back to the bench and resumes work. Joe finishes his tea. Rinses his cup and goes to his bench. They work away steadily. Tom hums and sings "The Blue Danube." After a few beats, Joe joins him by whistling. Tom glances across at Joe*)

TOM: You're getting the hang of it nicely now. I'd say you really have the knack for this work.

JOE: Thanks, Tom, It's coming along a little better now.

TOM: You're picking it up almost as fast as I did. When I started here ten years ago there were three of us. All temporary. When things got slack they laid off the other two fellers and kept me on.

JOE: You've been here ten years so?

TOM: Almost to the day.

JOE: And before that? You don't mind me asking?

TOM: (*Pause*) I've never told anyone before. The brother knows. Of course. I was in a different class of trade altogether. I was a turner and. . . .

JOE: What's that, Tom?

TOM: Working on a lathe. Served me time five years. It's a good trade, Joe, the best there is. You have to know what you're about in a machine shop.

JOE: The money would be good, I'd say.

TOM: One of the highest paid trades there is. I was renting, like I told you, but I had my eye on a house in Santry with a nice bit of a garden.

JOE: What happened to you, so?

TOM: I was a bit too fond of the old jar. Went on the skite once too often. I knew I'd be for the high jump if I stayed off the job again, so I went in of the Monday when I still had the shakes.

JOE: Ah, drink's a curse, so it is.

TOM: To make a long story short, I made a regular bags of the job I was on—a special kind of shaft that was worth a packet. I could never get a job in my own trade after.

JOE: We all have our troubles, Tom. But you're well fixed now. A nice steady job.

TOM: Yeah. I pulled myself together after I lost the missus. And I never take more than the odd jar now.

JOE: A pity about your old job all the same. I mean, after you serving your time and all.

TOM: A job is what a man makes it. There's a lot to this one, like I've told you. And I'm my own boss, like. I'm in charge.

JOE: I can understand now how you have the knack of it. You know, after having been a turner and everything. But I'll never get it.

TOM: Sure you will. It's just practice.

JOE: No. Not in a month of Sundays.

TOM: Well, if you don't do quite as good as me you'll be treading on my heels.

JOE: You think so, Tom?

TOM: I'm sure of it. It's a gift and I think you've got it, Joe. (*They work in silence for a while*) What's that room like of yours?

JOE: Not so hot. Why?

TOM: Well, I'll be looking for a room like I told you. I thought maybe if there was one going vacant in your house?

JOE: It wouldn't suit a man like you, Tom. Not one who's been used to his own house, and pigeons and everything. It's not up to much. Small and dark.

TOM: I'm sorry to hear that.

JOE: If I got steady work again I'd move out. Maybe near the sea. Then I could come in on a bike.

TOM: You have a bike, then?

JOE: No. But I could buy one on the never-never. If I had a steady job, that is.

TOM: If you don't get taken on here steady, I could keep my eyes and ears open for you. How about that now?

JOE: That's very good of you, Tom.

TOM: Did you ever try the buses?

JOE: I wouldn't be able for the stairs. Not up and down all day. Besides, I'd be scared out of my wits handling all that money.

TOM: Well, there's lots of jobs going, Joe. I'll look out for you. (*Pause. Looks at him critically*) You need to eat more. Meat and potatoes every day. You need more weight on you. There's not much nourishment in jam sandwiches.

JOE: I get a good feed pretty often at a café near the house.

TOM: Sausage and chips. I know them places. Not like a home cooked meal, Joe. I'll tell you one thing, Joe, the missus was only a grand cook. Cook anything, she could, but her specialty was meat puddings. I always said she could have opened her own café serving nothing else.

JOE: You're right there. The sister was only a wonderful cook. Make a real tasty meal, she could.

TOM: There's not much joy in living on your own. And that's a fact.

JOE: You never said a truer word, Tom. And yet you come and go as you please. All the quiet you want to read the papers or to have a bit of a snooze like. (*Two more bags come down the chute*)

TOM: Two of them! Let's go, Joe. (*They move to retrieve the sacks*) The pressure's on, boy. I'm glad you're here to help.

(*At the bench again*)

TOM: It looks like it could be good news tonight. If there's more than two sacks unopened at knocking off time, we're entitled to stay and do overtime. That's the rules. Sometimes there's two hours in it. At time-and-a-half.

JOE: That's great.

TOM: That'll pay your way into the zoo—and enough to buy your lunch. Plus a bag of buns for the elephants. What do you think of that?

JOE: Smashing. (*Pause*) I hope I'll be able for it, Tom. My legs are aching a bit.

TOM: Now never mind about that. Amn't I here? I'll lend

you a hand. I'll see you all right. Never fear. (*They resume work*) You know, Joe, I've never taken anyone home—for a bit of supper like. No reason why I shouldn't. I pay my whack. Regular. (*Pause*) Would you like to come back with me one night?

JOE: (*Pause*) I wouldn't want to put your sister-in-law to any trouble.

TOM: What trouble is in it now? I bet you don't eat more than a sparrow. (*Pause*) We could have a pint or two on the way home. Work up an appetite.

JOE: Thanks, Tom, all the same. But leave it over a bit, will you?

TOM: Whatever you say, Joe. No rush. (*Pause*) Be no harm if I took a look at the papers. Maybe I'd find a room that would suit us both. Near the sea, eh?

JOE: I often wished I'd been a sailor. The sea's the place.

TOM: And sharing with someone you get on with is the thing, I'd say. It's company. Many's the time I feel like a bit of a chat after reading something in the papers.

JOE: Or about a game in Dalymount Park.

TOM: That's it. A pint and a chat after the game is the best part. Do you watch soccer, Joe?

JOE: I always meant to go. A feller took me to Shelbourne Park once.

TOM: Nothing like a night out at the dogs. Now if we shared a room we could arrange all sorts of trips. God, there wouldn't be enough time left in the world to do all the things we wanted to do. Eh?

JOE: You're right there, Tom.

(*They work in silence for a while. Joe leans his elbows on the bench as he works*)

TOM: How's the legs?

JOE: All right.

TOM: Take a breather. Go over and sit at the table for ten minutes. No one will know.

JOE: I'm all right, Tom.

TOM: You'll get used to it. It takes getting used to. After all, this is only your first day. It must be hard on you. I mean, you're used to sweeping. Being on the move all the time. Right?

JOE: That's right, Tom.

TOM: You'll get used to it in no time. In a month you'll be doing it automatic like. And then you can think of other things. I often think about when I was a kid going to school. (*Laughs*) The teacher, Miss Molloy, used to poke through our hair with a pencil, looking for nits.

JOE: I don't think I'll get used to it at all. Ever.

TOM: Stop your talking! You will, of course.

JOE: (*Low*) I won't, Tom.

TOM: Why? Why do you say that?

JOE: I appreciate what you're doing all right. But it's no use.

TOM: What do you mean. No use?

JOE: Nothing.

TOM: You must mean something. You can't say things that mean nothing. (*Looks at him*) Huh? It doesn't make sense.

JOE: I know. That's just it.

TOM: What?

JOE: I won't be able to stick it. Now leave me alone, will you. (*They work in silence. Joe starts to speak several times. Tom sees this but waits*) I can't stick at anything and that's the gospel truth. It wasn't only on account of my chest I left the corporation. I couldn't stick it any longer. I've had dozens of jobs —maybe hundreds. I just can't stick at them. And that's the truth. Now you know.

TOM: But you could change. I mean, a nice job like this. Warm and dry and steady money and all.

JOE: It wouldn't work, Tom. I know. I'll never change. You could ask the sister. She got fed up with me. That's why she moved out and got married.

TOM: But you could try to stick it this time. You don't know until you try, do you now? Eh?

JOE: I don't know, Tom.

TOM: But isn't that what I'm after saying? You don't know until you try. Look at Napoleon!

JOE: Napoleon?

TOM: Yeah, Napoleon. He didn't know what he could do until he tried. He failed over and over again and then he succeeded. He kept on trying, Joe. Keep thinking of Napoleon. Eh?

JOE: I don't know much about him to tell you the truth. I've heard of him, of course.

TOM: I've told you all you need to know about him. He stuck at it. Like the spider in the cave, he watched when he was in exile; he kept on trying. He wouldn't give up. I wish I'd seen the film. Maybe if it comes 'round again we could go and see it together.

(*The door bursts open and Fergus enters. He is a burly man in his mid-thirties with a stupid, crafty face. He wears his cheap clothes with a certain swagger. His coat is belted and his cap is at a rakish angle. Joe looks at him with interest*)

FERGUS: The Labor sent me. I gave my cards to the gaffer upstairs in the office. (*To Joe*) Sorting rags, is it?

JOE: Yeah. Tom here will show you.

(*Fergus takes off his coat vigorously, looks around. Walks back to the door and hangs his hat and coat over Tom's raincoat which falls to the floor. Fergus moves to the bench*)

TOM: Watch it, feller! Watch what you're doing now!

FERGUS: (*Belligerently*) What's that? What are you on about, mate?

TOM: My coat. You knocked my coat down.

(*Fergus hesitates, then goes back to the door and roughly hangs up Tom's coat over his. Then he approaches Joe*)

FERGUS: All right, what do we do, eh?

TOM: The sacks come down. . . .

FERGUS: I wasn't asking you.

JOE: But Tom's the boss here. He knows. . . .

FERGUS: (*Examining Joe's pile of rags*) What are you sorting, cotton from wool?

JOE: That's right, but . . . .

TOM: I'll tell him, Joe. (*To Fergus*) You go over to the chute, see. . . .

(*Fergus picks up a full sack, rips it open and dumps contents on bench*)

TOM: That's not the way to do it!

FERGUS: What is it, then?

TOM: You take three handfuls. Place them on the bench.

FERGUS: (*Starting to sort*) All right. So I took ten handfuls, twenty maybe. What's the differ, eh?

(*Tom motions to Joe to move closer to him. Joe does so*)

TOM: (*Low*) Let him alone. He won't be here for long. I can tell you that for nothing.

JOE: It's a wonder he doesn't want to learn to do the job properly.

TOM: An ignorant lot altogether. I know his type.

FERGUS: (*Stopping work*) What's that whispering! Are you talking about me? (*Moves threateningly to Tom*) Because if you are I'll give you a puck in the gob in short order, mate! Make no mistake about that. (*He returns to his own bench*)

JOE. Don't bother about him, Tom. Let him alone.

TOM: A bowsie. An ignorant, good for nothing bowsie. That's what he is.

JOE: Shh!

FERGUS: Now I warned you! Don't say I didn't. (*Grabs handfuls of sorted rags. To Joe*) Where do I put these? They're cotton.

JOE: Tom will tell you.

FERGUS: I'm asking you. I won't ask twice.

JOE: (*Hastily*) Here. In this sack.

(*Fergus stuffs cotton in the sack indicated and then the pile of wool in the other sack. Tom goes to the sack and examines the rags. He walks over to Fergus with one rag in his hand*)

TOM: Cotton. This is cotton.

FERGUS: I can see it's cotton. What about it?

TOM: You put it in the sack with the wool.

FERGUS: (*Snatches it out of his hand and goes over to cotton sack and drops it in*) What differ does one lousy old rag make?

TOM: You're paid to sort. That's what you're here for.

FERGUS: Don't come that with me, mate! I'm warning you.

TOM: Listen you! I work here regular. Steady. I'm not a casual, by the hour. This is my job and I'm in charge. If you want to work here tomorrow you'd better remember that.

(*He looks at Fergus steadily then goes back to his place. Joe gives him an approving look. Tom goes to pile of empty sacks in corner, picks up two and drops them by Fergus. He marks one with a cross*)

TOM: Now, them are your sacks. The one with a cross is for the wool. See you don't make any more mistakes.

FERGUS: Frig off, will you!

(*They work in silence. Fergus looks occasionally across at Joe*)

TOM: (*Low*) I could have a word with the sister-in-law tonight. Maybe on pay night we could....

JOE: I told you, Tom, I'm not good in company. I get nervous eating with strangers. I never know what to say.

TOM: Right. I know a café. Near the quays. They put out a good feed. Reasonable. Plenty of meat and potatoes. How would that suit you?

JOE: Sounds good.

TOM: Well, will we make it a date, then? Straight after work.

FERGUS: (*Looking around*) Is there not a stool in this bloody place?

JOE: No, you see it wouldn't be right to....

TOM: Don't talk to him, Joe. Let him alone.

FERGUS: What do you mean it wouldn't be right? Why not? (*Lights a cigarette*)

TOM: No smoking in here.

FERGUS: I don't see no sign.

TOM: No smoking except during tea breaks.

FERGUS: Well, I'm taking my break now. All right? (*Tom resumes work*) Yeah, a stool would be just the job. (*To Joe*) Hey, haven't I seen you down at the Labor, signing on?

TOM: Don't answer him, Joe.

FERGUS: I remember you now. Your name is Joe. Joe something. Right? (*Joe nods*)

TOM: Ignore him.

FERGUS: You were talking to the feller behind the counter. The one with the glasses who gave you the card for here. He's a good pal of mine. Gets me lots of jobs. (*Walks to Joe and shakes his hand*) My name is Fergus.

JOE: Hi!

FERGUS: (*Resuming work*) He's going to fix me up in a good job next week.

TOM: Watch that fag. These rags are inflammable.

(*Fergus throws cigarette on floor and stamps on it with a flourish. He winks at Joe*)

TOM: (*Sews up bag and hands paint pot to Joe*) Here, you can mark the sack if you like. (*Joe does so*) Next time you can sew the bags up yourself.

JOE: Thanks, Tom.

TOM: Then you will have done everything. The whole operation. That's not bad for your first day on the job, is it now?

JOE: No, Tom.

(*They walk over to the lift*)

TOM: You see, Joe, you're willing to learn. To do the job proper. Not like some. You've got to have pride in your work. Right?

JOE: Right.

TOM: How's the legs?

JOE: Fair enough, Tom. Grand.

TOM: (*Loading the sacks onto the lift*) Now, you ring the bell. (*Joe does so. Tom listens with satisfaction. As they walk back to the bench Tom moves Joe to the other side so Joe is now at the bench to his left*) You work this side, all right? (*Tom is now working between Joe and Fergus. Fergus glares at him while he sorts carelessly*)

TOM: Watch it now! I've told you before. Don't mix them up.

FERGUS: Ah, what's the differ, eh! Who cares if you mix them up a bit?

TOM: It's the job. I told you.

FERGUS: It's no job at all. Not for a man, that is. Rag-picking! Only fitting for women.

JOE: If you'd take the trouble to learn the job proper....

TOM: Quiet, Joe! It's not ragpicking, it's sorting.

JOE: There's a knack to it.

FERGUS: Who're you codding? Knack! Sure, a child of ten could do it—with its eyes closed. (*Closes his eyes and elaborately sorts, tossing rags in the air*) See. (*Joe laughs. Tom hushes him*)

TOM: It's well to see you won't be here for long.

JOE: You won't be kept on steady.

FERGUS: I wouldn't want to be kept on here steady. Not if I was blind and crippled and starving. It's no job for a man. I don't work at nothing steady. Come and go as I please. I'm my own man. Listen. (*He moves his piles of rags to the next bench to his right so that he is next to Joe*) Do you know what I was doing last summer, eh? Give a guess.

JOE: I don't know.

TOM: And we're not interested.

FERGUS: Fruit picking. Over beyond in England. There was hundreds of students. Some smashing birds. You shoulda seen one I was knocking around with. Swedish, she was. Took a real fancy to me. Used to buy me pints in the local. And what do you think she did when she left? You know, at the end of the season when the job was over? Give a guess, Joe.

JOE: I don't know.

FERGUS: Gave me a fiver—for services rendered. (*Laughs*)

TOM: (*Low*) Don't mind him. Get on with your work, Joe. You're doing fine. How's the legs?

FERGUS: He needs a bloody stool, same as me.

TOM: I wasn't talking to you. Get on with your work and keep to yourself. (*Pause. They work*)

FERGUS: Hey! Is that steam escaping?

JOE: Yeah. No harm in it though.

FERGUS: Live steam! Hey boss, did you know the air is being polluted? (*Joe coughs*)

TOM: Get on with your work and not be bothering about a bit of steam.

JOE: It's good for you. Isn't that right, Tom?

FERGUS: Good for you! Do you know what I'm going to tell you? I could get the Health Department to close the whole shebang here like that. (*Snaps fingers*) One phone call from me and everybody out.

JOE: All the same, Fergus, it's warm. There's some fellers crucified with the cold and. . . .

FERGUS: Now if I had a stilson wrench, some compound and lagging, I could fix that up in a jiffy. I used to work for a plumber, you know.

TOM: We have our own maintenance crew here, so just forget it.

FERGUS: Well, see you get them down here or. . . . (*He makes dialing motion and winks at Joe. They resume work*)

FERGUS: I bet you don't know what these rags are used for, eh? I bet you don't know. I bet you a hundred quid. (*Tom concentrates on his work*)

JOE: Tell him, Tom.

FERGUS: He can't tell because he doesn't know. I won my bet.

TOM: The job here is sorting. That's my job. And teaching the casuals. That's my job, too. Them's that's willing to learn, that is.

FERGUS: You don't know! Well, I do. I've used them. Many and many a time. The cotton's used for polishing cars and things. And the wool is used in machine shops for mopping up the oil. You know, around the lathes and such like. I've used them both. So what the hell does it matter if you get one or two mixed up? Nothing! It doesn't matter a tinker's damn. Nobody notices.

TOM: The gaffer upstairs will have a different notion about that, I can tell you. You'll get your cards tomorrow.

FERGUS: So what! I'll be in another job by dinner time. No bother. Maybe I'll go down the country. (*To Joe*) Do you know I was with a circus once?

JOE: (*Interested*) Yeah?

FERGUS: For a year. Almost. Traveled every parish in Ireland. Putting up the tents, the booths and assembling the seats. Hard graft it was, too. A man's job, I can tell you. Not like this. Women's work.

JOE: What happened? Why did you leave?

TOM: Don't listen to him. It's only a pack of lies.

FERGUS: Lies, is it! Calling me a liar, are you! You want to have a bet on it? You go and ask anybody at O'Malley's circus if Fergus wasn't with them. They'll tell you. Ah, what do you know about anything anyway. Spent your whole life in this shagging kip ragpicking.

JOE: That's not true! Tom has . . . .

TOM: Never mind him.

JOE: But tell him you had your own house and all.

FERGUS: A corner in a public house is more like it.

TOM: I wouldn't waste my breath talking to that bowsie and I'd advise you not to either.

FERGUS: And that's not all, Joe. I was with the animals. The lions.

TOM: Here, let me check your work. (*He checks his piles*)

JOE: They're all right, Tom.

FERGUS: Yeah. The lions. Proper fierce they were, too. Not doped or anything, you know.

JOE: Gosh! Tom here goes to the zoo regular. Don't you, Tom?

TOM: Ah, don't be believing a word this feller says. Lions!

FERGUS: I told you before, mate. Ask anybody at O'Malley's. I wouldn't cod *you*, Joe. Want to hear how I got the job helping with the animals?

JOE: Tom, there'd be no harm . . . .

TOM: It's up to you, Joe. I can't tell you what to do. But I'd think you'd have more sense than . . . .

FERGUS: The regular feller who helped the trainer—his name was Lenihan—got sick. He was in the rats. You know, after too much booze. And because I was always interested, always watching them being fed, I got the job while he was drying out in Dublin. For three weeks.

JOE: What did you do?

FERGUS: Helped to feed them. Once a day. Pushed big hunks of meat through the bars. We had two lions, a tiger, and a bear. Then we had to get them from the cages into the ring. And back again. They'd roar and snarl something shocking when they had to go in the big cage in the ring, but they'd run back to their own cages like lambs.

JOE: Were you ever scared?

FERGUS: No. What was there to be scared about? I used to poke at them with a stick to hurry them along. They're animals, aren't they? *We've* got the brains. The old head power. It's them that was afraid of us.

JOE: Gosh! So why did you leave?

FERGUS: Ah well, there's a story there all right. I'll tell you sometime, Joe. I'm afraid it might shock your man there.

TOM: We don't want any of that sort of talk in here.

FERGUS: See! What did I tell you? Ah well, I would have moved on anyway. I don't like staying anywhere too long.

JOE: You mean you don't want steady work!

TOM: He couldn't keep a job for more than a few months. That's easy enough to see.

FERGUS: Wrong again, me old segocia. Wrong again. I was working in a lumberyard in Limerick once and the boss begged me to stay on. Said he'd make me foreman. Not for me! I've been a gaffer in my time, though you might not believe it.

TOM: We wouldn't.

FERGUS: Unloading coal at a siding in Arklow. There's backbreaking work for you. Takes a man to handle a shovel full of coal right. (*Fills his two sacks. To Tom*) What do I do with these?

TOM: (*Sewing them up*) Put them on the lift over there. (*He points. Fergus grabs both sacks under his arms and takes them to the lift. Joe helps him to load them on*)

JOE: Will I ring the bell, Tom?

TOM: Go ahead. I don't see why he shouldn't do it himself. If he can tame a pack of lions, I can't see why he can't ring his own bloody bell.

FERGUS: I never said I was a lion tamer. All I said was I helped the trainer. Right, Joe?

JOE: Yeah. (*To Tom*) You have to be fair Tom, he never . . . .

TOM: Ah, shut up! Sorry, Joe. I didn't mean it. That feller gets on my wick. That's all. (*They resume work*) Did you say you were thinking of going down to Carlow to see the sister?

JOE: She asked me down all right but . . . .

TOM: But what, Joe?

JOE: I think she was only asking, you know. We had a bit of a barney before she left.

TOM: But that's all dead and gone now. She'd be pleased to see you, I'm sure.

JOE: You think so, Tom?

TOM: Why wouldn't she, so? Blood's thicker than water, you know. And who can you trust if you can't trust relations— and friends, eh?

JOE: True enough, Tom.

TOM: A day out in the country would do you the world of good. I could go down with you. Oh, I wouldn't go with you to your sister's. I could have a pint or two while you visited. I'd enjoy the bus ride.

JOE: That'd be nice all right. (*Pause*) Were you ever in Killarney, Tom?

TOM: I was. Years ago when I was a kid.

JOE: Maybe we could go there on the bus and I could visit the sister some other time.

TOM: Fair enough.

FERGUS: Would you ever check these for me, Tom? (*Indicating piles*)

TOM: Why?

FERGUS: Just to make sure I've got them in the right piles. You're the boss.

TOM: Aren't you just after saying that it doesn't matter?

JOE: Do it for him, Tom. He wants to do it the proper way now.

TOM: Ah, Janey Mac! Can't you see . . . (*He checks Fergus's work quickly then goes back to his own bench*)

FERGUS: All okay, Tom?

TOM: Yeah. (*Fergus grins and winks at Joe*)

FERGUS: I was in Killarney once. Worked for the Council. On the roads. All summer. I bet you I seen more of the lakes and scenery than any shagging tourist.

JOE: I'll say you did. I worked for the corporation once. Sweeping.

FERGUS: Is that right? So did I. Just for a week to fill in. In Rathmines. Rained every bloody day. I packed it in.

JOE: It's hard in winter all right.

FERGUS: How long were you at it?

JOE: Over three years.

FERGUS: You stuck it that long! Me, I wouldn't want anything that steady.

JOE: It all depends.

FERGUS: On what?

JOE: What you're doing. A steady job you know, a good job somewhere . . . .

TOM: That's right, Joe. Security. That's what you want.

FERGUS: Security me eye! Not for me. I like to come and go as I please. I'm my own man. I thought of going to Australia once.

JOE: Australia! Did you not go?

FERGUS: I could have. As easy as snapping my fingers. There was a feller wanted to give me the loan of the money but I changed my mind.

JOE: Were you ever in Australia, Tom?

TOM: I would have told you if I was.

JOE: That's right, Tom, you would have.

FERGUS: Remember that job I was telling you about—the feller at the Labor is fixing me up with?

JOE: Yeah.

FERGUS: You'd like it.

TOM: He has a good job here. Right, Joe?

JOE: That's right, Tom.

FERGUS: This is a factory doing assembly work. You don't have to be in the union. It's easy work, sitting down and the pay is good.

TOM: You wouldn't want to work in one of them big factories. Some foreman watching you all the time. Speed ups and things like that.

FERGUS: What's wrong with a big factory? They've their own canteen. A good feed at dinner time, dirt cheap. Always lots of people to have a bit of crack with. You don't work as hard as you do here. And there's always lots of birds. Some of them dead-easy.

TOM: That's just the sort of place Joe wouldn't want to work in.

JOE: I like a bit of company now and then. And sitting down.

TOM: Now, if it's only a stool that's after bothering you . . . .

FERGUS: They'll be taking on half a dozen men. I could put in a quiet word for you if you want.

TOM: He's not interested. He has a good job with the chance of being steady.

FERGUS: I'm not talking to you, mate. I'm talking to Joe. How about it, Joe?

JOE: I don't know.

TOM: But you do know. You know when you're well off.

JOE: I wouldn't want to work in a factory—not for long.

FERGUS: Janey Mac! Who says it'd be for long? It's only a month. That's why the pay is so good. It's temporary. I wouldn't want it for longer than a month. Not with summer coming up.

JOE: Summer?

FERGUS: Yeah. Summer's no time for working inside in shagging dumps like this. (*Gestures*) I know a bloke in South Kerry who'd give us a start.

JOE: Would you be going near Killarney?

FERGUS: And why not? I'm my own man. I've got connections there. Ah yes, they all remember Fergus in Killarney.

TOM: The guards too, I bet. Now listen to me, Joe . . . .

FERGUS: No reason you couldn't come along with me. We could stop over in Killarney a few days. As long as we liked.

TOM: You wouldn't be able for it, Joe. Traveling is terrible hard on your legs.

FERGUS: Looka, mate, I've traveled the length and breadth of Ireland and never had to walk more than a couple of miles. (*Lifts thumb*) Beats shanks' mare, that does.

JOE: It'd be good to see a bit of the country, all right.

FERGUS: Go where you like, when you like. Good grub on the farms. All you want. You work a day here, a day there. If it don't suit we move on.

TOM: Yeah, like some tramp or tinker. That sort of life wouldn't suit you at all, Joe.

JOE: I don't think I could do farm work, Fergus. I'd like to all right but, well you know, lifting and things like that . . . .

FERGUS: And who says you'll have to lift a finger? Not when you're with Fergus. Amn't I strong enough to do two men's work and no bother?

TOM: Look who's talking! He can't even do one man's work here.

FERGUS: I told you, mate, this isn't a man's job. Besides,

it's different when you're on the road. It's share and share alike. Nobody ever said Fergus didn't take care of his mates.

TOM: (*Low*) Now, Joe, like I told you, I'll see the gaffer in the morning about you staying on here. You're getting the hang of it and tomorrow will be easier.

FERGUS: Woman's work!

TOM: Give it a trial for a couple of weeks. *Then* if you don't like it—and I'm certain sure you will—I'll see about getting you fixed up somewhere else in Dublin.

JOE: Yeah, maybe it'll be easier tomorrow. It's nice and warm down here anyway.

FERGUS: Too shagging hot. Takes all the energy out of you. That's why you're tired, Joe. But suit yourself. I'm used to traveling on my own.

TOM: And don't forget I'll keep an eye open for some place, say near Dollymount, eh?

JOE: And I could get a bike, eh?

TOM: Why not? (*To Fergus*) You'd better pick up your cards tonight. We won't need you tomorrow.

FERGUS: That's what I was going to do. I don't need you to tell me. Hump you and your shagging job!

JOE: Let him stay, Tom. It's only his first day. Give him a chance.

TOM: He's not fitted for this work.

JOE: But he could settle in. He works very fast when he wants to. Faster than me. Maybe if I spoke to him?

TOM: No. Leave it be. He'll go and good riddance.

JOE: (*Pause*) Give him a chance, Tom. I mean, he's good company for us.

TOM: A bowsie. That's what he is. Nothing more.

FERGUS: Whispering again, eh? Well, it's no skin off my nose.

JOE: Would you not think of staying on here, Fergus? Say, for a couple of weeks?

FERGUS: Not me, Joe. I've a great life waiting for me outside. (*The whistle blows*)

TOM: That's it. Knocking off time. (*To Fergus*) You can go now. (*To Joe*) Let's make a cup of tea. (*He looks across at chute. There are two bags there*) We'll get one hour's overtime anyway. (*Fergus puts on his coat and cap and looks across at them*)

JOE: I can't tonight, Tom. Thanks all the same.

TOM: What! Are you turning down the extra?

JOE: I'm not able for it tonight, Tom. My legs, you know. I'm a bit tired like.

TOM: Look, you sit down and have a cuppa. I'll carry on. When you're rested up a bit you can give me a hand. No rush. (*Fergus strolls back*)

FERGUS: Coming, Joe?

TOM: He's not. We've overtime to do.

FERGUS: Suit yourself. (*To Joe*) I'm going up to the Labor tomorrow to see that pal of mine. If you come with me he can fix you up at the same time.

JOE: I'd be sitting. Is that right, Fergus?

FERGUS: Gospel truth. Ask my pal yourself. I wouldn't take it otherwise. And then after that I head south for Kerry.

JOE: (*Puts on coat and cap*) I think I'll go now, Tom.

TOM: Listen. I'll get a stool. One of them barstools. It'll be just the right height. I know a feller. You could sit on the stool all day. No one will know.

JOE: I don't know, Tom. Honest.

TOM: But we were getting on fine. I was going to take you up to the brother's for supper one night. Any time you liked.

JOE: I know, Tom. I'm sorry.

TOM: And the zoo. You said you wanted to go to the zoo.

JOE: I do. We'll go together one day. I'd like that, Tom.

FERGUS: Coming, Joe?

JOE: It's no use, Tom. I told you. I'm not able for—a steady job. Thanks. Thanks for everything.

(*He walks slowly to the door. He and Fergus exit. Tom goes back to the bench and sorts in a dispirited fashion. As he throws a rag onto one of the piles he stops suddenly*

*and examines it. It is clear that he has put a cotton rag
onto the wrong pile. He starts as if to correct himself and
then changes his mind. Almost savagely he throws it
back on the wrong pile and continues sorting listlessly)*

Curtain

Bill Morrison

SAM SLADE IS MISSING

Bill Morrison

Bill Morrison was born in 1940 in Ballymoney, a small town in Northern Ireland. He studied at Queen's University, Belfast, during which time he became deeply involved in running a dramatic society for which he wrote, directed and acted. After graduation he concentrated on acting for a couple of years and then returned to writing in 1966 with his adaptation (with William Chappell) of George Farquhar's Restoration comedy, *Love and a Bottle*. It was a major success of the Dublin Festival that year and subsequently was presented both at Belfast and the Nottingham Playhouse.

In 1968, Mr. Morrison moved to England and shortly thereafter, he was commissioned to write a children's play for the Arts Centre, University of Sussex, which he both played in and directed. During that same year, he married actress Valerie Lilley who was then a member of the Victoria Theatre Company, Stoke-on-Trent, which commissioned him to write a new dramatization of the Thomas Hardy novel, *Tess of the D'Urbervilles*. Both play and production proved to be one of the most outstanding successes in the history of that theatre and in April, 1971, he became its resident dramatist. Since then, Mr. Morrison has had a number of plays produced there and in London on stage, television and radio.

In May, 1972, Bill Morrison made his American debut as a playwright with *Patrick's Day*, a drama staged at the Long Wharf Theatre, New Haven, with Fritz Weaver and Nancy Marchand in the principal roles. *Variety*, as indeed did others, found the play to be "a well-written work by an author to be reckoned with."

Now, with *Sam Slade Is Missing*, published for the first time anywhere in this anthology, Mr. Morrison is making his initial appearance in print in this country.

Characters:

SAM SLADE
PORTER
A. J. PATTEN
ROSEMARY

Scene One

*A room in a large hotel in Dublin. It has its own bathroom.
It is furnished in the usual anonymous hotel style, with a
single bed, one armchair, a bedside table with telephone,
dressing table, etc. It has an electric fire linked to a 5p meter.
There is one window. It is about seven o'clock of a May
evening.*

*Sam Slade enters behind a Porter who is carrying a
single suitcase.*

*Sam is a dark man of about thirty-two, dressed in a
smart dark raincoat, a suit and a rollneck sweater. There
is something in his very stillness and restraint which hints
at some barely controlled passion beneath. He is a man
who has been living too long on the marrow of his nerve.*

PORTER: Here we are, sir. (*Puts down suitcase*)

SAM: Thank you. (*Gives a tip*) Ah . . . (*This stops the
Porter as he begins to leave, but Sam seems to have forgotten
what he was going to say. Finally*) Are you busy at the moment?

PORTER: Fairly so. Always a crowd these days, can't complain. (*Waits for the comment that doesn't come*) It's all expense
accounts, you know. Different from the old days.

SAM: Yes. (*An awkward silence*)

PORTER: Anything else you want, sir?

SAM: Eh? Oh, yes, there is. I'm sorry. I've just seen someone in the bar, on the way up. Gave me a bit of a surprise. An
old school friend. As a matter of fact I haven't seen him for
years. (*Digs in his pocket for some money as if coming to a*

decision) I wonder . . . would you tell him—Patten's his name—tell him Miss Thomphson would like to see him urgently in . . . (*Checks the key in his hand*) . . . in room 114. (*Hands over tip*) Would you do that?

PORTER: Miss Thomphson?

SAM: Yes, it's a . . . (*Smiles*) . . . well, he'll understand. Mr. Patten.

PORTER: In the bar, sir. Right, Mr. Thomphson.

SAM: Thank you. (*The Porter leaves, Sam takes his overcoat off and snaps open his suitcase. He takes out an almost full bottle of whiskey and, taking a glass, wanders about the room*) What am I doing? It's too late to ask questions, Sam. (*Pours a drink, looking in the mirror*) Say when. You are as high as a kite. (*Drinks. It helps*) Perhaps it's all a dream. And I, being desolate in a lonely place of stones panicked and ran. (*He laughs and then breaks into song and dance*)

Oh, I do like to be entirely free, sir,
Oh, I do like to be entirely free
There's no one here to see,
No longer you, just me,
Oh, I do like to be, entirely free. Hey!

(*The euphoria passes*) Very sensible. (*He goes to the bedside table and lifts the water carafe, then heads for the bathroom. He stops and goes back to the open suitcase and lifts out a blue nylon slip that has a large dark stain. Shrugs. Drops it*) Why don't you come up, old school friend? I've got my own civil rights campaign. (*He goes into the bathroom. Sound of running water. There is a knock and he comes out with the filled carafe*) Ah. (*Imitates a woman's voice*) Just a moment. (*Sets carafe down. Stops by door*) Listen, oh great white chief, sitting up there pretending we're not good enough for you, I'm just in the mood, so don't stop me. (*Woman's voice*) Coming.

(*He opens the door and Armour John Patten is standing there. He is a Unionist M.P. about the same age as Sam, but plumper, sleeker, more assured. He is very well dressed, almost a dandy within his conventional limits. And surprised*)

A.J.:   Miss . . .

SAM: Ah, A.J., the very man I didn't want to see.

A.J.:   Slade!

SAM: Who? I don't think I know anyone of that name. Or want to. But come in, come in. Give me a clue. I might remember him. Enter, sit down, you seem to have the odd crack in your composure at the moment.

A.J.:   I got a message about a Miss Thomphson who wanted to see me.

SAM: (*Consulting his watch*) And you made it in two minutes flat. You wouldn't think it to look at you. Ah, the hidden fires raging down below. Close the door, have a drink.

A.J.:   (*Closes door cautiously, but remains standing by it*) Is this some kind of a joke?

SAM: Not yet. Whiskey?

A.J.:   No, thank you. I have one downstairs. (*Puzzled*)

SAM: I think I will. First today. (*Pours*)

A.J.:   The message was yours?

SAM: Yes.

A.J.:   Very funny. What are you doing here anyway?

SAM: There's no escape.

A.J.:   Sam, I have some people downstairs waiting for me. Do you have anything to say to me? If not I'll . . . .

SAM: Why did I do it?

A.J.:   Do what?

SAM: Entice you up here.

A.J.:   I haven't the faintest idea and I'm sure I wouldn't be interested if you told me. Now if you'll excuse me. Maybe all that socialism has parted you from your last titter of wit. Either way, I haven't time to find out.

SAM: Okay, forget it.

A.J.:   (*Irritated. Stops as he reaches the door*) It was just a joke.

SAM: I don't see anybody laughing.

A.J.: Now listen, you drag me up here on some pretext of a woman wants to see me. I think I'm entitled to some explanation, Slade.

SAM: Thomphson.

A.J.: What?

SAM: Thomphson. That's my name. Harry Thomphson.

A.J.: Since when?

SAM: Will you have that drink?

A.J.: Yes. Yes, I will.

SAM: Your friends won't mind?

A.J.: Not for one drink.

SAM: Splendid. (*Pouring*) Water?

A.J.: Just a little. (*Pause*) Are you all right?

SAM: Don't I look all right? I do my best but it's a hopeless struggle.

A.J.: (*Walking about*) You just booked in?

SAM: (*Giving him his drink*) That's right.

A.J.: Under the name of Thomphson.

SAM: Harry Thomphson, please.

So he floated up to Heaven
And fell down on his knees,
Can I have a word with Comrade God,
I'm Harry Thomphson, please?

Remember?

A.J.: No.

SAM: No, I don't suppose you got any closer to the Boy Scouts than the motto.

A.J.: Can I know why you're here?

SAM: Well, I said to myself, Harry, I said, it's time you got away from it all. It is undoubtedly time you left. And when I get here to this foreign clime just thirsting to don my panama hat, sling my camera 'round my neck and rush out to photograph the wine and the country, who is the first charmingly original peasant that I see but yourself, large as life and twice as ugly. Do you speak English?

A.J.:   You're drunk.

SAM: Maybe. But also left.

A.J.:   How do you mean?

SAM: Left. Left as in Harold Wilson, although he's more a shade of tinned pink. Bend sinister as in Georgie Brown. Not that you'd know about things like that. From your lofty eminence on the right hand of Paisley you probably can't even see the left, let alone know what it's doing. The seed of many a downfall. Or if you prefer, left, meaning vamoose.

A.J.:   I'm afraid, Sam, you can change the name but you can't disguise the style. Instantly detestable.

SAM: I always end up as the eccentric at the party.

A.J.:   I still haven't grasped this. Why am I standing in a Dublin hotel room with you of all people? There isn't any story for you in Dublin at the moment. Why aren't you in Derry?

SAM: I ask you the same. Why aren't you up there handing out the blackthorn sticks, crying wolf and I.R.A. alternately?

A.J.:   That's no way to speak to me. (*Very cold*) Did you want to see me about something?

SAM: No. Well, yes, I did. It's a deadly secret. I have been sent with a message. I struggled—God, how I struggled, through fire, famine and ferocious bands to reach you. The message is that you are to return at once. I am to tell you that Ulster has taken the logical step and declared herself an independent monarchy and they want you for Prince Charming. You'll excuse me for not bending the knee but I'm paralyzed with boredom at the prospect.

A.J.:   I take it you will be court jester.

SAM: They could do worse. If I ever leave Northern Ireland, which is unlikely, since I am too afraid of the great real world which exists outside our little asylum, it will be for one reason and one reason only. I am deathly afraid that I might begin to believe that God is on our side. Or any side for that matter.

A.J.:   I'm glad you told me. If you'll excuse me I have better things to do.

SAM: I don't think you have. Since chance has thrown us

together and finally proved to me that chance is not blind but truly malicious, I may have to confess.

A.J.: Confess what?

SAM: I haven't decided yet. It was as big a surprise to me as it will be to you.

A.J.: That you've left, is that it? I don't think that would surprise me very much at all. It's exactly the kind of damn silly thing you would do. Unless, of course, you've left the newspaper, in which case we'll all give thanks. But we wouldn't be so fortunate, would we?

SAM: Not yet.

A.J.: I see. Then . . . you've left . . . *her*. (*A pause*)

SAM: Were you going to say something?

A.J.: No. No.

SAM: I arose this morning from my usual restless night. I should explain that I have not slept easy in my bed since I discovered that King William was a homosexual. I mean, one does not cross the threshold of an Orange Hall with the same light and innocent tread—one begins to wonder just where he is exhorting us to follow as he beckons from his gay white steed. But I digress. I arose this morning and knew, with the same dread certainty of a visit to the dentist that can no longer be avoided, that on this day my life was changed. So I packed at last this suitcase that you see and fled. By way of numerous bars, I will admit.

A.J.: On a bender or for good?

SAM: I'm always on a bender these days.

A.J.: What a damn silly thing to do.

SAM: Oh, I haven't got a problem. I mean, I'm not an alcoholic or anything, just a social drinker.

A.J.: I mean leaving her.

SAM: Oh that. There's more than you ever dreamed of, A.J.

A.J.: I'm glad, if that's the word to hear it. You would have been most foolish to leave her just because of me.

SAM: What was that? What was that? Are you insinuating there has been some—and forgive me if I err in my description—some hanky-panky between you and my wife?

A.J.: You know damn well there has been. (*Angry*) I knew it, I knew from the look of you. And you run away. Here, to Dublin. Under an assumed name?

SAM: And who should be here ahead of me but my wife's erstwhile lover. Pretty ironic, don't you think?

A.J.: So.

SAM: (*Finishing his drink*) Goodbye, Harry Thomphson, refugee. I was beginning to be quite fond of you.

A.J.: Can I have another drink? (*Sits*) Yes. Perhaps it's not such a malicious chance after all. Perhaps it's time we had a talk. At least I've got hold of you before you do something really foolish. Now listen to me, Sam.

SAM: (*Handing over a drink*) Of course.

A.J.: I appreciate how you must feel, believe me I do. I can't pretend it's not a regrettable situation. But we know each other well enough to talk straight. In fact, I've been thinking for some time of speaking to you. Because I know I can talk to you, Sam. We understand each other, you and I. You know, it has always been a matter of some regret to me that our friendship has been allowed to drift apart over the years. Although given our respective political positions . . . .

SAM: And our beliefs. Or isn't that important?

A.J.: Oh yes, I meant our jobs. Journalists and M.P.'s have a peculiar relationship, like . . . like . . . .

SAM: Snakes and ladders?

A.J.: Listen, if *we* took the liberties with the truth that you newspapermen take, the people would chuck us out on our ears, and they'd be right. But on a personal level, we have avoided each other.

SAM: Have been.

A.J.: We used to be friends.

SAM: But that was long ago and far away. Let's say we had something in common.

A.J.: (*Walking about*) So you left her. I'd like to help you on this, Sam, if I can. The important thing is not to be hasty. Why did you make the decision? Why don't you tell me what happened?

SAM: Why not? Why not indeed? So be it. Relax, enjoy yourself, have another drink, I shall tell you all in good time. But now that we're signed on for another term as blood brothers, how shall we present it fairly? We must at all costs be impartial. What is it you Unionists do when you want the dust to settle? What does that little black book entitled *How to Win Power and Manipulate Voters* say? Rule three, put away the big stick, but not too far away, see rule five, and appoint an inquiry —note, the procedure for this is simple: you give them the answers and they have to find the questions. Why don't we do that? Why don't we have a little inquiry, wouldn't that be nice?

A.J.: My offer of help stands but I don't have time to play games.

SAM: A.J., with respect, you will want to hear this. Right. In the absence of an independent third party, we shall from the present assembly elect a temporary presiding magistrate, which shall be me.

A.J.: Elected by whom?

SAM: By me. You as defendant don't have a vote.

A.J.: Then you don't either.

SAM: Quick. You can see he's a lawyer. I have a residential qualification. Even you must have heard of plural votes; the Unionist Party flourished on them.

A.J.: (*Laughs*) Still trying to throw the same old mud. It won't stick, Sam. You socialists are all the same, running yourselves ragged looking for a revolution that's already happened. Can't you see you're irrelevant? Incidentally, I object to the description of defendant; this is an inquiry to establish certain facts only.

SAM: Objection sustained. That's bloody fair-minded, isn't it?

A.J.: I'll have that drink now.

SAM: (*Taking his glass*) Of course. It's a very civilized court.

A.J.: Make it a small one. I don't have much time.

SAM: (*Deliberately pouring a large one*) Anything you say.

A.J.: And let's be civilized about it. I know you have to get whatever it is out of your system and I'm quite prepared to be patient. Basically, I see my part in the problem. But hurling abuse isn't going to solve anything. Agreed?

SAM: (*Handing him his drink*) Indubitably. (*A yell*) Read out the charges!

A.J.: They're not charges.

SAM: (*Ignoring him*) That on the twenty-second of January last at 11 P.M.—after the pubs had shut—the defendant, Armour John Patten, Member for Down Central, elected with the assistance of the Orange Lodges and an electoral register composed only partly of people, to the wee Parliament on the big hill, otherwise known as the Stormont Follies, the longest running show on earth—did seduce, albeit without noticeable resistance, and, as may yet be shown, full cooperation—did seduce and keep on seducing over a period or periods of eighteen months the wife of the aggrieved Sam Slade, known to his friends as Harry Thomphson.

A.J.: Harry Pollock.

SAM: What?

A.J.: I've remembered in the song he was called Harry Pollock.

SAM: You're right. My God, I've been going under an alias.

A.J.: How did you know it was the twenty-second?

SAM: I know everything—and if that doesn't worry you it should. And that the aggrieved, upon possession of certain information, did wilfully remove his person to points distant and remote, there to ponder his next move, if any. How's that?

A.J.: I don't deny it, just get to the point.

SAM: That the aggrieved did, in this balmy month of May, commit the heinous and most dreadful crime of upsetting the status quo, thus turning sanity loose upon the wind.

A.J.: In my bleaker moments I do tend to feel that a policy of free education is very dangerous.

SAM: Sweet Rosemary, the wife, told me it was the twenty-second. While I was at a Labor Party séance the enemy attacked me in the rear. Didn't you keep it as an anniversary?

A.J.: She told you.

SAM: What, no flowers, no cards with loving verses?

No matter where you wander,
No matter where you roam.
Remember, please, remember,
The dumb bastard's still at home.

A.J.: It wasn't like that.

SAM: I don't suppose it ever is.

A.J.: Are you finished? Maybe I can get a word in edgeways. I'll be frank. I'm not going to deny the situation. I could say I regret it, but you wouldn't believe me. I might be the same in your position, although I doubt it. But let's be practical. It's quite clear you haven't thought about the consequence of this. You can't just pack a bag, change your name to Harry-whatever and run. You've got a job, a house, a wife. You can't afford to stay here long. As I see it you haven't an idea what you're going to do next.

SAM: That's easy. I point the finger and say he's the dirty little boy we always thought he was.

A.J.: Ah yes, I wondered when we'd get to that.

SAM: Page One headlines.

A.J.: Be your age. Divorce scandals went out with Charles Stuart Parnell. It doesn't scare me. But think of Rosemary. It won't just be my reputation that you'll be trying to drag down.

SAM: I know that.

A.J.: What sort of reputation will *she* end up with?

SAM: The sort you gave her. (*Pause*)

A.J.: Believe me, Sam, it's a mistake.

SAM: The bitch deserves it.

A.J.: You can't mean that.

SAM: Why not? Just because I married her, lived with

her, nearly had kids by her, doesn't mean I now have to like her, or even care what happens to her.

A.J.: Then why did you marry her?

SAM: I don't know anymore, and that's the truth. It seemed to be the thing to do at the time, but it's all changed. I've changed. I married her because I loved her, what does that prove. (*Suddenly upset*) You want another drink?

A.J.: Yes. Let me phone downstairs. Keep talking.

SAM: When I consider what I was like in those days, well, you know what I was like. Like a garden rake with a fever. A grown-out crew cut and a suit out of Burtons, able to buy whiskey once a week and thinking I was a big fella. And, oh, the dreams. When the revolution comes.

A.J.: I remember. (*On the phone*) Can you page Mr. Brady in the bar for me. 114. Thank you.

SAM: I married her because . . . because I slept with her before we were married and she wasn't ashamed of it, because she had blonde hair. But then she's not ashamed to sleep with anything, it seems, and anyway it was a rinse. I was too innocent even to know that. It must seem unbelievable now, but then . . . you cannot imagine how the sheer abject gratitude for her gift of sex deprived me of my senses. I existed in a dream. It was after all my total and only experience.

A.J.: Joe . . . Armour. Look, I'm going to be tied up for a little while . . . Yes . . . Can you go on, I'll join you where we arranged. All right? Fine. Bye. (*Hangs up*)

SAM: Because my family approved, and for them to approve of anything was so rare, so cruelly rare, that I reacted like a whore to a ten-pound note. Because I was admired for having such a fine bird, and how big a part did that play? Because it is the outward and visible proof, I am told, of growing up. Jesus! Those seem to be a part of it now, but then I only knew, or thought I knew, I loved her.

A.J.: I know.

SAM: When we were at university I used to envy you, did you know that?

A.J.: Me? I find that hard to believe.

SAM: Oh, yes. We all have a secret shaming love for the smell of power and money. It is like an aphrodisiac to our worst instincts. I sometimes think all the socialists are just inverted snobs. It is the reaction to what they have not that impels them. But secretly they don't want to change a thing, they only want to reverse it, so that they may be on the top and you on the bottom. And the tragedy of that is that their ambition is so small, so mean, that when they turn it on its head they show, not another and different head, but, inevitably, the hole in the arse of their trousers. It is sad that what they stand for precludes them from any style in the exercise of power. So I envied you your ten-guinea cavalry twills and thought the possession of a sports car akin to a state of grace.

A.J.: (*Laughing*) That's good.

SAM: What are you laughing at?

A.J.: The fact that I used to envy you.

SAM: Why?

A.J.: Because you always seemed to have the best girls.

SAM: I still do. (*Pause*) Why aren't you married?

A.J.: Do you expect me to answer that?

SAM: I mean, isn't it a handicap in those campaigns? No wife for all those mothers' meetings and church prayer circles and Unionist bun worries? Are you sure you can rely on the support of the flower-arranging committee? But I suppose they're all mad for you; you send a respectable shiver down their corsets. Parliament's most eligible bachelor, hooray! God, my neck is stiff.

A.J.: (*Getting up and going to the dressing table and writing on a card*) Sam, I want you to do something for me.

SAM: They'll be spreading rumors about you.

A.J.: What rumors?

SAM: Oh, just people that don't like you. There are a few. But no really evil tales, no being seen up an entry with a Boy Scout troupe. (*Sam seems suddenly very tired, too drunk. But there is some hard evil entering his soul*)

A.J.: My advice is—and it's good advice—is not to do

anything rash. You're far too upset, naturally. Ring this number. It's Billy Briggs. He's a good lawyer and a good socialist so you won't be contaminated.

SAM: I know him.

A.J.: Incidentally, does anybody at all know you're down here? (*No reply*) Rosemary doesn't know.

SAM: How do you know that?

A.J.: I phoned Belfast this morning.

SAM: While I was out?

A.J.: While you were supposed to be at work. Does anyone know?

SAM: Why should I tell you?

A.J.: I want to help.

SAM: I would suggest, A.J., that it's too late for that.

A.J.: Why?

SAM: I warned you there was more.

A.J.: Yes?

SAM: Why did you tell me a lie? You didn't phone her; she wasn't there.

A.J.: I did phone.

SAM: Why did you tell me she was there?

A.J.: What is this?

SAM: You may have phoned but you didn't get any reply, did you? Did you?

A.J.: There was no reply.

SAM: I know. That's because I've killed her.

(*There is a shocked pause. A.J. for a moment almost believes him. Sam watches his reaction intently, a little surprised himself. Then Sam laughs and A.J. laughs also in relief*)

SAM: Ah, A.J., I could almost grow to like you. Again. Don't go, sit down, have another drink, talk me out of it. (*Gets drinks as A.J. sits*) Yes, she told me. I get my information straight from the horse's mouth. That's the trouble with tumbling a journalist's wife. It's not like you to take that kind of risk. I mean, if I stand up in court there and open my mouth, you never know what might come out.

A.J.: I do wish you wouldn't keep calling me A.J. It makes me sound like an auctioneer or something.

SAM: Ah, I forget you're one of the landed gentry. (*Handing over a drink*) But now that we're so nice and cozy, tell me, what did happen between you?

A.J.: She fell in love with me.

SAM: Just like that? Amazing.

A.J.: It happens. Far too often.

SAM: And she dragged you protesting into the bushes?

A.J.: The bedroom actually.

SAM: Sensible Rosemary.

A.J.: This must be painful for you.

SAM: Not more than I can enjoy. Anyway you're not the only one.

A.J.: What?

SAM: I thought you'd jump. No, you are the only lover that sleeps cherished in my wife's saggy bosom. I think. (*Pause*) Just for the record. What do you mean by love?

A.J.: A desire to have someone to the exclusion of everything else.

SAM: That's lust.

A.J.: Not if it's exclusive.

SAM: God help us all if that be true. Are you in love with my wife?

A.J.: I wish I knew, Sam, I wish I knew.

SAM: Okay, given that the wife required other amusements, why not a one-night stand, a quick tumble in the electric blanket, then tea and sour grapefruit and a lift to the bus in the morning?

A.J.: Loneliness, perhaps.

SAM: You mean you'd nobody better to do.

A.J.: Her loneliness.

SAM: Shall I light the fire? (*He crawls under the furniture to the meter*)

A.J.: She was very lonely; she never saw you. You were not hard to deceive, Sam, for you were never there.

SAM: I need a shilling. I mean five pence.

A.J.:   I may have one. (*Fumbles in his pocket*) I'm not making excuses, but if it hadn't been me, it would have been somebody else. I didn't take her from you; you drove her away. (*He is dropping his small change on the floor, one at a time, seven pennies*) That's what you have to face. Just pennies.

SAM: (*Still on the floor*) I have one. (*Fire goes on*)

A.J.:   Pick them up. (*They look at each other, then Sam lifts the pennies and puts them in his pocket*) Those are mine.

SAM: (*Returning them*) They're just pennies. Do continue, I'll refresh your glass. (*He goes to the bottle, pours a little more into A.J.'s glass. Finds the carafe almost empty and heads for the bathroom to fill it as A.J. talks*)

A.J.:   I found her interesting, exciting to be with. I shouldn't have to tell you that she has a lot to offer any man. We enjoyed—can you hear me?—enjoyed . . .

SAM: (*In the bathroom*) Enjoyed.

A.J.:   That's the important thing. How can it be wrong to bring a smile to a sad woman, to make her feel alive again? When I came to know her, she used to spend hours in that bungalow, in that state, just staring out of the window. She had nothing in common with . . . I felt sorry for her, any man would. So, it developed. I can't live like a monk. I'm not married because, until now, I haven't felt that I could be fair to a wife. I've been too busy with my career. And one must be careful—as you said yourself, she has to fit in. It's part of the price you pay in politics. I mean, if one were callous about it, I'd probably end up marrying the Prime Minister's daughter whether I fancied her or not.

SAM: (*Off*) Sad.

A.J.:   But in the meantime, there was much we could share. Trips to London, meeting people, some fun. You must understand, Sam, that this is what she wants.

SAM: (*Coming back*) And she got it?

A.J.:   Yes.

SAM: And what did you get?

A.J.:   A great deal of pleasure.

SAM: (*Clutching the filled carafe*) Water?

A.J.: Please.

SAM: (*Not pouring. Seeming to forget*) Despite the secret meetings, the driving twenty miles into the country, to a place neither of you liked, for the dubious hope of being unobserved.

A.J.: It's easier than that.

SAM: Separate registrations, false names, the drunken tiptoeing down a hotel corridor at three in the morning, three hours sleep and up before the chambermaid.

A.J.: Has that been your experience?

SAM: The careful, meticulous, deadening game of hiding. Not from an avenging husband, he'll get drunk with his artistic friends in a stow of liberal indecision. No, the threat of gossiping colleagues and nosy newspapermen waiting for the first mistake. Everybody knows, and everybody will do sweet-damn all so long as they don't have to reveal they know, but they lurk in the shadows like quiet wolves and slobber in anticipation of the inevitable fall. What a fine balance, eh?

A.J.: That's a very dramatic view.

SAM: I am a journalist; isn't that the danger?

A.J.: Sam, grow up. We are not talking about scandal or the inside of politics. I stand on my record there, that's what counts. We are talking about emotions. About a lonely woman with a husband who comes home drunk in the early mornings, about a marriage which is not even convenience. Face it. It's your fault, not mine. The affair wouldn't have happened, but for your behavior. Promising to take her out on her birthday and she sits there, all dressed up, waiting, till you roll home at three, stinking, clutching three stolen daffodils. Christmas day, off to play Santa Claus to the shipyard kids. Very noble. But it doesn't take two days. The information cuts both ways. Is it any wonder she looked elsewhere? Hell, I'll say it anyway, do you care at all about your wife?

SAM: Yes, in spite of all. She sits in my belly like a pain. When she smiles my thighs tremble. Even now. Yes, oddly enough, I love my wife. How much water?

A.J.: I find that very sad.

SAM: No, it's rather funny. Not a belly laugh, more a kind of constricted giggle. And you?

A.J.: What?

SAM: Do you love my wife?

A.J.: I told you.

SAM: And if I let her go, would you marry her?

A.J.: Marry her? You must be joking.

SAM: I didn't think I was.

A.J.: How could I in my position?

(*Sam is standing above him clutching the carafe as A.J. sits. He pours the contents slowly and deliberately all over him*)

SAM: Your water.

A.J.: (*Leaping up*) What the . . . you bloody fool!

SAM: It was an accident.

A.J.: You did it deliberately! Look at it, the suit's ruined.

SAM: I wouldn't go as far as that.

A.J.: What the hell is the matter with you?

SAM: It just sort of slipped from my paralyzed grasp. If you see what I mean.

A.J.: Soaked! Of all the . . . why? (*Sam shrugs*) I should never have stayed to talk to you.

SAM: You'll have to stay a little longer. I'll hang your coat to dry.

A.J.: (*Taking it off*) I suppose I haven't any choice. How long will it take?

SAM: (*Hanging the jacket by the fire*) Not long. It is only water.

A.J.: It's the trousers—it's right through them!

SAM: Well, it'll cool you down.

A.J.: It's too ridiculous! What am I going to do?

SAM: I'll take them down and get them dried and pressed.

A.J.: I haven't time. I have to meet someone.

SAM: Who?

A.J.: None of your business.

SAM: Be like that. But you can't entertain a lady with a stain all down the front of your trousers.

A.J.: What lady?

SAM: The one you're knocking off down here. After all, you're not a monk.

A.J.: I won't forget this, Slade. Never.

SAM: Right, let's have 'em.

A.J.: What?

SAM: Drop 'em.

A.J.: I will not.

SAM: You'll catch cold. Anyway I'll close my eyes.

A.J.: (*Going to rummage through Sam's case*) If I had known what this would end up like I would . . . haven't you got a spare pair? (*Finds the slip*) What's this?

SAM: Nothing . . . a mistake. Put it back. (*Stuffs it back in the suitcase*)

A.J.: What do you do, dress up in it? (*Finds a pair of slacks*) These'll fit me, I suppose.

SAM: Yes, it's my secret life. Samantha Slade, ring the bell and walk right up.

(*A.J. hands Sam the new trousers while he takes his own off and throws them over the back of the chair. Sam at once picks them up so that he has both pairs*)

A.J.: How long do you think they'll take? I'd better make a phone call. It's absurd. What a stupid, childish thing to do! Give me them. (*Holds out his hand for the dry trousers*)

SAM: (*Makes no move*) I like your underpants. Feel free to use the phone. (*Walks to door with both pairs*) I'll be right back.

A.J.: Where are you going?

SAM: To get them pressed.

A.J.: But I want to wear those!

SAM: They could do with a press.

A.J.: Give them to me.

SAM: I wouldn't like to see you looking anything but your best.

A.J.:   You think I couldn't take them off you? (*Advancing*)

SAM: I'd be out this door and down the stairs before you got near me. And then what would happen if you were caught in the corridor in your stripey drawers? I can just see it. Ulster —no, Six Counties—M.P. caught with trousers down in Dublin hotel corridor. (*Goes out*) See you.

A.J.:   Sam, for . . . . (*He is alone*) What did I ever do to deserve this? (*Goes to the telephone*) Hello. Room 114. I want to place a call to Lisburn 2049. Yes. In the meantime get me the Russell Hotel. If only I knew what he means to do. At least slow him down. Hello. I want to leave a message for a Mrs. Lynch. I was to meet her in the bar. Tell her I'm unavoidably delayed; she'll know who it is. Thank you. (*Hangs up. Lights a cigarette*) I should have realized he was ready to leave her. (*Phone rings*) Yes? What? No reply. Then I'll send a telegram. Let him pay for it. To Rosemary Slade, 17 Harmony Villas, Lisburn. Message: Found Sam here. Come at once. Signed, Armour. Room 114. Thank you. (*Hangs up. Looks at the case*) Why, why, why? He's not that drunk. (*Lifts the stained slip*) It makes no sense. No. But then . . . .

SAM: (*Entering and collapsing in a chair*) Did you make your call? I'm exhausted.

A.J.:   Where's the trousers?

SAM: Well, you can't go down with two pairs of trousers and hand one in. I mean the man would think I was mad—so they needed a press anyway. My neck is stiff. (*Massages it*)

A.J.:   Why?

SAM: I've been sitting in a draught. You should keep your mouth shut.

A.J.:   I've just phoned Rosemary. There was no reply.

SAM: I could have told you that. Oh, it's so good to relax, let all my worries fall away.

A.J.:   How do you know I'd get no reply?

SAM: I just knew. I am tired.

A.J.:   I sent her a telegram.

SAM: You did? Saying what?

A.J.: That we were here and to come down.

SAM: Christ! You didn't? (*Very agitated*) Well, that's it! That is it, goodbye. I take my eyes off you for two minutes.

A.J.: What can be wrong with a telegram?

SAM: It has both our names and address on it. The end is nigh. Of all the dumb . . . I need a drink. Stupid, that's what you are. What are you? Stupid.

A.J.: What has happened between you?

SAM: (*Very guilty*) Nothing.

A.J.: (*Holding up the slip*) What's this stain?

SAM: Coffee. She has shaky hands, especially in the mornings.

A.J.: You've hurt her in some way, haven't you?

SAM: Have I?

A.J.: Sam . . . Oh, sweet God, if what I think is true, you'd better tell me everything, every detail.

SAM: Drink?

A.J.: (*Yelling*) Stop evading! We've no time for that. When was it? Last night, this morning? Who knows about it?

SAM: You, me and Harry Thomphson.

A.J.: The phone wasn't answered this morning or now.

SAM: And you sent a telegram.

A.J.: I wish I knew when you were telling me the truth.

SAM: You'll have to work that out for yourself.

A.J.: (*Very decisive*) Sit down. Now I want you to start at the beginning and leave nothing out.

SAM: What are we going to play. Hunt the loophole?

A.J.: Your neck is stiff because she hit you?

SAM: Yes. I've got nothing to lose now.

A.J.: Why did she hit you?

SAM: Well, you see, your honor, she's the heavyweight champion of Sandy Row and she needs the sparring.

A.J.: I am trying to help you.

SAM: I almost believe you. We had a row, the seven hundred and forty-seventh.

A.J.: Did you hit her?

SAM: I used to believe in words.

A.J.: How did the row start?

SAM: We don't have rows, *she* has rows. I don't fight. I think that makes her worse. The more I try to be reasonable, the more infuriated she gets. She actually came up behind me once and hit me over the head with an encyclopedia just to provoke a reaction, which she did. I was out cold for ten minutes. Do you think, counselor, if I had fought we might in some curious way have been happier?

A.J.: I doubt it.

SAM: I see. It was over money. Isn't that a poor reason? She's always running up bills, charge accounts, for ridiculous things. I told her I wouldn't pay anymore.

A.J.: How often have you said that?

SAM: Often.

A.J.: Have you ever done it?

SAM: No.

A.J.: Would you have done it this time?

SAM: No.

A.J.: Then don't you understand that she hated the fact that you never actually went through with anything you said?

SAM: She's my wife. But this one was for forty-seven pounds thirty-six. I didn't have the money; she knew that.

A.J.: That's why she did it.

SAM: I meant it at the time. I said I'd ring up all the managers and say I wouldn't be responsible for her debts and . . . all the usual came out—I was mean, I spent all my money on other women, on drink, I wasn't faithful to her so she saw no reason why she should be faithful to me, why didn't I go away and leave her alone.

A.J.: Where is she now?

SAM: Let me tell it in my own way. She has been continually delighted to tell me about you. In great, even revolting detail, even the impressiveness of your erections.

A.J.: But you always put up with it.

SAM: I did my best. Hell, what can you do, hit her, beat her, chain her up, lock her in the house? We try to be rational adults. As long as we are able.

A.J.: (*After a pause*) Go on, there was a row.

SAM: Yes, she was a bit drunk, so was I.

A.J.: This was last night, Sunday night.

SAM: Yes, I'd been in the club; God knows where she was.

A.J.: Wasn't she there when you got home?

SAM: No. I don't know if she has anyone else. I wouldn't put it past her.

A.J.: Nor, I suppose, would I.

SAM: Do you care?

A.J.: Yes, yes I do.

SAM: Maybe we're on the same side after all. Anyway, when she came in she invoked you again as all that was bright and beautiful compared to me. And I . . . I wish I hadn't . . . .

A.J.: What?

SAM: I brought up the other thing. She hit me. She kept on hitting me. I left her, she ran after me, yelling, hitting me, she was . . . she'd lost her head completely, called me all the names . . . you know . . . Jesus, it was ugly.

A.J.: And what happened? Was it an accident?

SAM: (*With passion*) An accident? That's all you want to know! How much easier if it was. We'd all be in the clear. That's all you care about, the angle, the way out, spread the blame until it is no one's fault, especially not yours.

A.J.: Whatever you have done, you have done, not me.

SAM: True. I could give myself up, throw myself on the mercy of the court, play the injured husband. You needn't come into it at all, just another man of a whole succession of them. Looks better for me, too. You bastard! That would suit you very well. I've been suiting you for eighteen months; I've suited Rosemary for five years. But not anymore. The moment comes in all things when we must refuse to cooperate.

A.J.: Sam, we are talking about your wife whom you have harmed in some way.

SAM: We are talking about my wife that I have killed. Past tense. Academic speculation.

A.J.: Oh, my God!

SAM: Present tense, we are talking about your skin. My life's unimportant now, but you are in it up to your neck.

A.J.: If you don't care what happens, why didn't you stay?

SAM: I . . . I panicked. I ran. What else have I ever done, all my life?

A.J.: How could you . . . ? I need a drink; I've got to think. (*A cry of agony*) Why?

SAM: I know. The money, the drinking, all those sordid, seemingly unimportant details, not heavy enough to support the finality. Such poor justification for that cataclysmic act. But then, then I shall explain, when they come for me, and don't think I cannot prove it because I can.

A.J.: But those are the reasons, aren't they?

SAM: How could I not know when she came home shaved and blank and tired? You paid for it, didn't you?

A.J.: Is that . . . ? Yes, yes I did.

SAM: One abortion, signed, sealed and delivered, thank you very much. It saved me the money.

A.J.: But it was the only thing to do! She wanted it; she asked me for the money; it was her decision.

SAM: So you did the contemporary version of the decent thing.

A.J.: I did the sensible thing. She hadn't any choice. How would you have reacted if she had had my child?

SAM: I would have loved it. It hadn't any choice.

A.J.: How did you know?

SAM: She told me, one night when she was drunk and feeling sorry for herself. She told me that she was carrying a child, a child she did not want, and that she was going to have it cut out like a cancerous growth. It was in the way. And I offered, I pleaded with her to keep that child, and she told me I was too late. It was arranged and paid for, a far better job than I could afford, which is probably true.

A.J.: But you took her back afterwards. It was months ago.

SAM: Yes.

A.J.: Then don't you see, Sam, that wasn't the "why?" It was because she was attacking you. You had accepted the abortion; you kept on living with her. It's not because of *me*.

SAM: You never thought about it as long as nobody knew —a minor indiscretion. It doesn't impinge. We talk about responsibility but it doesn't mean anything because we never experience the results. It's like poverty, it doesn't impinge. No one belonging to us goes hungry.

A.J.: No, I am not responsible. It was the row, the fight, you were both drunk. It was about money not about me. Those are the facts.

SAM: That child, that thumbnail sketch of a person she began to nurture was mine, not yours.

A.J.: I didn't know. (*Sam towers over A.J. as he sits huddled on the bed*)

SAM: I wanted that child she wouldn't give me. I thought, God help me, that it might change both her and me. And it was mine, which you paid for. She came home shaven and asked me to forgive her—easy to ask when the job's done. But I saw and watched, as incapable as any of some action. I brought it up again, the question of the child, and she laughed and said she knew it was my seed, and that was why she was so determined not to have it. What cruelty, you think, or what honesty. And then . . . then it all snapped, and when the boil burst, at that moment I went beyond love and I took her as I had never taken her in love . . . like this . . . (*He seizes A.J. by the tie and on his knees behind him hauls him up in a mime of strangulation*) . . . and I strangled her, Armour John, like this, and she lies now on the tiled kitchen floor—a pattern of sea stones in many mosaic colors. She lies, curiously twisted with her skirt up to her navel, revealing all to the curious policemen's eyes, with a swelling where her throat was, parted only by that thin red line where the plastic, mundane wash line slices her life away. And her hair is trapped to the floor by spilling milk and a little blood which came from her mouth and nose and which I cleaned as best I could in my haste with a blue nylon slip that you have touched. She is dead, irrevocably dead. No life. With her eyes bursting. Amen. (*He allows the limp A.J. to sag back onto the bed and, exhausted, moves away*) I wish I could tear this body up and start again.

(*A little silence. A.J. is shattered. Sam, slack, drained of tension. It has got dark in their little room*)

A.J.: We . . . we never think of where it may lead to. Just one casual thing, a little wrong, and then the next casual thing, and then the next. I said to myself there's no harm done, but that's no different from a hell of a lot of other people. I couldn't foresee. . . .

SAM: (*Kindly*) Take it easy. Have a cigarette.

A.J.: Rosemary . . . dead.

SAM: (*Lighting two cigarettes and giving him one*) It's over. It's done.

A.J.: And I have to face it.

SAM: (*Coughing*) I smoke too many of these damn things. They're killing me.

A.J.: I can't believe it. I can't believe it's happening.

SAM: Did I hurt you?

A.J.: Yes. Yes, you did.

SAM: I'm sorry.

A.J.: Don't say that. (*Stands up*) Sam, I am responsible.

SAM: I don't blame you.

A.J.: We must face it. You'll have to go back. At once. (*There is a loud knock on the door. It paralyzes both of them. Sam moves first, gesturing to A.J. to hide in a corner. He goes to the door. Tenses himself. Opens it*)

SAM: Yes?

PORTER: (*Off*) I've brought your trousers, sir.

SAM: Oh, thank you. (*Finds a tip*) Thank you.

PORTER: Not at all, sir. Good night now.

SAM: Good night. (*He closes the door. Throws A.J. his trousers. Sits down*)

A.J.: (*Dressing*) You'll have to go back. It'll be much worse if you don't.

SAM: Tomorrow. I'm too tired. I have to sleep.

A.J.: Perhaps. They know where we are.

SAM: Tomorrow. (*Begins to undress*)

A.J.: I should never have done it. I cannot say I didn't know it was wrong. But I'm only human. How very easy to make excuses. Now it's all gone—all the plans, all the hard work. I was going to be a minister in a few years, and I'd have been a good one. It's not all personal gain and corruption, the taste of power. It's a practical business. Ideals are so much chaff in the wind without pounds and pence. Too slow for you, I know. But God, I can't believe it! That's past tense! Academic speculation. What's it like outside? (*Sam, by now with his trousers off and his shirt open, is standing by the window*)

SAM: Dark, quiet, dry. Just a little wind in the tops of the trees. One car. And the lamplight melting over the pavement. I shall have a hangover in the morning. I'm stoned now. All of us, flabby, aging, and imprisoned in our doubtful lusts. Trapped and can't break out. Frightened. You'd be lucky if you broke a leg.

A.J.: (*Joining him*) What?

SAM: If you jumped out of the window.

A.J.: Yes.

SAM: It would be too ironic.

A.J.: No point in thinking about it. (*Pause*) Sam?

SAM: Yes?

A.J.: If we go back, I'll tell them how it was. It'll be some help.

SAM: Off the roof?

A.J.: No. Anyway, I can't stand the Prime Minister's daughter.

(*A long pause*)

SAM: Has it occurred to you, that you might be next?

Blackout

Scene Two

*It is about six in the morning. A cold, cold dawn. A.J.
is asleep in the bed. Sam is crawling about the floor in his
pajamas trying to get at the meter. Clothes lie on the
floor. The whiskey bottle is empty but there is now
another one, half-full.*

SAM: Gone. And nobody has a shilling. (*Stands*) Oh,
I'm cold. Dare I have another drink? Would you care for another drink, Harry? Harry Pollock answers, "Please." Doesn't
sound right. It's not Pollock, it's Pollitt, two *t's*. This is a right
mess. (*Drinks*) Oh, that's . . . (*Almost sick*) It's probably the
quickest, alcoholic poisoning. Light a fag, complete the damage.
Heart, liver, kidneys, lungs, all grotesquely swirling about in
there, diseased, slowly breaking up. Here's to civilization.
(*Coughs*) That's it. Strangulation, asphyxiation, lovely words.
Pajama cord? Not strong enough. Nothing's easy. A belt. (*From
his trousers*) But where? (*Looking for somewhere to suspend
it*) Experiment and experience shows that it is impossible to
strangle yourself. You pass out before death and thus cannot
maintain the vital pressure. Doorway's too low. (*Stands on chair,
belt around neck*) No, even if I jumped, like so, (*Jumps*) the
force wouldn't be enough to break the neck. They don't make
rooms right. We are only equipped for spiritual self-destruction.
I've thought of a razor. I can't understand how people do it.
(*Mimes the action*) I mean, I can see taking it carefully in . . .
and deliberately but decisively slashing the veins of the left
wrist, but then to transfer . . . appalled, strength, blood and
determination flowing out. One too hasty jab and then slump
and watch the thick red blood creep out and faintly bleed to
death. Too long Someone would come, too weak to protest,
rushed to hospital, transfusion, nothing to show for it but two
strips of plaster. Could have been done sharpening a pencil.
The best you could hope for would be if they gave you the

wrong group blood. It's not easy. (*Looks despairingly around*)
Imagine hacking away with a bread knife. Ugh. Pills! The
modern answer. (*Drags his case forward and rummages in it*)
Just to sleep, to drift away, with the mumbled vision of a dream-
invited naked lady to bid me gone. (*Holds up a bottle*) Alka-
Seltzer. I ought to take a couple of those for the morning.
Oh, it's so cold, six in the morning cold when the men in the
parks shift and waken and curl their newspapers around them
and know . . . (*Another bottle*) What the hell are these? . . .
know, that no matter how drunk the night before, they will not
sleep again until the afternoon like dead men among the public
daisies. Must be some kind of laxative. What does she have that
for? Jesus, what a way to go. Relieves all aches and pains. You
can't relieve my heart. Wait. Everybody leaves a note. How
remiss I am. But what would I say? It's all been said before!
Ah . . . (*Another bottle*) This is it. Sleeping pills, I knew she
had some. I should arrange it properly, laid out like Garbo.
(*Closes his eyes and clutches the bottle*) Dawn. What do I
feel? Tired. I can hear the wind investigate the trees. I can see
a dozy woman poke up the overnight fire and make the first
sleepy morning moves. The tea will soon be steaming in the
thick blue and white cups, and the children will leap straight
into their clothes in one bound to stay warm and complain and
clatter on the stairs. Not my children. I have no children.
(*Empties the contents of the bottle into his hand and looks
down*) Two! Two lousy pills. Charming. Work yourself up to
it, and then the tide's out. (*There is a knock on the door. Sam
looks up, pleased but not surprised*) What a picture. Couldn't
be better. You're right on cue. (*He surveys the room. Another
knock*) Be calm.

> (*He opens the door and his wife, Rosemary, is standing
> there. She is simply and expensively dressed in a trouser
> suit, but tired from much driving. The impression we
> have is of a woman of spirit and sensuality who has not
> met her match in either case*)
> ROSEMARY: Hello, Sam.

SAM: Shhhh.

ROSEMARY: Are you going to leave me standing in the corridor?

SAM: Come in. You must be cold and tired. What you need is a drink.

ROSEMARY: I'd prefer a cup of coffee. (*Comes in*) Who's that?

SAM: (*Looks at figure on bed*) I don't know. He came in here looking for a priest. Very embarrassing.

ROSEMARY: Oh, it's him. This place looks as if a bomb hit it. Does the fire work?

SAM: Have you got a shilling? One of those?

ROSEMARY: Yes, I have.

SAM: Ah, Rosemary, sweet Rosemary. I'll put it in.

ROSEMARY: (*Sitting, warming herself*) Do you want a cigarette?

SAM: Yes. Thank God for heat. I was freezing to death.

ROSEMARY: Have you been to bed at all?

SAM: Sort of.

ROSEMARY: You look terrible.   (*Pause*)

SAM: How are you?

ROSEMARY: How do you think, driving through the night?

SAM: (*Coughing*) At this rate I have about six months to live.

ROSEMARY: A bad night?

SAM: It's not over yet.

ROSEMARY: Well?

SAM: Well what?

ROSEMARY: This. (*Dangles telegram before him*)

SAM: Ah . . . well . . . I'm glad to see you. Very glad.

ROSEMARY: That makes a change. The last time I saw you, whatever number of days ago it was, you were trying to make a bed on the floor out of all my coats, swearing never to share a pillow with me again. That was after our little argument which you probably don't remember.

SAM: I do.

ROSEMARY: It didn't last long, do you remember that? Within five minutes you were in beside me complaining you were cold.

SAM: Betrayed by my body once again.

ROSEMARY: Sam, what's going on?

SAM: In a minute. Don't you feel any remorse?

ROSEMARY: About him? Why should I?

SAM: True.

ROSEMARY: Sam, we have been over and over all this. It's not as if you don't know what's been going on. And it seems not to make the slightest difference to you. You have been an impossible husband. I don't know why I didn't leave you years ago.

SAM: Why didn't you?

ROSEMARY: As I was driving here, I began to imagine all kinds of things. After all, it was a summons in the middle of the night from the last person to . . . you know. I began to think you were hurt, or ill, or . . . I don't know what. You'd tried to . . . I thought you might need me. That's why I came.

SAM: I'm touched.

ROSEMARY: I still don't know what you two are doing here. Nor did I know that you are on such intimate terms that you could share a bedroom.

SAM: What I just said—I didn't mean it.

ROSEMARY: I would like an explanation. How long has this been going on?

SAM: (*Laughing*) It was an accident, I swear it was. (*Pause*) I love you, you know that. (*She makes no reply*) Is he . . . ?

ROSEMARY: If he's asleep an earthquake wouldn't waken him; I should know.

SAM: Please believe me.

ROSEMARY: You give me no reason why I should.

SAM: We met by accident. You must understand that I didn't plan it.

ROSEMARY: But what were you doing here?

SAM: I left you.

ROSEMARY: No, Sam, be serious.

SAM: I left you.

ROSEMARY: (*Looking at him closely*) I believe you.

SAM: He was worried. Naturally. Tried to talk me out of it. It had its comic moments. Rosemary, I couldn't go on. I wakened and I thought, "What am I?" If they cut me open I would be ringed with hangovers, like a tree. Leave her, make her free, perhaps—and this is the first time I faced the thought —perhaps she is happy with him, that is what she wants. I could even make myself feel generous, forgiving, benevolent, as I packed the suitcase. But then, you see, presented with the opportunity, I had to know how *he* felt.

ROSEMARY: He would only tell you if you forced him.

SAM: What would have become of my grand gesture?

ROSEMARY: But why did he send me a telegram?

SAM: To talk me out of it, I suppose. After that I got carried away. (*He begins to laugh. Then cough. Then laugh*)

ROSEMARY: Why are you laughing?

SAM: (*Controls himself with difficulty*) You see . . . you are supposed to be dead.

ROSEMARY: *What?*

SAM: I'm afraid so.

ROSEMARY: Me?

SAM: He thinks you're dead.

ROSEMARY: But how?

SAM: I confessed.

ROSEMARY: How am I dead?

SAM: I killed you. (*Pause*)

ROSEMARY: But that's ridiculous!

SAM: Yes. I strangled you in the kitchen.

ROSEMARY: How sick.

SAM: I told you I got carried away.

ROSEMARY: And he believed you?

SAM: I was very convincing.

ROSEMARY: And he's lying there asleep.

SAM: I think it's very callous too.

ROSEMARY: (*Laughs*) I don't know why I'm laughing. I can't believe it! What did he say?

SAM: It was a great shock to him.

ROSEMARY: I'm sure he was worried. What's he going to say when he wakes up?

SAM: *If* he wakes up.

ROSEMARY: (*Her laughter sliding into tears, catching him in her arms*) Oh, Sam, what have I done to you?

SAM: (*Gently making her sit*) Nothing. I did it all myself. (*Sits himself on the floor*) I was thinking of a weekend when you went away with him, one of the first. I spent most of it in bed, just lying, staring at the wall. But I went out on the Saturday evening, with the intention of being drunk. We were all drinking, a large group of us, 'round a table in one corner of the lounge bar. All people you know, responsible, educated, family people. I was sitting next to Barbara, Jack's wife. We were all high, I more than the others. As you know, she is the most respectable of ladies, offended by coarse jokes, an assiduous worker on committees. And on some sulphurous impulse I reached underneath the table as we sat side by side, talking, laughing, and I slipped my hand—deliberately and slowly, so that she could not mistake it for an accident—between her knees, under her hem, and steadily climbed her thighs. She did not blink or turn or even pause in her flow of talk. Nor did she try to disengage me. And I talked, as, like some agent of the devil neither of us owned, my hand crept along—to discover . . . to discover that she wore nothing. She was naked beneath the tweed. And thus entangled we sat as if nothing had happened. It was then that I realized, for the first time, that we observe no boundaries any more between ourselves. I left before them and we remain the casual friends we always were.

ROSEMARY: I think you're sick, Sam.

SAM: No, I'm free. We are all free. So free.

ROSEMARY: But why?

SAM: I don't know. I've never fancied her.

ROSEMARY: Nor she you. No, what I meant was why did you tell him you'd ... you know ....

SAM: Say it.

ROSEMARY: I won't.

SAM: That I strangled you? It just came into my head.

ROSEMARY: And he believed you?

SAM: That's how his mind works.

ROSEMARY: Could you?

SAM: No. (*Looking at A.J.*) But there he lies.

ROSEMARY: I don't think I believe a word of this. Oh, I mean, all right, you met by accident, but the rest of it, no, I won't swallow that. Sam, what are you up to? What game are you playing?

SAM: The truth, so help me.

ROSEMARY: Did you meet him accidentally on purpose? Did you follow him?

SAM: I left you.

ROSEMARY: You couldn't leave a launderette without explaining why! It would have to be discussed, analyzed, picked at until you couldn't act at all. I know you.

SAM: Please.

ROSEMARY: If you think, for one moment, that by arranging some sordid little confrontation you will make any difference, you have another think coming. That would be the last thing. I suppose you sent the telegram in his name.

SAM: I knew it wouldn't work.

ROSEMARY: May God forgive you.

SAM: I thought of it while I was taking his trousers to the cleaners.

ROSEMARY: What?

SAM: We had a little accident.

ROSEMARY: You can't mean you had a fight?

SAM: It wasn't exactly Marquis of Queensberry.

ROSEMARY: Who was *he*?

SAM: He made the rules of professional boxing.

ROSEMARY: I can't imagine you two fighting. The two of you together wouldn't be a match for a man.

SAM: I had the evidence, you see.

ROSEMARY: What evidence?

SAM: This. (*Holding up the stained slip*)

ROSEMARY: I've been looking everywhere for that. I was going to wash it. That's the one I spilled coffee down.

SAM: I knew that.

ROSEMARY: But it's just a coffee stain. Anyway I thought I was strangled.

SAM: You bled a little; it was very messy.

ROSEMARY: Ugh. No, I don't want to hear anymore.

SAM: In the kitchen.

ROSEMARY: Sam, what are you trying to prove? What is there in that twisted, savage little mind of yours? You've got us here.

SAM: Because it's up to you two.

ROSEMARY: Oh, for God's sake!

SAM: But isn't it? Isn't it? You two are up there driving. I'm just an interested bystander. For a while, you see, it was bearable. More than bearable, it was even fashionable. I could have wished you had chosen better. But leaving that aside, we pretend to the civilized view that couples may not be forever coupled. In the litany of the new morality, boredom is the enemy. So have your fling, I will do likewise, said I. But you had at least the postures of love. I had none.

ROSEMARY: I'm sorry for you.

SAM: I cannot bear it any longer.

ROSEMARY: Don't tell me that you sat back in virtuous isolation. If anybody would have had you, you'd have been off like a shot. But nobody would put up with you, except me. God knows why, for I don't.

SAM: I don't think that is true.

ROSEMARY: If you can't bear it, then do something about it.

SAM: What?

ROSEMARY: You see. You ask me. Me! If you ask me once more what I want, I'll be sick.

SAM: But you want him.

ROSEMARY: Oh, Sam, I don't. Why does it have to be al-

ways what *I* want? Why do you have to be so goddamn understanding? Yes, he's been good to me; yes, if I didn't like him
it wouldn't have gone on; yes, it was my fault; yes, I was unfaithful to you. Oh hell, I'm not going to make excuses. I promised myself I wouldn't, but I'm like one great gaping sore because of you. I don't like what I have become, Sam. I want to be
rescued from myself. I listen to myself sometimes and I sound
like the all-time bitch. I am terrified by some of the things you
make me say. I don't want to be so cruel, so much of a bitch,
so much of a coward. I didn't used to be like this. I need help,
Sam, I know I do. Sometimes I think I will lose my reason.
You have to help me, Sam, for I can't help myself.

SAM: He'll save you.

ROSEMARY: Oh, God! (*Pause*) You mean I can take my
pick. Between the jelly and the spoon. All right. Let's get
it over with. Let's find out.

SAM: (*Between her and A.J.*) No. Wait.

ROSEMARY: You've made yourself perfectly clear, Sam.

SAM: Darling . . . .

ROSEMARY: Keep away from me. (*She crosses to the bed
as Sam hovers*) Armour. Armour. Get up. (*He doesn't move*)
What arrangement have you two come to?

SAM: Eh?

ROSEMARY: I'm not fooled. Get up. Oh, get up, you fat
. . . Armour. (*She hauls the clothes back. A.J. stirs and curls
himself up*) Armour. Get up. (*He blinks and raises his head*)

SAM: Morning, A.J.

A.J.:   *Rosemary?*

ROSEMARY: Who do you think it is?

A.J.:   But . . . but . . . .

ROSEMARY: Get up and put some clothes on.

A.J.:   What . . . you . . . you're all right?

ROSEMARY: There was never anything wrong with me.

A.J.:   But . . . he . . . Sam . . . where is he?

SAM: Yes?

A.J.:   You said . . . you told me . . . .

ROSEMARY: You were a fool to believe him. You should never believe him.

SAM: Quite right.

A.J.: He told me you were dead.

ROSEMARY: You actually did.

SAM: I have this urgent need to go to the toilet. Anyway I know when I'm not wanted.

A.J.: Sam ... (*Too late. Sam has slipped off to the bathroom*) It's like a dream.

ROSEMARY: You look terrible. At least comb your hair.

A.J.: I don't understand what's going on. He said he'd killed you.

ROSEMARY: I know.

A.J.: Is this some kind of plot?

ROSEMARY: No. I got this telegram.

A.J.: *My* telegram.

ROSEMARY: Oh? Yours. And he told me when I got here. I didn't believe him.

A.J.: I did. I believed him. How you were strangled. How could anybody do such a thing? I'd accepted the responsibility of ....

ROSEMARY: Aren't you glad it isn't true?

A.J.: Of course. Can I have a glass of water? He told me a lie.

ROSEMARY: Perhaps he saw it as a fair exchange.

A.J.: (*Swallowing water*) Thank God, you're all right.

ROSEMARY: Feeling better?

A.J.: (*Getting up*) No. The man is mad. I mean, I can't grasp it. He told it all in such vivid detail, I had to believe it.

ROSEMARY: Oh come on.

A.J.: He had his reasons.

ROSEMARY: What reasons?

A.J.: Look, I can't think straight. (*Going to her*) I'm just so glad you're safe.

ROSEMARY: What reasons?

A.J.: Well ... the baby ....

ROSEMARY: So that was the story.

A.J.:   It was his.

ROSEMARY: You bloody men. It was mine. Mine! Thinking of yourselves. All because of one tiny ill-timed spurt. I had to think of the child. I carried it; I heaved up my heart every morning. He doesn't know if it was his; I don't know; it could have been either of you. What chance could it have had? You can't use a baby like cement to pour into the cracks of a marriage. That's what he wants it for. Oh, the romance of it. Have you taken precautions? Good, then we'll begin. I think I will go mad.

A.J.:   Darling . . . .

ROSEMARY: Why did you send a telegram if you thought I was dead?

A.J.:   It was before. I couldn't get you on the phone all day.

ROSEMARY: I was visiting my sister. Sam knew that.

A.J.:   He can't have planned it!

SAM: (*Reentering*) Now, shall I tell you all what really happened?

ROSEMARY: No, Sam.

A.J.:   Slade, why the hell . . . .

ROSEMARY: Shut up, Armour! (*He does, surprised by her vehemence, and begins looking for his clothes*) Sam. Just get it over with, whatever it is.

SAM: It was on the spur of the moment.

A.J.:   Where are my trousers?

SAM: What?

A.J.:   My trousers.

SAM: Under the bed. (*To her*) Would you like some breakfast?

ROSEMARY: After.

SAM: (*Turning to look at A.J. on his hands and knees grovelling under the bed*) You like it?

ROSEMARY: No.

SAM: Hey, A.J. . . . .

A.J.: (*Putting on his trousers*) Listen, Slade, you've had your fun; you have made me look ridiculous. That's not hard to do anymore, but most people wouldn't see the point. But I'm not humiliated. I, at least, have my self-respect.

SAM: Baby....

ROSEMARY: Sam!

SAM: Of course. Well. I couldn't help overhearing, perhaps because I had my ear pressed firmly to the door. And let's be honest, we have made a deal.

A.J.: Don't listen to him.

SAM: Has he ever said he'd marry you?

ROSEMARY: Once.

SAM: Good. Just checking. He has a very noble character, if you dig on the surface. And he, passionately, nay, desperately, wants to marry you. I had to agree. After all, I couldn't stand in the way of your happiness.

A.J.: It's ....

SAM: Are you going to deny it?

A.J.: I have no need to.

SAM: I'm just conducting negotiations. What do you think?

ROSEMARY: I'm glad you finally asked me.

SAM: He has some good points. Money. Ahm . . . well, some good points. He'll go through with the divorce.

A.J.: Has anybody seen my shoes?

SAM: Well, sweet wife, what do you say?

ROSEMARY: What does *he* say?

SAM: He...I don't know. What do you say?

A.J.: Nothing. This is neither the time nor the place. I, personally, have had more than I can take. Rosemary, I think it would be best if you came back to my hotel. He doesn't even recognize the truth any more.

SAM: I want to hear your answer.

A.J.: There's nothing to answer.

SAM: (*A yell*) Tell her!

ROSEMARY: And then I'm supposed to make a choice between you, is that it, Sam? Between you two. Well, look at you. Half-dressed. Unshaven. Little boys, dirty little boys. I'm just like some favorite toy you've quarreled over. Of course, it's all in the name of freedom. To choose. Dear God, is there no tenderness any more? I could have three heads for all you care. All you want ... all you want is to bury your little pride inside me and if I groan and cry out on cue it comforts you. We have a relationship; you own me; I can keep proving to you what you are—like a badge of membership. Well, to hell with you. Both of you. To hell with you. I am better on my own. (*Pause*)

SAM: Rosemary ....

ROSEMARY: Leave me alone. (*Rushes into bathroom*)

SAM: You heard her.

A.J.:   I could have told you. I'll go. I'm grateful to you, Slade. I, at least, have learned that it could happen. I will not make such a mistake again.

SAM: (*Very painfully*) There is one more thing, A.J. ... sorry, Armour.

A.J.:   What?

SAM: Have you ever thought where I get my information?

A.J.:   I know.

SAM: I am a very well-informed journalist and there is a lot I can't print.

A.J.:   What do you mean?

SAM: Don't pretend. It was the first thing occurred to you. Isn't that right?

A.J.:   I don't know what you mean.

SAM: Then I'll spell it out for you. You get drunk, you boast to her, she tells me. Every secret. Now, they'll forgive you anything up there on the big hill, except a big mouth.

A.J.:   Prove it.

SAM: It just needs a word in the right ear. Your friends will always be prepared to believe the worst about you, and I can't say I blame them.

A.J.:   What do you want?

SAM: I still need the information. I'm a bit particular who runs my life.

A.J.: It's a fair society.

SAM: We can't always bear the truth, but somebody has to know it, besides the authors of it. It may as well be me.

A.J.: I'll tell you what I can. Sometime in those bleak early hours I faced up to the fact that my career was over in the muddiest way imaginable. That life was going to be impossible. I was able to accept it because I recognized it was my own fault. It still is. I suggest you ask yourself the same questions.

SAM: We'll be back. Nothing changes that much. We prefer to forget, we blur the edges. The pain is in knowing what you ought to be and not being able to do anything about it.

A.J.: Too easy.

SAM: Yeah, maybe. Take care.

A.J.: Goodbye. (*He leaves and Sam closes the door quietly*)

SAM: A drink. (*Pours it; goes to the bathroom door*) You can come out now. He's gone. (*No answer*) Rosemary? (*Tries the door*) Rosemary. Rosemary. (*Rattles the door*) For God's sake. Rosemary, what are you doing? Rosemary, please. Open the door. (*Rattles again*) What are you doing? I didn't mean it, whatever it may be. It was not my intention to be cruel. Believe me. (*No answer*) Then I admit I cannot be so pure that . . . I didn't get carried away. All right, I was vindictive. But I only wanted to cleanse. (*Contemplates forcing the door. Doesn't. No answer from within*) Oh, the desire to be re-born, to begin again, to be like a snake sliding out of an old skin, leaving it like a mossy tomb, emerging shiny and new. Rosemary? What are you doing? (*No answer to his knocks*) I so want to begin again. I know it's impossible but I want to try. Rosemary? (*Silence*) Say something.

ROSEMARY: (*Off*) Go away.

SAM: Thank God. No, I won't. I've paid for this room. (*Silence, as he waits*) Come out and talk to me. I'm lonely.

Please. (*The door opens and a pale Rosemary comes out*) Hello.

ROSEMARY: Hello, Sam.

SAM: What are you doing here?

ROSEMARY: We're on holiday, aren't we?

SAM: Of course, that's it. Just a few days. A pause in the daily struggle.

ROSEMARY: What makes people stay together, Sam?

SAM: I don't know.

ROSEMARY: I keep thinking about that. I've always been afraid of being alone. I know that now and I know why. Because my parents left me alone so much as a child. That's the reason; I don't have to be very clever to work that out. It's what the books would say. And I know it's silly to still feel resentful when I'm left alone. But I can't help it. I just don't want to be alone. It frightens me. All the boys. I used to pretend—I mean, I know that now—that I was pretending that I loved them. Just while I was with them really.

SAM: You've told me before. I don't mind.

ROSEMARY: Yes, but Sam, do you think I'm just . . . a whore, really? That I . . . sometimes I think so. It's usually in the afternoons. In fact very often in the afternoons, almost all the time now. I'll sit down, alone, and then I can't sit any longer. I'm too restless and . . . .

SAM: What?

ROSEMARY: It's such a shameful feeling. I get so desperate that I almost faint, become giddy, swaying and light-headed with . . . you know . . . and then I have to go and lie down. I feel so dreadful afterwards. But I can't help myself. It's then I think maybe I'm just made like that. That I can't ever be satisfied. Am I like that?

SAM: No.

ROSEMARY: I wish you'd tell me what you think. It's not because I'm thinking about it all the time, Sam. I could be doing the shopping list or the laundry. It's as if my body and myself can't work together. It keeps betraying me.

SAM: I know.

ROSEMARY: Do you?

SAM: Yes. Abuse of self. Our peculiar sickness. You're not alone. It taints us all now. I can't imagine my parents . . . I mean I don't know, I had little awareness of their private life together. They didn't show it much at all, in fact. But they too must have been overcome with passion and its aftermath. Yet it was but one plank in their lives. They existed in a frame, a society, that gave them some sense of themselves. We don't.

ROSEMARY: What can we do?

SAM: I don't know. It's up to you.

ROSEMARY: I don't want to play that game.

SAM: But it is. It's your life. I'm not much of a bargain. I don't want to influence you. You have to decide for yourself.

ROSEMARY: I don't want to decide for myself, that's the last thing I want. I want you to do it for me. It is not my life. It is our life. Ours. Ours.

SAM: Then I want us to go on.

ROSEMARY: Then we will.

SAM: If that's what you want.

ROSEMARY: (*Almost a scream*) What *we* want!

SAM: Shhh. For Christ's sake! It's still early morning. This is a hotel. There's people still asleep.

ROSEMARY: I don't care about other people.

SAM: Rosemary, we'll get thrown out.

ROSEMARY: I don't care.

SAM: Shhhhh.

ROSEMARY: I wish you had killed me, strangled me, whatever you said you did. I wish you had.

SAM: Don't say that.

ROSEMARY: Are you ashamed of it now? It would be better than this, at least it would all be over. Why don't you do it?

SAM: Because I love you.

ROSEMARY: Oh, Sam, why is it so hard to say?

SAM: Because I'm afraid, that's why.

ROSEMARY: Afraid of what?

SAM: Of the pain. That same emotion that means I cannot do it made me want to kill you. It is the most virulent, diabolical, confining, frustrating, stupid, violent, marvelous, ridiculous emotion in all the world. I have no control over it or who it chooses to attack. I am it's slave, outlaw, executioner and mindless acolyte. I am possessed. I am putty in its grasp. I look at you and I do not see just Rosemary Wright, a girl, a girl I married. I see my dreams and their fulfilment, my secret habits and my not-so-secret lusts, my disgrace and my hope, my shame and my salvation. I see my love like a moth sees a flame and blunders to it, knocking on its glass to be admitted to delight unimaginable, one exquisite immolation. If only you would have me.

(*Silence*)

ROSEMARY: I will.

SAM: Good, then we'll go home. (*Silence*) Tell me that you're not afraid.

ROSEMARY: But I am.

SAM: Good. That makes two of us.

Curtain

Martin Duberman

THE COLONIAL DUDES

Martin Duberman

A prominent historian as well as playwright, Martin Duberman was born in 1930 in New York City and grew up there and in Mount Vernon, New York. He received his B.A. from Yale University and his M.A. and Ph.D. from Harvard. He is the author of two distinguished biographies: *Charles Francis Adams, 1807–1886,* which was awarded the prestigious Bancroft Prize in 1962; and *James Russell Lowell,* a nominee for the National Book Award in 1966. A collection of his essays, *The Uncompleted Past,* was published in 1969 (*The New York Times* defined it as "a remarkable intellectual autobiography") and in 1965, he edited *The Antislavery Vanguard: New Essays on the Abolitionists.*

Although Mr. Duberman admitted to a newspaper interviewer that "there are times when I have trouble deciding which I am, historian or playwright," he successfully has juxtaposed both careers by discovering "there is a feedback between history and the theatre" and the cord that binds his two selves is "curiosity about the inner worlds of people."

The author first became enamored with the theatre at the age of seventeen when he performed the juvenile lead in a summer stock rendering of Thornton Wilder's *Our Town.* "At any rate, I wound up at Yale, where I did some acting and directing and where I also became fascinated by American history."

Mr. Duberman's first play, *In White America,* opened in October, 1963, at the Off-Broadway Sheridan Square Playhouse. It enjoyed a run of 500 performances, two national tours, a large number of foreign productions and won the 1963–64 Drama Desk-Vernon Rice Award. His short play, *Metaphors,* was presented as part of *Collision Course* at the Café au Go Go in 1968; *Groups* was given a workshop production at the Loft Theatre, 1969; and in 1971 his full-length play, *Payments,* was staged at The New Dramatists, an organization that has been assisting in the development of outstanding new playwrights since 1950.

The Colonial Dudes, published here for the first time, also was seen at The New Dramatists and later, in August, 1972, was presented at the John Drew Memorial Theatre, East Hampton, Long Island, under the auspices of Edward Albee and Richard Barr. It is the second work by Martin Duberman to be included in *The Best Short Plays* annuals. In the 1970 volume, the author was represented by *The Recorder: A History,* one of two related plays dealing with the elusiveness of truth and the enigma of history. Bearing the overall title of *The Memory Bank,* *The Recorder* and its companion piece, *The Electric Map,* opened in January, 1970 at the Off-Broadway Tambellini's Gate Theatre to considerable praise spearheaded by Clive Barnes of *The New York Times* who declared that "it is good to spend the evening with a professional playwright of Mr. Duberman's quality."

A former professor of American History at Princeton University, the author recently was appointed Distinguished Service Professor of History at the Herbert H. Lehman College of the City University of New York. His newest book, *Black Mountain: An Exploration in Community,* was published in 1972.

Characters:

ALEX FOLEY

WAYNE FROBER

Scene:

The office of Alex Foley, professor of English literature, and, separated by a wooden partition, the corridor that leads to his office.

Foley is at his desk, typing. He lights a cigarette, types some more, then sits back, looks disgustedly at his type-writer and mutters: "Von schmaky putz."

Foley is about forty-five, burly, tough, bearded, dressed in the sort of informal, somewhat adventurous style which makes it clear that he is not a standard academic.

Wayne Frober is sitting up against the wall of the corridor, eyes closed as if asleep. He is nineteen, long-haired, wearing a leather jacket with fringe, bell-bottom blue jeans, no socks, and sneakers. He has bad skin. The neck of a pint bottle sticks out of his jacket pocket.

Foley gets up from his desk, walks to the office door, opens it and steps into the corridor. He begins to stride purposefully down the corridor when he sees the figure of Wayne and stops. Wayne has not opened his eyes.

FOLEY: Oh. Are you waiting to see me? (*Wayne barely opens his eyes*)

WAYNE: No.

FOLEY: (*Surprised*) You're not?

WAYNE: No.

FOLEY: Oh. (*Pause*) Mine's the only office up here, you know. There's no one else around. (*Wayne doesn't react*) You're not waiting, then, for anyone else?

WAYNE: Yeah, I am.

FOLEY: (*Confused*) But as I said, mine is the only office up here.

WAYNE: Yeah, I know. I'm resting.

FOLEY: Okay. (*He starts down the corridor*)

WAYNE: Hey!

FOLEY: (*Stops, turns around*) Yes?

WAYNE: Where's Hale?

FOLEY: Hale who? (*Wayne starts laughing*)

WAYNE: Hale who! Oh, I like that. You made a poem: Hale who. Sounds like haiku. Hey, we can put the two together:

Hale who
Haiku.

FOLEY: Not bad. At least for eight in the morning.

WAYNE: Man, is it that late!

FOLEY: Late? Nobody else has arrived in the building yet.

WAYNE: What are *you* doing here?

FOLEY: That's just what I was going to ask you.

WAYNE: I already told you. I'm waiting for Hale.

FOLEY: Hale who . . .(*Interrupts himself*) No, let's try it this way: who is the Hale you're waiting for?

WAYNE: She-e-t! That's no poem.

FOLEY: Poems don't get answers.

WAYNE: Right! They get questions.

(*Foley waits for a second, shrugs, then starts down the corridor again*)

WAYNE: (*Yelling after him*) Hale Riker!

FOLEY: (*Stops, turns around*) Oh—Mr. Riker.

WAYNE: Is that what you call him—*Mr.* Riker?!

FOLEY: (*Embarrassed*) Well, no, as a matter of fact. I call him Hale.

WAYNE: So do I.

FOLEY: Are you a student?

WAYNE: 'Course. Isn't everyone?

FOLEY: I mean, are you enrolled in the college?

WAYNE: I guess so.

FOLEY: You don't know?

WAYNE: Yeah. I'm a beginner, a freshman.

FOLEY: I see. And Mr. Riker—Hale—is your teacher?

WAYNE: No. He's a buddy. We shoot the shit together.

FOLEY: (*Staying cool*) That's nice. Where do you shoot it?

WAYNE: Oh man, I don't *shoot* nothin'. I'm too young to shoot. I'm barely at the pill stage. (*He laughs at what he thinks is a private joke*)

FOLEY: Shooting is bad news. Especially if it's speed.

WAYNE: (*Impressed*) Oh—you know what shooting is?

FOLEY: Doesn't everybody? I'm sure Hale does.

WAYNE: Well, Hale—he's a kid. Not much older than I am. But you ... you're a ... a ....

FOLEY: Go ahead. I'm a what?

WAYNE: You're a regular Rip Van Winkle! (*Wayne laughs; Foley smiles*)

FOLEY: I guess I am pretty ancient.

WAYNE: Naw, that just came out. I often say things I don't mean. To hear how they sound—in case I ever really want to say them.

FOLEY: Why are you waiting for Hale *here?*

WAYNE: I don't like his corridor. It's got too many doors in it. I can't concentrate.

FOLEY: He probably won't be in for hours.

WAYNE: That's okay. It's nice up here. How come you get a corridor all to yourself?

FOLEY: (*Smiling*) It's what they call seniority.

WAYNE: Aha, you're a big shot!

FOLEY: No, just a survivor. (*Pause*) Well, I hope you find Hale all right. (*He starts to leave*)

WAYNE: Do you really?

FOLEY: (*A little exasperated*) There are things I care about more, it's true, but ....

WAYNE: I don't even know if I *want* to find him. I don't know if I'm in the mood for Hale. He can be a butternut.

FOLEY: What's a butternut?

WAYNE: (*Smiling broadly*) Gee, I don't know. Nice

sound though. (*Savoring the word*) B-U-T-T-E-R-N-U-T. Well, not that nice. It's got too many meanings already; butter, nut— all that stuff. You got to think of words that are brand new. Like stropeldean.

FOLEY: The "dean" part means something. You know— Dean of the College and all that.

WAYNE: (*Frowning*) Right. You see what happens? This atmosphere messes up your mind. I haven't been here two months and already I'm using words that mean something. (*Shakes his head*) It's a bummer. (*He looks dejected*)

FOLEY: (*Trying to cheer him up*) If all the words you use are new, nobody else will understand you.

WAYNE: So?

FOLEY: You do want to communicate with other people, don't you?

WAYNE: Oh, sure. But that's not what words are for. Words are for disguise. Or for games. Disguise, when you're talking with someone. Games, when you're alone. Now, like here ... (*He reaches into his jacket and takes out three or four hand-written pages*) ... here's a new game I wrote last night while I was sitting here.

FOLEY: You've been here all night?

WAYNE: No. Since about four.

FOLEY: The building is locked at night.

WAYNE: Only the doors. (*Suddenly enthusiastic*) Hey, what are you doing? (*Foley looks down at himself, self-consciously*)

FOLEY: Doing? Nothing.

WAYNE: I mean, why'd you leave your office? Where are you going?

FOLEY: To get a drink.

(*Wayne reaches into his jacket and takes out the fifth of rum, which is almost empty*)

WAYNE: Here. (*Holds out the bottle to Foley*) Here's a drink.

FOLEY: Thanks. It's a little early for me. I was going to get a drink of water.

WAYNE: Suit yourself.

FOLEY: Is that rum?

WAYNE: Yup.

FOLEY: Seems a strange thing for you to be drinking. I think of rum as a skid row drink. Sort of end of the line.

WAYNE: You can't drink rum on skid row. It's too expensive.

FOLEY: That's a point.

WAYNE: Rum is a colonial drink. Molasses Act of 1733 and all that. Very big in the history books.

FOLEY: (*Confused*) What is?

WAYNE: (*Deadpan*) The Molasses Act. The British put a tax on molasses, which meant the colonists didn't have enough to make all the rum they needed. They needed a lot of rum. For corrupting the Indians and that sort of thing. So they got sore as hell at England and started dumping tea in the harbor. (*Pauses; scratches his head*) Seems to me I left something out. (*Shrugs*) Oh, well. Anyway, the British got scared and introduced salutary neglect. But that didn't work either; they didn't neglect enough. So the colonists finally said, "the hell with it," and Paul Revere roused the Minute Men, who fired at a statue at Lexington. And before long we were the United States of America.

FOLEY: And that's why you drink rum.

WAYNE: Something like that.

FOLEY: You're one of the corrupted Indians.

WAYNE: (*Pleased*) Yeah! Here's to that! (*He hoists the bottle of rum, then uncorks it*) Here's to the Molasses Act! (*Drinks*) Hey, you know, you're a pretty good dude!

FOLEY: You're mixing the historical metaphor. No dudes in the eighteenth century.

WAYNE: Here's to the colonial dudes! (*He drinks again*)

FOLEY: It looks like you've finished most of that pint.

WAYNE: Yeah—well, I'm sicka grass. Puts you too far out. You know what I mean? Makes you vague, foggy.

FOLEY: I don't much like it, either. Once in a while, maybe, at a party.

WAYNE: That's when it's worst. You *think* you know

where everybody's at. But you're miles away. (*Pause*) So, what are you doing?

FOLEY: After my drink of water?

WAYNE: Right.

FOLEY: I came in early to finish a piece I'm writing.

WAYNE: A piece of what?

FOLEY: A book review.

WAYNE: Hey, I'll tell you what—I'll read yours if you'll read mine.

FOLEY: You mean *now?*

WAYNE: You don't wanna. I can tell.

FOLEY: My review isn't finished.

WAYNE: Oh. Too bad. Whenever I stop, I'm finished. I get bored easy.

FOLEY: I'd be glad to read *yours,* if you want.

WAYNE: (*Pleased*) Groovy!

FOLEY: Why don't you come in the office?

WAYNE: Sure thing, Mr. Foley.

FOLEY: (*Surprised*) So you know who I am!

WAYNE: Oh, yeah. You're the cat who digs *Steppenwolf.* (*Foley opens the door to his office. They walk in. Wayne looks around at all the books*)

WAYNE: Uh-huh! Is that how you got to be a survivor?

FOLEY: One way.

WAYNE: I like books.

FOLEY: So do I. The feel of them.

WAYNE: Yeah! They're neat little packages. I mean, to hold.

FOLEY: What's your name?

WAYNE: Wayne. Wayne Frober. What's yours?

FOLEY: I thought you knew mine.

WAYNE: All I know is Professor Foley.

FOLEY: Alex. Alex Foley.

WAYNE: Hi, Alex.

FOLEY: Hi, Wayne. (*He starts to sit down behind his desk*)

WAYNE: You gonna sit *there?*

FOLEY: Why not? This is where I sit.

WAYNE: Aw no, Alex. That'll make the vibes all wrong, man.

FOLEY: The vibes?

WAYNE: The vibrations.

FOLEY: Oh. All right. Then *you* sit there. (*He points to the desk chair*)

WAYNE: That's no better. It's *positions* I don't like.

FOLEY: Now look, Wayne. If I can't sit down, how am I going to read your story?

WAYNE: You sit when you read, huh? That's a groove! I lie down when I read. Or, if it's a poem, I walk around. But never sit; it bends me the wrong way.

FOLEY: Well, we all have our peculiarities. And one of mine is that I like to sit when I read. (*He starts to sit*)

WAYNE: (*Casual*) Okay. If that's what you dig. Why not? Sure! By the way, it's not a story, it's a poem. So you might want to walk around a little bit.

FOLEY: I sit when I read poems, too.

WAYNE: No kidding? I'll have to try that.

(*As a concession, Foley moves the chair to the side of the desk*)

FOLEY: I'm full of ideas.

WAYNE: (*Serious*) Yeah, you're terrific. (*He hands Foley the poem. They smile at each other. Foley begins to read*) I don't like what we said about books. (*Foley looks up from reading*)

FOLEY: We didn't say much.

WAYNE: That's just it. Superficial. We said we "liked" them. Now what does that mean?

FOLEY: You said you like the feel of them—you like to hold them.

WAYNE: Yeah, but what's to like? It's only cloth, or paper; you can get to feel that any place—like up a Spanish girl's skirt.

FOLEY: What?

WAYNE: They put paper up their skirts so when they walk it swishes like silk.

FOLEY: Never knew that.

WAYNE: Only poor Spanish girls. The rich ones wear real silk. Anyway, it can't be the weight, either. I mean, books. Shit, if all you want to do is hold a couple of pounds, you could grab two pounds of anything. Like hamburger meat.

FOLEY: (*Confused*) Uh-huh.

WAYNE: 'Course, hamburger meat doesn't have a very nice texture—in the naked hand, that is. Especially if you mix it with egg yolk, which is how my mother prepares it. She's a good cook, even though she isn't Jewish. Are you Jewish?

FOLEY: No.

WAYNE: Imagine—two non-Jews talking about books.

FOLEY: What's strange about that?

WAYNE: Jews have got the book bag sewn up. Which makes it even weirder for us to like books so much. You got any ideas on that?

FOLEY: (*A little arch*) Could it be we enjoy the *contents* of the book, what's inside of it?

WAYNE: Could be, but I doubt it. Because I like holding books I haven't read. I often like those more. Reading a book can ruin it. No, I think it's a symbol thing. Like you hold these books or you stare at them and you think, "Wow! there it is, the world all wrapped up and ready to be eaten. Like a hamburger to go." (*Pause*) That's the second time I mentioned hamburgers. Funny. I must be homesick. (*To Foley*) My mother, you know, and the egg yolk.

FOLEY: Miss the home cooking, huh? You're living in a dorm, I suppose.

WAYNE: No, I'm not living anywhere right now. Corridors, that kind of thing. The old man threw me out.

FOLEY: Oh? I'm sorry to hear that, Wayne.

WAYNE: He'd throw you out, too. You know: *Hair.* The big threat. It's so goddamn boring—that's what *everybody* gets thrown out for. Why couldn't he come up with something original at least? Like getting pissed off because I forgot my orthodontia exercises. (*Bares his upper teeth, like a horse about to whinney*) You see, it's these two. They're buck for good. Too late now. And all because I forgot the exercises. (*Shrugs*) Oh well, I guess there are worse things. (*Pause*) Trouble is, I got those, too. (*Points to his face*) Like this acne. The chicks sure don't dig it. Guys, it's okay. Like it makes you approachable. I guess they figure they got one up on you at the start in the competition for *girls* and *power*, so it's okay to be friendly. But chicks—forget it! They take one look at this eruption and run like it's Vesuvius. (*Pause*) That's what the poem's about. Chicks and acne. What we call the enduring adolescent themes.

FOLEY: You only write about the universal.

WAYNE: You got it! I'm a kid for all seasons. (*They laugh*) Well, why don't you read it?

FOLEY: Well, why don't you give me a chance?

WAYNE: So, okay, here's a chance. (*He puts his elbow on the desk, leans his chin on it and self-consciously stares in the direction away from Foley*)

FOLEY: (*Reading aloud to himself, almost inaudible*)

Silent falls the tamarack,
Out of reaches,
Out of sorrows
Nearer men than you must tell.

WAYNE: (*Mumbling to himself*) How could I ask the guy if he's Jewish, with a name like Foley? Stupid!

FOLEY: You talking to me?

WAYNE: No. Keep reading.

FOLEY: Yes, sir!

WAYNE: Oh, sorry—I didn't mean it like that.

FOLEY: (*Smiling*) I know. Anyway, I like the four lines I managed to read. A dramatic beginning.

WAYNE: (*Beaming*) Oh, yeah? You mean, like it catches your interest?

FOLEY: I could hardly put it down.

WAYNE: You're making fun of me.

FOLEY: (*Contrite*) I'm not! Look, Wayne, it's *very* good. I'm leveling with you. Come to think of it, I should be offended. You're suggesting I'd say it was good if I didn't think so. Why would I?

WAYNE: To be pleasant.

FOLEY: People are pleasant because they want to be liked. I don't give a damn if anybody likes me or not. Including you.

WAYNE: No shit? That's very impressive. (*Pause*) I think. (*Pause*) I want *you* to like *me*. I suppose that's a defect in my character.

FOLEY: It depends on what you're willing to do to get me to like you. You don't strike me as the kind of person who'd prostitute himself. (*Wayne looks shocked*)

WAYNE: (*Softly*) Jesus!

FOLEY: What's the matter?

WAYNE: (*Hesitant*) Well, it's . . . it's . . . (*Blurts it out*) Are you queer?

FOLEY: Good God! You move a little fast!

WAYNE: You want to build up to it slow, huh?

FOLEY: I mean, you can be hard to follow—the way you jump from one thing to another.

WAYNE: It was perfectly logical. You talked about what I'd do to get you to like me; whether I would prostitute myself.

FOLEY: Now look! I never thought I'd have to explain this, but let me be very clear. I'm a married man with . . . .

WAYNE: You married to a woman?

FOLEY: (*Exploding*) Of course I'm married to a woman, for Christ's sake!

WAYNE: (*Quietly*) Well, lots of people aren't. I know lots of men who are married to men.

FOLEY: Is that so?

WAYNE: Sure. It's a big thing. Besides, some men who *are* married to women also like tricking once in a while with a man. It's a very "in" thing. You know, sample all the varieties of human experience and all that jazz.

FOLEY: I wouldn't know.

WAYNE: You've never tricked with a man?

FOLEY: What does "tricked" *mean*?

WAYNE: Wow, what a groove! There aren't many of you guys left, you know? (*Low whistle*) You're a find!

FOLEY: Now who's making fun of whom?

WAYNE: Okay. I'm putting you on.

FOLEY: Thank you. Now what does "tricked" mean?

WAYNE: Ball. Hit the sack.

FOLEY: I get it.

WAYNE: I think it's nice you've never made it with a man. I admire that.

FOLEY: You're putting me on again.

WAYNE: No, I mean it. You don't try to keep up. Buddy-buddy it with the kids. That's good, man. You stay you.

FOLEY: Thanks.

WAYNE: I don't mean you're square either. No; I got a whole theory about that. I think the squarest thing somebody your age can do, is try to keep up.

FOLEY: I do have a beard.

WAYNE: How long have you had it?

FOLEY: Only a year.

WAYNE: (*Subdued*) Hmm. Well, that is disappointing. (*Brightening*) But at least you haven't tricked with a man.

FOLEY: You have, I gather.

WAYNE: (*Disgusted*) Yeah—had to. I was fifteen. Still interested in the status bit—you know, following the crowd. So I hit the sack with a couple of buddies. Just to keep up. Never again. Men aren't my bag. It's against my nature. (*Pause*) But, you know, you ought to try it once.

FOLEY: You just said you admired me for *not* trying it.

WAYNE: Well, I'm of two minds about it, to tell you the truth. I'm worried you didn't make a real choice; that you were too paranoid to consider it.

FOLEY: I've been asked, if that's what you mean.

WAYNE: No—I know you've been asked. Hell, everybody knows the faculty is full of fags.

FOLEY: Now look, Wayne!

WAYNE: Don't faint. I won't name names. You probably know 'em all anyway.

FOLEY: It happens I don't. And I don't want to.

WAYNE: Bullshit. You're dying to know if *Mr.* Riker and I are making it.

FOLEY: I am not. Besides I already know. You said you only tricked once with a man—when you were fifteen.

WAYNE: I might have been lying. To spare you. You gotta go slow with the oldsters on the unisex theme.

FOLEY: You weren't lying. I think you tell the truth most of the time. And what's more, I'm not sure that's a virtue.

WAYNE: (*Interested*) No kidding! I thought the one thing all you types liked about us was our "truth-telling."

FOLEY: Only very young children and very old people always tell the truth and only because they can't help it.

WAYNE: Hey, I dig that! It's almost an epigram. (*Pause*) But I'm not sure what it means.

FOLEY: It means if you tell the truth all the time, you're either infantile or senile. Everybody else knows "truth-telling" is usually an excuse for cruelty.

WAYNE: Hmm. I'll have to think about that. (*Pause*) You don't mean I should go around telling lies?

FOLEY: Sometimes. White ones. Not out of deceit; out of kindness.

WAYNE: I need an example. I have a very concrete mind.

FOLEY: Wayne, I think you have a mild case of acne.

WAYNE: You *what?*

FOLEY: That's a white lie. Your acne is not so mild. But I like you. I don't want to hurt you.

WAYNE: Well, you have.

FOLEY: See! You tricked me into telling the truth and now you're angry.

WAYNE: You're getting fond of that word.

FOLEY: What word?

WAYNE: Tricked. (*Pause*) So you don't like my acne?

FOLEY: I didn't say that.

WAYNE: So you like it?

FOLEY: I don't have a strong opinion one way or the other. I merely *described* your acne.

WAYNE: Oh, boy, there it is! The classic liberal remark! "I don't have a strong opinion one way or the other, I merely described an objective situation, my dear fellow—i.e., your acne." You know damn well you have an opinion of my acne, so let's have it!

FOLEY: (*Pause; accentuating each word*) I don't like your acne. (*Wayne slumps dejectedly in his chair*)

WAYNE: (*After a pause*) I knew it. I knew it the minute you invited me into your office. You wanted to stare at my pimples.

FOLEY: Well, that's an improvement. Ten minutes ago you thought I wanted to sleep with you.

WAYNE: My genius, my art—what does it all matter? It always comes down to the same thing. They want to freak-out over my blemished pores.

FOLEY: Wayne, are you putting me on again?

WAYNE: I'm not sure. It's a very depressing topic. I mean, I get genuinely depressed about my acne. But I don't know if I'm depressed now. I thought I should go into my routine anyway—my *Sorrows of Werther* bit. If you don't keep practicing a role, you forget it. And that role I really need. It's the only one that brings the chicks back after they go "ecch" at my face. You see, they feel guilty for going "ecch." And that leaves 'em wide open. So you got to be sorrowful. You got to play hurt-young-genius. Then they can comfort you. It makes them feel like Florence Nightingale among the Zulus. It can lead to some beautiful things. Like miscegenation.

FOLEY: Sounds like acne has its advantages.

WAYNE: Only if the girl is nice—capable of guilt. But there aren't many of those any more. It's a new generation: without guilt. (*Depressed*) It's what we call progress. It's all in the poem, if you'd only read it.

FOLEY: It's not in the first four lines.

WAYNE: Of course not. I'm a subtle cat. I don't telegraph my moves. A slow cadenza in the beginning—like the beach at dawn, or . . . .

FOLEY: (*Interrupting*) A cadenza is a flourish that comes at the *end,* not the beginning.

WAYNE: (*Pause*) You're a pedant. (*Foley jumps up*)

FOLEY: (*Half-serious*) Now you've gone too far!

WAYNE: (*Delighted*) Oh, yeah? Terrific! So that's where you live, huh? You hate being called a pedant!

FOLEY: Especially for the wrong reason. Someone who uses words with accuracy is *not* a pedant.

WAYNE: Who says the way you use "cadenza" is accurate?

FOLEY: The dictionary.

WAYNE: The *dictionary!* Oh, you're too much!

FOLEY: (*Formal*) The dictionary tells us what a particular collection of sounds—like *ca-den-za*—means to most people. In other words, how you can make yourself understood.

WAYNE: Most people never heard of *ca-den-za.*

FOLEY: That's not the point.

WAYNE: I don't care what most people think.

FOLEY: Don't you want them to understand you?

WAYNE: They can't.

FOLEY: Wayne, you're an elitist.

WAYNE: (*Aroused*) Hey, watch that!

FOLEY: Aha! So now we know where *you* live! Well, you better face it: you want to create a private language accessible only to the few. That, my boy, is the sign of an undemocratic mind.

WAYNE: Don't call me "my boy."

FOLEY: Did I?

WAYNE: Yes. And it's not the racial overtones I object to.

FOLEY: You're creating a diversion. Deal with my main point.

WAYNE: Words change their meaning. People who use words in a new way keep the language alive.

FOLEY: People like you.

WAYNE: Yeah. (*Smiling broadly*) Maybe even you. Like take the word "dig." Five years ago the majority of people used "dig" to mean shovel a hole. Then a few people started using it to mean "like" or "understand." "I dig you, baby," now means "I like you, baby, and I get what you're saying." Now if we'd stuck to the dictionary—to the majority's authority (*Suddenly struck by his own phrase*) Hmm—the "majority's authority." That's rather nice. Haiku again. (*To Foley*) What was the first haiku we thought of?

FOLEY: Stick to the argument.

WAYNE: I'm getting tired. Too much logic depresses me.

FOLEY: You're copping out.

WAYNE: There's *another* example. Now what did "cop-out" mean five years ago? Nothing!

FOLEY: If it had meant nothing, it could never have come into common usage. "Cop" and "out" already had meanings; they were combined in a new way, that's all. You can't talk gibberish and think you're being inventive. (*Pause*) Von schmaky putz.

WAYNE: *What!*

FOLEY: See! It's gibberish. Doesn't mean a thing.

WAYNE: Say it again.

FOLEY: Von schmaky putz.

WAYNE: (*Belligerently*) Is that so! You think I'm some kind of a dope? I know when I'm being cursed at.

FOLEY: Wayne, for God's sake!

WAYNE: Don't tell me! I heard it! *Putz!* Just like that he calls me a putz, and then says, "For God's sake, Wayne!" like he'd never meant it. What really hurts is that you're not even Jewish. I call that underhanded.

FOLEY: Wayne . . . .

WAYNE: Don't Wayne me.

FOLEY: Are you really angry? (*Pause*)

WAYNE: (*Quietly*) Yes. (*Then, louder*) I will not be called a putz! That's worse than "boy"—I mean, since I'm white.

FOLEY: I don't even know what putz means!

WAYNE: Sure, sure.

FOLEY: I swear!

WAYNE: Listen, you people may not know much, but putz you've got to know—it's a literary convention.

FOLEY: (*Bursts out laughing*) Where the hell did you hear the phrase "a literary convention"?

WAYNE: That's the only thing I've heard since I got here. *Everything's* a literary convention. (*Brandishes his bottle of rum*) This bottle! (*Waves it around his head*) This office! Your desk! Your name! Literary conventions. Agreed-upon symbols, that's all! Should we fail to sign the convention, we wouldn't know what to call anything. Everything would be a cop-out. Or a cadenza. Well, I've decided not to sign. I will not agree to the symbols. You are no longer Alex. You are Cadenza!

(*The telephone on Foley's desk rings. Foley jumps involuntarily. Wayne retreats to his chair*)

FOLEY: (*Timidly*) Excuse me. The day seems to have begun.

WAYNE: Now there's a good phrase. I'm sure we can make a literary convention out of it. (*Foley frowns, picks up the phone*)

FOLEY: Hello . . . Oh, it's you . . . Yes, I *am* surprised. You're usually not in this early, are you? . . . Oh really? What's wrong? . . . (*He looks furtively at Wayne, who gets up and starts wandering aimlessly around the office*) Yes, it happens I do know him . . . (*Wayne takes a cigarette from the pack on Foley's desk. Sarcastically, to Wayne*) Help yourself. (*Into the phone*) Not well, no. But well enough to understand what you're saying . . . Uh-huh . . . Yes . . . Uh-huh . . . That's right. It's difficult for me to talk . . . (*Wayne reacts by stuffing his fingers into his ears*) Can you hang on just one minute? (*Foley puts his hand over the receiver*) Will you please take your elbows out of your ears. There's nothing I have to say that you can't hear. (*Wayne removes his fingers*)

WAYNE: Meaning you won't say anything.

FOLEY: (*Responding to the challenge*) Is that so! (*He

takes his hand off the receiver and speaks into it) Sorry ... No, it's all right ... I can talk. Now, what is it you're worried about exactly? ... *You're* worried, or his family is? ... Yes, I know about his father ... (*Wayne reacts sharply*) ... Yes, his hair ... All right, then, his general appearance ... I agree with you.

WAYNE: (*Interrupting*) What do you agree with?

FOLEY: (*His hand over the receiver*) If you wait a second, you'll find out. (*Into the receiver*) As I started to say, I agree with you. There's nothing wrong with his appearance. Sure it's different. But I happen to like it. ... Well, that's his father's problem ... (*Wayne returns to his chair*) What else did he have to say? (*Suddenly looks concerned, even frightened*) Oh? No, no, I didn't know that ... Yes ... uh-huh ... Right.

WAYNE: Should I put my fingers back in my ears?

FOLEY: (*Going on with the phone conversation*) I'll talk to you later about it. I'll call you when I get free ... No, it shouldn't be long ... Yes ... Right. Goodbye. (*Hangs up receiver; trying to sound expansive, jolly*) Well! Guess who?

WAYNE: Hale who.

FOLEY: That's right. How'd you know?

WAYNE: His voice has resonance. It carries.

FOLEY: Oh, does it?

WAYNE: Don't panic. I couldn't hear the words, just the tone.

FOLEY: He's worried about you. Been looking for you half the night.

WAYNE: And I've been looking for him half the night. So, we're both nuts. (*Pause*) Why did he call you? You're not supposed to know me. I'm a lowly freshman.

FOLEY: He didn't think I knew you. He wanted my advice. In general.

WAYNE: Must have been surprised.

FOLEY: He was.

WAYNE: He thinks I'm his discovery. His protégé. He's probably pissed off at you. No one else is supposed to know the Child Genius.

FOLEY: Meaning you, I gather.

WAYNE: 'Fraid so. It's my cross.

FOLEY: (*Looking at Wayne's poem on his desk*) Well, the first four lines are good.

WAYNE: Which is more than I can say for your book review. You know, that was pretty rotten of you, not letting me read it.

FOLEY: It isn't finished.

WAYNE: Neither is my poem. You're too self-protective.

FOLEY: Could be.

WAYNE: That's the easiest way to get hurt. (*Wayne suddenly gets out of his chair. Foley involuntarily jumps, revealing fright*)

WAYNE: Wow, man! Those coffee nerves! I was just reaching for my poem. I gotta split. (*He holds out his hand for the poem. Foley doesn't offer it*)

FOLEY: Wayne, I want to talk to you.

WAYNE: Man, we been rapping for three days! It makes me nervous to talk so much. I worry about being too verbal. I'll end up like you—an expounder.

FOLEY: Look, I'm worried about you.

WAYNE: (*Embarrassed; pleased*) Oh, boy, another daddy. Just what I need. I hope you're better than the original.

FOLEY: Cut the sarcasm. I want to talk straight to you.

WAYNE: Who ever heard of a straight Cadenza?

FOLEY: The name is Alex.

WAYNE: (*Hesitates, then shakes his head in mock self-disgust*) A man of my sophistication should be beyond the appeal of brute sincerity. (*Shakes his head again*) But what can I tell you? (*Sits in his chair*) I know why you're worried. I also know why you jumped just now. I'm a smart kid. I'm also storybook gentle. So don't worry. (*Pause*) You're still worrying.

FOLEY: Umm.

WAYNE: Will you feel better if you look at it, if you actually see it?

FOLEY: (*Nervously*) I don't think so.

(*Wayne digs in his pocket and takes out a switch blade. He throws it, unopened, on the desk*)

WAYNE: Here. Look at it. Big deal. (*Foley gingerly picks up the knife and examines it*) Not much to see, right? Standard brand. (*Pause*) Except for one little thing.

FOLEY: What's that.

(*Wayne gets out of his chair and leans across the desk*)

WAYNE: Gimme. I'll show you. (*Foley hands him the knife. Wayne flicks it open, leans close to Foley, while pointing to the bottom of the blade*) Here. See this?

FOLEY: (*Apprehensive*) No. See what?

WAYNE: Jesus, man, if you'd stop shaking, you'd be able to focus your eyeballs!

FOLEY: I am not shaking.

WAYNE: I mean, I'm very hurt! What do you think I am, a *killer*?

FOLEY: *I don't like knives.*

WAYNE: Neither do I.

FOLEY: Then why do you carry one?

WAYNE: You make it sound like a papoose, my lifetime companion. I've been "carrying" this knife for a big eight hours.

FOLEY: You shouldn't carry it at all.

WAYNE: (*Pointing to the bottom of the blade*) You want to see these initials or not? I mean, don't do me any favors. I'll take my blade and go. (*Pause*) And my poem, too.

FOLEY: (*Leaning forward*) I can't see any initials.

WAYNE: They're here—way down in the corner—real tiny. Like he was ashamed of them.

FOLEY: (*Squinting*) F.F., right?

WAYNE: Good, man! It's always a comfort to find a professor who can read.

FOLEY: Who is F.F.?

WAYNE: You're allowed five guesses. But make them imaginative.

FOLEY: (*Thinking*) Franz Ferdinand.

WAYNE: What?

FOLEY: Franz Ferdinand, Archduke of the Austro-Hungarian Empire, was assassinated at Sarajevo in the year 1914—thereby precipitating the First World War.

WAYNE: (*Impressed*) That's a pretty good guess.

FOLEY: Fannie Farmer. The candy lady.

WAYNE: Concentrate on the second F.

FOLEY: Farouk . . . Faust . . . Fillmore.

WAYNE: It's a person, not an auditorium!

FOLEY: Fillmore *was* a person. He was president of the United States.

WAYNE: You expect me to believe he was a person on that kind of evidence?

FOLEY: Haven't I used up five yet?

WAYNE: No—not near it. You're terrific!

FOLEY: (*Pause*) Freneau.

WAYNE: Who?

FOLEY: Philip Freneau. American poet.

WAYNE: No kidding!

FOLEY: You ought to know him. He's one of your predecessors.

WAYNE: I don't have any.

FOLEY: On that note of arrogance, I quit!

WAYNE: Aw, come on, just one more.

FOLEY: Frost.

WAYNE: It's got to be a real person.

FOLEY: *Robert Frost* was a real person!

WAYNE: Oh, *Robert* Frost! I thought you meant Jack. (*Pause*) Who else?

FOLEY: (*Mock iciness*) I will not say the obvious.

WAYNE: Go ahead, say it.

FOLEY: Fuck!

WAYNE: No—*Frober!*

FOLEY: What?

WAYNE: *Me!* Wayne Frober, remember?

FOLEY: Wayne does not begin with an F.

WAYNE: Fred Frober. The old man. It's Fred Frober's! Fucking Fred Frober's fucking war knife!

FOLEY: He gave it to you as a going away present?

WAYNE: Fat chance! I took it.

FOLEY: Why?

WAYNE: I hate knives.

FOLEY: I see—you took it because you hate it.

WAYNE: I took it because the old man's crazy about it! It's like a voodoo thing with him. He takes it out and stares at it. Remembers the good old days—zapping it to the Japs.

FOLEY: I was in the Second World War, and the army did not issue switch blades as standard equipment.

WAYNE: He bought it himself. Had some deep American thing about sticking it in the belly of the Orient. Claims he did, too. Says he gave it to some Jap on Okinawa. I'll bet it was after the guy was dead. He's a mean bastard, my old man. He should be in Washington.

FOLEY: How did Hale know you had the knife?

WAYNE: I told him. I called him yesterday, right after I left home. Said I was in possession of a death weapon and that I felt very strange.

FOLEY: That was thoughtful. You have him pretty worried.

WAYNE: He loves to worry about me. He gets bored with Jane Austen. (*Pause*) You think he's in his office?

FOLEY: He's waiting for me to call him back.

WAYNE: I can see him down there, fingering his *Pride and Prejudice*. Just another colonial dude. (*Gets up*) I guess I'll go see him. Tell him I've been talking the higher metaphysics with a full professor.

(*Foley laughs. Wayne leans over, takes the knife off the desk and starts to pick up the pages of his poem as well*)

FOLEY: Hey, aren't you going to let me finish it?

WAYNE: I figured I'd quit while I was ahead. You might not like the fifth line.

FOLEY: Then you can make a four line poem out of it.

WAYNE: (*Grins*) Yeah—maybe I'll get lots of little poems out of it. Lots of haiku. Then we'll publish 'em as a slim volume, and two weeks later I'll commit suicide. (*Pause; Foley suddenly looks grim. Cheerfully:*) That way I'll be a legend. "Brilliant young man falls on sword," et cetera. If you wait too long, then they can't say you were a "promising young poet." I think twenty—maybe twenty-two—is the cut-off point. (*Pause*) Anyway, you can read it, if you like.

FOLEY: I would like.

WAYNE: (*Pleased*) Okay. (*He puts the poem back on the desk, then starts toward the office door, the knife still in his hand*)

FOLEY: Why don't you come by tomorrow, and I'll tell you what I think of it?

WAYNE: Sure. About eight a.m.?

FOLEY: Uh-no. It's not when I'm at my best.

WAYNE: *I* thought you were pretty good.

FOLEY: Thanks.

WAYNE: I mean, I'm a handful.

FOLEY: (*Very serious*) I think you're a delight.

WAYNE: (*Embarrassed; sincere*) Gee, thanks Mr. Foley.

FOLEY: *Mr.* Foley! Now where did that come from! Suddenly I'm back in your old man's generation!

WAYNE: (*Quietly*) I wish you were. (*He starts to open the office door, then turns back toward Foley*) You gonna let me read your book review?

FOLEY: Definitely.

WAYNE: Tomorrow?

FOLEY: I'll have a carbon waiting for you. How's eleven in the morning?

WAYNE: Groovy.

FOLEY: Good. See you at eleven.

(*Wayne again starts to leave, then hesitates for a moment, turns back towards Foley, and tosses him the closed knife*)

WAYNE: Hang onto this for me, too, will you? I can pick it up some time. (*Foley catches the knife*)

FOLEY: Sure. (*Pause; He opens the top drawer of his desk*) Look, I'll put it in here. Then if you ever want it, you can come get it. Okay?

WAYNE: Far out! (*He opens the office door and steps into the corridor*) See you tomorrow, man.

FOLEY: Say hello to Hale for me.

WAYNE: Aw, he'll probably give me up after this. I'm losing all my mystery. (*Pause*) Does that drawer have a lock on it?

FOLEY: No.

WAYNE: (*Sadly, shaking his head up and down*) Good. Good. (*Pause*) Well, so long, Alex.

FOLEY: (*As Wayne leaves*) See you tomorrow, Wayne.

Curtain

Terence Rattigan

HIGH SUMMER

Terence Rattigan

The year 1971 was a momentous one for Sir Terence Rattigan: already a Commander of the Order of the British Empire, he was raised to knighthood by Queen Elizabeth II and on the occasion of his sixtieth birthday he was widely honored by his countrymen with galas, revivals of his plays and special showings of his films. It was a singular tribute to one of the most successful and popular of England's modern playwrights.

Sir Terence was born in London on June 10, 1911. Educated at Harrow and Trinity College, Oxford, he sprang to prominence in 1936 with his comedy *French Without Tears* which ran for over a thousand performances in the West End. Seven years later, he was to duplicate this theatrical feat with *While the Sun Shines,* a West End landmark for 1,154 performances.

Among Sir Terence's other noted plays are: *Flare Path; Love in Idleness* (retitled *O Mistress Mine* for Broadway where it was performed by Alfred Lunt and Lynn Fontanne for almost two years); *The Winslow Boy* recipient of the Ellen Terry Award for the best play produced on the London stage during 1946, it won the 1947–48 New York Drama Critics' Circle Award as the season's best foreign play); *The Browning Version* (the Ellen Terry Award play for 1948); *Adventure Story; Who Is Sylvia?; The Deep Blue Sea; The Sleeping Prince; Man and Boy; Separate Tables;* and *Ross.*

At one of the anniversary galas, Sir Terence was lauded for his "mastery of craft, high entertainment values, compassion, care for clarity, and concern for human beings as individuals." A staunch defender of craftsmanship, he has expressed his thoughts on the subject in a preface to the edition of his collected works: "The school of thought that condemns firm dramatic shape derives, I suppose, originally from Chekhov, an author who, in my impertinent view, is not usually properly understood either by his worshippers or his active imitators. I believe that his plays are as firmly shaped as Ibsen's. The stream that seems to meander its casual length along does so between strong artificial banks, most carefully and cunningly contrived by a master craftsman.

To admire the stream and ignore the artifice that gave it its course seems to me a grave oversight, and may well have led over the years to the present critical misapprehension by which laziness of construction is thought a virtue and the shapelessness of a play is taken as evidence of artistic integrity."

In addition to his works for the stage, Sir Terence has written more than fifteen major films and a number of original television plays, one of these being *High Summer,* here published for the first time. A dramatic portrait of a life-style that dwindled away in a changing world, it was originally presented on British television in 1972 with a company headed by Margaret Leighton, Roland Culver and Christopher Gable.

The author's most recent work for the theatre was *A Bequest to the Nation,* produced in London in 1970 and which presently is being filmed with Glenda Jackson, Peter Finch, Anthony Quayle and Margaret Leighton in the starring roles.

Characters:

LORD GEORGE FRANKLYN-PEARCE

COLONEL ARTHUR (BAGS) DONOVAN

MARCHIONESS OF HUNTERCOMBE (LETTIE)

LADY MARGARET BALLARD

CROWN PRINCE

LANGHAM

AMY SPROTT

MARQUESS OF HUNTERCOMBE

LORD FREDERICK FRANKLYN-PEARCE

MASHAM

GUESTS

FOOTMEN

MRS. CHAPPEL

Scene:

A summerhouse on the grounds of White Manly, the country seat of the Huntercombes. It is an eighteenth century gothic pavilion, built on a small prominence to command a view, surrounded by trees and approached from the level of the lawn by a few short steps. To the right there is the corner of a marquee, gaily striped in red and white. The year is 1906 and the time about 5:45 P.M. of a day in late July.

Outside the pavilion there is a group of five people. Taking them in strict order of precedence we find: first, an elegantly dressed young man fast asleep in a deck chair, with his hat over his eyes. We will later hear him referred to as "The Crown Prince"—though of what country it will not be necessary for us to discover. The sole clue to his nationality will be his accent, which is German, and his manner, which is melancholy.

In the deck chair next to the prince and nearly as comatose is the Marchioness of Huntercombe. She is a woman in the middle fifties and from her clothes and bearing is plainly aware that she was once—and not so long ago—regarded as one of the great beauties of her age. A sunshade shields her delicate complexion from the sun.

On the other side of the Crown Prince, also in a deck chair and reading The Times, *is Lord George Franklyn-Pearce, a plump old gentleman with an expression that is gentle and benign and therefore highly misleading. He has a half empty glass by his side.*

Lady Margaret Ballard is leaning against the stone balustrade of the pavilion regarding something that is happening out of our view through field glasses. She is in the early twenties, admitted to be pretty but lacking both the buxomness and ingenuousness of expression which might otherwise have earned her from her contemporaries the acknowledgement of beauty.

Finally, standing behind Lady Huntercombe's chair and clad in blazer, white flannels and cricket boots is Colonel Donovan, known to everyone by his nickname of "Bags." He is a large, red-faced, jovial-looking man of powerful physique. He is also looking intently in the same direction as Lady Margaret.

Nothing happens for a moment or two, save that George takes a gulp of his drink and Lady Huntercombe smothers a yawn. Then, from the direction of the marquee comes an outburst of applause, taken up by Donovan and Margaret. George lowers his Times.

GEORGE: What's the hullabaloo about?
DONOVAN: Freddy's made his fifty.
(*Lady H. taps her palm lightly with her fingers, producing no sound but granting the unseen batsman a delicate gesture of approbation. The clapping from the marquee dies down*)
GEORGE: I detest cricket. I don't know why you asked me this weekend.

LADY H: I didn't ask you. You asked yourself.

GEORGE: Well, you might have warned a fellow of the miseries in store for him.

LADY H: You are in a bad mood, George.

GEORGE: Yes, I am.

(*Langham, the butler, heads a slow and stately procession of three footmen and a pageboy, all in livery, behind the pavilion towards the marquee. They are carrying jugs of champagne cup, cider cup, sherbet, etc.*)

GEORGE: Oh, Langham. Bring me another hock and seltzer.

LANGHAM: Very good, my Lord. (*The procession goes off*)

LADY H: (*To George*) I do hope you're not going to be as grumpy as this all weekend, George, or I shall have to send you back to London.

GEORGE: Can I rely on that, my dear?

LADY H: (*Quietly*) No, now I come to think of it, you can't go back. I'm very glad you've come as it happens, because you can help with our poor friend here. (*She indicates the sleeping form beside her*)

GEORGE: Certainly not! I'm notoriously bad with royalty.

DONOVAN: Oh good shot, sir! (*He applauds, Margaret joins in*) By jove! Young Freddy improves every time I see him. Lady Margaret, I wouldn't be at all surprised if your future husband doesn't play for his county one day.

MARGARET: (*Looking through her field glasses*) Poor dear. He looks so terribly hot.

(*Langham has come back with George's hock and seltzer which he hands to him. He then approaches Lady H.*)

LANGHAM: My Lady, Mr. Wilkins, who is scoring for the town, would like to know if you are going to say a few words this year.

LADY H: Oh dear! I'd forgotten all about that. (*To Donovan*) Henry used to make a speech, didn't he?

DONOVAN: Just a few words of welcome, that's all. It's rather expected, you know.

LADY H: (*To Donovan*) I think you'd better do it this year. After all, you're captain of our side.

DONOVAN: Yes, if you think so.

LANGHAM: Excuse me, My Lady. I hope you will forgive me for saying so, but as regards our relations with the town I believe it would have a better effect if your Ladyship made the speech.

LADY H: Yes, Langham. You're perfectly right, as always.

LANGHAM: Thank you, My Lady.

LADY H: You can tell Mr. Wilkins I will be glad to say a few words.

LANGHAM: Very good, My Lady. (*He goes towards the marquee. Lady H. rises, assisted by Donovan*)

LADY H: I think you'd better come with me, George.

GEORGE: Is that a hostess invitation or a sister-in-law's command?

LADY H: (*Tactfully*) Neither, my dear. You can please yourself, of course. But there's going to be a lot of champagne.

GEORGE: I'll follow you down there in a minute.

LADY H: See that he does, Margaret.

MARGARET: Yes, Lady Huntercombe.

LADY H: (*Pointing her parasol at the somnolent Prince*) Shall I—or would it be lèse-majesté, do you think?

GEORGE: No, Lettie. Leave the poor fellow in peace. Don't wake him up to the torments of cricket week at Manly.

LADY H: It's true. I've never known anyone more puzzled by anything. It seems no good telling him it's only a game.

GEORGE: You shouldn't have mentioned it *was* a game. You should have told him we'd arranged some local peasant dances out there in his honor. He'd have been delighted.

LADY H: Well, leave him for a moment, but if he wakes up, you must bring him along. The townspeople would appreciate it. (*To Donovan, who has taken the field glasses and is watching the game*) Come along, Colonel Donovan.

DONOVAN: Yes, Lady Huntercombe. (*He offers her his arm and they go off towards the marquee*)

MARGARET: (*After a pause*) Is that for my benefit?

GEORGE: What?

MARGARET: Colonel Donovan, Lady Huntercombe.

GEORGE: (*Absently*) Oh, no. They always surname each other, even in front of me. (*He puts down his paper suddenly and regards Margaret sternly*) You're far too young even to know about such a thing, let alone to speak of it.

MARGARET: But I've known about it since I was a school-girl. I've always thought it was an accepted fact.

GEORGE: Acknowledged, perhaps. But not accepted. And never, never mentioned—least of all, to the lady's own brother-in-law. My dear girl, I am utterly appalled.

MARGARET: Did your brother know?

GEORGE: (*Impatiently*) Yes, of course he did.

MARGARET: Didn't he do anything?

GEORGE: Well, I suppose he must have made a fuss at some time or another. Centuries ago, when he first found out.

MARGARET: Nothing more drastic?

GEORGE: Fighting a duel or something?

MARGARET: There's always divorce.

GEORGE: For stock brokers.

MARGARET: But did nothing ever happen?

GEORGE: Nothing ever does happen in this family. It's not allowed to. That's something you should know, as you intend to marry into it. Anyway, stop all this rattling of family skeletons. It shocks me profoundly.

MARGARET: Nonsense, it doesn't shock you at all, Lord George, and you know it. No one likes a little bit of gossip more than you. Besides, Freddy's a positive clam. I can never get a thing out of him—not even about that fascinating brother of his. Tell me, is he really such a sinner?

GEORGE: Now, you're not going to draw me out on that, my dear girl. I tell you, on the subject of the present Marquess of Huntercombe, I too am a clam—one that bites.

MARGARET: Oh, of course I know all about him being sent down from Oxford, and the dud check to Lord Grantham, and being turned out of the Diplomatic and the pro-Boer article he wrote for the *Berlin Magazine,* and his being cut out of the will—and the lady who shot herself for love of him and the rest of it.

GEORGE: Is there a rest of it?

MARGARET: What's he like, really, Lord George? Do tell me.

GEORGE: I will not be badgered in this way. I refuse utterly to say a word, except that Jack Huntercombe is not a name we ever mention in the house. Now, is that understood? (*Margaret nods*) Good. (*Looking at cricket field*) Ah, thank goodness, they're coming in. And now, young lady, you will pray proceed to the marquee and announce in a fairly distinct voice that I have a touch of sunstroke and have had to take refuge indoors.

MARGARET: What about the champagne?

GEORGE: I have other arrangements for that, in more congenial company—my own. (*Applause breaks out for the incoming batsman. Margaret and George join in*)

MARGARET: (*Shouting*) Well done, Freddy! Well done! (*The somnolent Prince stirs and emerges sleepily from beneath his hat*)

PRINCE: What is it, please? (*Looking around happily*) Ah! It is over. Tell me who has won?

GEORGE: No one, sir.

PRINCE: No one? They make an equal score.

GEORGE: No. The game isn't finished yet.

PRINCE: (*His face falling*) Not finished?

GEORGE: No, sir. (*Unkindly*) The game goes on all day tomorrow.

PRINCE: (*Brightening*) At least it is finished for this evening, then?

GEORGE: Yes.

PRINCE: And now what do we do? Return to the house?

MARGARET: I think our hostess suggests we should go down to the pavilion, sir, and meet some of the players and their supporters.

PRINCE: (*After a faint pause, with a little sigh*) That will be delightful. (*He offers his arm to Margaret. To George, who is retiring*) You are not coming?

GEORGE: I must ask you to excuse me. A slight touch of the sun. Nothing very serious. A sip of champagne will soon put it right.

PRINCE: I have no doubt. You are a rascal, Lord George. Tell me, is our host not expected?

GEORGE: (*Puzzled*) Our host? Our host, I suppose, is Colonel Donovan. Honorary host, of course.

PRINCE: I meant your nephew. I should so much like to meet him.

GEORGE: (*Still puzzled*) You have already met him, sir.

PRINCE: No. Not Lord Frederick. Your other nephew, I mean—Lord Huntercombe.

GEORGE: (*Catching Margaret's eye, uncomfortably*) Oh, that nephew.

PRINCE: I read yesterday in *The Times:* "The Marquess of Huntercombe has returned to London from Paris and is staying at the Ritz Hotel."

GEORGE: Oh, you read that, did you, sir?

PRINCE: Certainly. (*Puzzled*) What is the mystery?

MARGARET: Yes, what is the mystery, Lord George?

PRINCE: This house does belong to him and not to his mother, I take it?

GEORGE: It does, sir, yes.

PRINCE: Then I am his guest, am I not?

GEORGE: Yes, in a sense. In a sense, we're all his guests.

PRINCE: Perhaps I have said something I should not have said. I am sorry.

GEORGE: No, sir. It's perfectly all right. It's only that he's been abroad for a very long time—indeed since two or three years before his father's death—and the family have quite lost touch with him.

PRINCE: I see. But it is then likely that he will come to Manly after being away so long?

GEORGE: No. I venture to think it is very *un*likely.

MARGARET: My guess is that the present Lord Hunter-combe quarreled with his father some time ago and was disinherited. Though what the cause of it all was I couldn't, of course, have the faintest idea.

PRINCE: I see. But if disinherited, how is it that he still owns Manly?

MARGARET: (*Innocently*) I should imagine, sir, that it was entailed, to the holder of the title.

PRINCE: Of course. (*After a pause*) I am sorry, Lord George, that I have so embarrassed you. Shall I see you later? After dinner, perhaps—a quiet game of billiards?

GEORGE: I'm afraid that will hardly be possible. I see you haven't heard that the program for the evening includes a three-hour session of amateur theatricals.

PRINCE: Oh, how delightful! (*Margaret suppresses a laugh*) What are we to have? Some country dances, perhaps, with maidens and boys from the villages?

GEORGE: No, sir. A four-act play by the Dean of Hamble, some conjuring tricks from Colonel Donovan, and a flame dance by a certain Mrs. Chappel. What a pity I have this sunstroke.

PRINCE: You do not think, perhaps, that it might not be possible for us *both* to develop sunstroke?

GEORGE: Sir, I am shocked. Your Royal Highness's absence would give the greatest possible offense.

PRINCE: My friend, you are a treacherous dog.

GEORGE: I am pained that you should choose to insult a very sick and infirm old man, who is constrained by respect for your exalted position from replying in kind. However if you'd like a glass of champagne before dinner . . . . (*He goes off towards the house*)

PRINCE: What a rogue! Well, shall we go to meet the cricket players?

(*They go out in the direction of the marquee, whence now comes the sound of polite applause. And from a distance we hear the sound of Lady Huntercombe's voice, though we are too far away to distinguish her "few* words." *A footman comes on from the direction of the house in some agitation*)

FOOTMAN: (*Calling*) Mr. Langham! Mr. Langham!

(*He goes off towards the marquee. Amy Sprott appears from the house. She is in her late twenties, very fashionably, though rather unsuitably, dressed. She looks—as indeed she is—"got up" for the occasion*)

AMY: (*Looking at the pavilion*) What's this, Jacko? A church or something?

(*Jack Huntercombe follows her on. He is a rather cadaverous young man, a little older than Amy, dressed with a bohemian air that looks—and indeed is—rather studied*)

JACK: No. It's the East Pavilion.

AMY: Pavilion? Oh, for the cricket.

JACK: No. There are four of these. Two hundred years ago, when they were built, they each commanded a vista.

AMY: A vista? Like a view, you mean?

JACK: Sort of.

AMY: (*Suddenly grasping Jack's hand*) Oh, Jack, what are we doing here? Let's get out quick—before the fireworks. Let's go back to town.

JACK: Scared?

AMY: Of course. Aren't you?

JACK: No, Amy, I'm sorry. I've got a job to do.

AMY: Oh, all right. But it's not only I'm scared; it's these bloody shoes. They're two sizes too small.

(*She takes one shoe off and slips it on as Langham and the footman come from the marquee. He wears the air of someone who has been fetched in a hurry to deal with a crisis*)

JACK: Hullo, Langham. How are you? (*The footman disappears. Langham comes forward*)

LANGHAM: Very well, thank you, my Lord. (*They shake hands*) May I say how very good it is to see you again, after all this time?

JACK: Thank you, Langham. You're looking very well. Put on a bit of weight, I think, haven't you?

LANGHAM: Just a little, I suppose—six years . . . .

JACK: I thought I'd surprise them.

LANGHAM: Ah, you'll do that, my Lord, I'm sure.

JACK: Langham, what's being done the stables?

LANGHAM: They're being pulled down, my Lord, to make garages for the motor cars.

JACK: Pulled down? But that's sacrilege. (*Violently*) Good God! Has he no taste at all? Doesn't he realize it's Inigo Jones?

LANGHAM: (*Gently*) *He,* my Lord?

JACK: My mother, I mean. Doesn't she realize she's going to smash up an architectural masterpiece?

AMY: (*Taking his arm*) What on earth are you getting so excited about, Jack? Aren't you forgetting the reason we came down?

JACK: (*After a pause, more quietly, to Langham*) I'm sorry, Langham.

LANGHAM: I regret it myself, my Lord.

JACK: Where is everybody?

LANGHAM: They're mostly in the marquee, my Lord, with the teams. Her Ladyship is there with Colonel Donovan and His Royal Highness.

JACK: What Royal Highness?

LANGHAM: I forgot the name of the country. He is the Crown Prince of it, as I understand. Shall I inform her Ladyship?

JACK: No, don't. I'll go down there myself.

LANGHAM: Which room shall I get ready for you, my Lord?

JACK: Any will do.

LANGHAM: It should be your father's, of course, but Colonel Donovan is there.

JACK: I'll have my father's room.

LANGHAM: But the Colonel?

JACK: Whatever he likes.

LANGHAM: It will probably have to be a dressing room.

JACK: Then it shall be a dressing room.

LANGHAM: Very good, my Lord. (*Glancing at Amy*) And the lady?

JACK: The Queen Anne room.

LANGHAM: The Duchess of St. Olphert's is in there, my Lord.

JACK: She'll have to move then.

AMY: (*Hastily*) No, Jack, move a duchess! (*To Langham*) It's all right. I can sleep anywhere—really. (*Jack suppresses a laugh. Glaring at him*) I'm not at all particular. Put me wherever you like.

LANGHAM: Very good, M . . . (*He hesitates*)

AMY: Miss Sprott. Miss Amy Sprott.

LANGHAM: Yes. (*To Jack*) I do trust that you have come back to us for good now, my Lord, after all your travels.

JACK: No, Langham, I'm afraid not.

LANGHAM: Your grandfather, I remember, went off abroad saying he'd never come back. But he did in the end.

JACK: Only to die.

LANGHAM: Dinner is at eight, my Lord, and the dressing gong will be going in twenty-three minutes exactly. (*He goes off*)

AMY: Do you think you'd come back to this place to die, Jack?

JACK: No.

AMY: I'd die of boredom if I had to live in it.

JACK: You won't have to, my dear. We'll be back in Montmartre tomorrow night. Now, *en avant*. Let's face the firing squad. (*He takes her arm and moves towards the marquee. Amy draws back*)

AMY: No. I can't. My legs won't move. I'm paralyzed.

JACK: Darn it, Amy! I brought you down here to give *me* courage. Come along, now.

AMY: Did you hear what he said about a Royal Highness?

JACK: Mother collects them. They don't bite, certainly not if Langham doesn't even know who they are.

AMY: It's all right for you, Jack. You were brought up to this kind of thing.

JACK: Worse luck.

AMY: (*She fondles his hand*) Why did you run away from all this, Jack?

JACK: I didn't run away. I was turned out.

AMY: Yes, I know, but you didn't need to stay out. All you ever needed to do was to write to your old dad and say you were sorry. That's all he wanted, I expect.

JACK: Why should I? I wasn't sorry. Besides, I wanted to stay out. I'm out of place here.

AMY: What you're born to is usually right for you. You can't deny it.

JACK: I can deny it. I can deny it passionately!

(*He breaks off as Lord Frederick, a pleasant looking young man in blazer and flannels, and Margaret come from the marquee side. They do not, at first, notice Jack and Amy*)

FREDDY: (*To Margaret*) It's only the one that goes with his arm that you have to look out for.

JACK: Hullo, Freddy.

(*Freddy stands rooted to the ground in sheer amazement. Margaret takes in the situation more quickly and utters a little sigh of satisfaction*)

MARGARET: Ah.

FREDDY: Jack! I can't believe it. When did you arrive?

JACK: A little while ago. How are you? My God, I don't know what I expected to see, but not a six-foot Apollo. Do you realize you were a scruffy little fourteen-year-old when I last saw you?

FREDDY: Yes, I suppose so.

JACK: Did you make any runs?

FREDDY: Sixty-seven not out.

JACK: Congratulations.

FREDDY: Oh, thanks. I say, I'm most terribly sorry, this is Lady Margaret Ballard—my brother, Jack. We're engaged, Margaret and I—unofficially, of course.

JACK: Congratulations again. (*To Margaret*) How do you do?

MARGARET: I'm sure you don't remember, Lord Huntercombe, but you and I have already met. It was at a dance, about five years ago.

JACK: Oh, yes, of course. I remember perfectly.

MARGARET: Whatever your other qualities I can see you're a most unconvincing liar.

JACK: Oh, forgive me. This is Miss Sprott—Lady Margaret Ballard, my brother, Freddy.

AMY: How do you do? (*Standing rather in the background, she gives a distant formal and evidently rehearsed bow*)

FREDDY: (*To Jack*) You live in Paris now, don't you? What do you do there?

JACK: Learn to paint.

FREDDY: Oh, yes. That's your forte, isn't it?

JACK: Or my weakness. I haven't earned any money yet.

FREDDY: (*Surprised*) Money? (*Then, uncomfortably*) Oh, yes. Of course all that's a lot of rot, you know. I'm glad you've turned up, because we can settle all that in a jiffy. I mean, we just have to go to the solicitors, that's all.

JACK: Thank you, Freddy, but I've already been to the solicitors.

FREDDY: Oh? What did they have to say?

JACK: I'll tell you later.

FREDDY: I say, I do think you might have let us know you were coming, old chap. Mother's going to get the most awful shock.

JACK: Yes. I expect so. (*Donovan strolls on, and Jack, in turning, comes face to face with him. (Quietly) Hullo, Bags. (Donovan, after the first show of surprise, glares at him. There is no attempt on either part to shake hands*)

DONOVAN: Why didn't you warn us?

JACK: I'm a creature of impulse. You know that.

DONOVAN: This is a stupid and rotten trick to play. However, I suppose we should have expected it of you for precisely that reason.

JACK: Exactly. This is Colonel Donovan, an old friend of mine and my mother's—Miss Sprott.

AMY: How do you do? (*Donovan looks her over curiously and nods curtly*)

DONOVAN: What do you expect to do here?

JACK: Enjoy myself, talk a little business and perform my duties as host to what looks like a delightful party.

DONOVAN: Have you no consideration for your mother at all?

JACK: Oh, yes. Quite a large consideration for her, though I can't, of course, flatter myself that it's quite as large as yours.

DONOVAN: If you're serious in your intention of staying in this house, I'd better warn you that I'm equally serious in my intention of leaving it tonight.

JACK: Oh, no, you mustn't leave. I'm sure my mother wouldn't hear of it.

(*Lady H., arm in arm with the Crown Prince, walks on from the marquee side*)

LADY H: (*To Prince*) No, the terrace was added later— about 1780, I think. Hullo, here you all are. Why are you all staring at me like that?

(*Jack comes forward quietly*)

JACK: I think I'm the cause.

(*Lady H. relinquishes the Prince's arm and comes forward, peering shortsightedly at Jack*)

LADY H: Jack? Is it Jack?

JACK: Yes, mother.

LADY H: I . . . we . . . didn't expect to see you . . . .

JACK: I should have warned you, I'm sorry.

LADY H: (*With a little sob*) Jack! (*She embraces him*) Oh, Jack! You shouldn't give me shocks like this! Now let's have a look at you. (*She takes out a pair of lorgnettes*) I've got awfully shortsighted, you know. (*Looking at him*) You don't look very well. Have you been eating enough?

JACK: Yes, I think so.

LADY H: Oh, Jack, how terribly typical of you to play a trick like this! (*She embraces him again*) But then, you always were such a silly boy. How do you think I look? Have I changed at all?

JACK: No.

LADY H: No older?

JACK: No older.

LADY H: It's six years, you know. Jack, I do think you might have come home for the funeral.

JACK: I do think you might have told me that he'd died.

LADY H: How could we, when none of us have the faintest idea where you live? (*Jack nods*) They surely get *The Times* in Paris?

JACK: They get it. I don't read it.

LADY H: But of course it must have been in the French papers, too. Now don't tell me you don't read the French papers either.

JACK: Not the kind that would be bothered to record the death of an obscure English Marquess.

LADY H: Obscure? There aren't any obscure English Marquesses. There are quite a lot of obscure English Dukes. (*Jack laughs*)

JACK: Oh, mother, I do so love you when you're doing your Burke's Landed Gentry.

LADY H: And I do so love you, Jack—whatever you're doing. Why have you never got that into that skull of yours? (*Turning to Amy*) Please introduce me.

JACK: This is Miss Sprott.

(*Lady H. bows and levels her lorgnette at Amy, who is plainly nervous*)

LADY H: Charming.

AMY: How do you do, Lady Huntercombe? I've heard so much about you from your son.

LADY H: I'm glad he still talks of me occasionally.

AMY: Oh, all the time. He never stops.

(*Lady H. accords her her hand and a warm smile. Then she turns to the Prince, who has been with her tactfully admiring something that Inigo Jones once did, in the middle distance. Only Freddy and Amy are hovering in earshot. Also, of course, Donovan*)

LADY H: (*With something of an air*) Your Royal Highness, may I present my son.

(*Jack shakes hands and gives him the customary nod*)

PRINCE: I am most happy, dear Marquess.

JACK: May I present Miss Sprott?

(*Amy, now almost paralyzed with fear, moves forward slowly and takes the Prince's outstretched hand*)

PRINCE: Most pleased.

(*Amy glances helplessly at Jack, who isn't looking at her, but at his mother. She decides that she should imitate Jack's experienced, squareshouldered, quick nod of the head. The Prince looks surprised. Lady H. is quick to rescue, and takes Amy familiarly by the arm*)

LADY H: Miss Sprott is a close friend of my son.

PRINCE: Of course. (*Politely*) Who of us would not give much to be a close friend of Miss Sprott?

FREDDY: Look, hadn't we all better be going indoors? (*To Margaret, who is suppressing giggles in a low voice*) Stop it, Margaret. (*To Prince*) Shall we go in, sir?

PRINCE: Certainly.

LADY H: Come and see me in my room, Jack. After you've changed. You're staying, of course?

JACK: For tonight at least.

LADY H: Good, but I don't know where on earth I'm going to find you a suitable room.

JACK: That's all right, mother. I've already found myself one.

LADY H: Have you? How clever. Which?

JACK: Father's.

LADY H: Oh. But ... (*She glares at Donovan*)

JACK: Bags won't mind turning out for a night—will you, Bags?

DONOVAN: As a matter of fact, Lady Huntercombe, I'm afraid I shall have to go back to London tonight. I had a wire this afternoon. I'm terribly sorry.

LADY H: (*Sharply*) No, you mustn't! (*With an instant recovery*) I can't possibly let you go, Colonel Donovan. How on earth do you think our team will get on without its captain? I won't hear of it. (*Beckoning him*) Come along.

DONOVAN: If you don't mind, Lady Huntercombe, I'll follow you in. I'd rather like the chance of a few words with your son before I leave.

LADY H: But you're not leaving.

DONOVAN: We'll discuss that after dinner.

LADY H: Very well. (*Offering her arm to the Prince*) I was saying about this East Terrace, sir, if you remember, that it was added towards the end of the Eighteenth Century. Some of it is Nash, but not, I'm afraid, Nash at his best. (*They go off together. Freddy turns to Margaret*)

FREDDY: Come along.

MARGARET: Are you coming with us, Miss Sprott? (*Amy looks towards Jack for guidance and gets a nod*)

AMY: Yes, all right. That'd be nice.

(*They go off, Freddy following, after a shy friendly smile at Jack. Jack lights a cigarette*)

DONOVAN: Well?

JACK: (*Indifferently*) Yes, Bags?

DONOVAN: What do you want?

JACK: In general or specific terms? In general terms my wants are not very different from the rest of the human race. I want happiness, a quiet life and the fulfilment of my ambition.

DONOVAN: And in specific terms you want money.

JACK: You could say that money is one of the reasons for my visit. I mean it comes into the matter.

DONOVAN: What have you done this time? It could hardly be a dud check to one of your clubs, seeing you've been turned out of all of them.

JACK: No, not all of them. Some let me resign.

DONOVAN: Why do you want money then?

JACK: Why does anyone want money? To spend it.

DONOVAN: Listen, Huntercombe. Thanks to your mother's generosity you've got all the money you need to keep you out of the gutter where you belong. I'd be damned if you get a penny more.

JACK: In exactly what capacity are you making that prophecy, Bags? As an old acquaintance of mine or as my mother's financial adviser?

DONOVAN: As your future stepfather.

JACK: Tell me, Bags, where are you and mother going to live after you're married? (*There is a pause. Donovan stares at him and then laughs shortly*)

DONOVAN: I see. So, that's your game. Well, it won't work, my lad. We have your letter assigning Manly to Freddy absolutely and for life.

JACK: (*Nodding*) The point is immaterial anyway, since I've revoked it.

DONOVAN: You can't. It's a legal document.

JACK: No. It's an illegal document. So, at least, my solicitors say. They are not, by the way, the ones you employed to draw up that document and who forced me to sign it.

DONOVAN: Forced you? For forty thousand pounds?

JACK: Bribed me, then. The point—the only point is that you can't break the law of entail with a letter, nor induce a man to part with his legal property for a small fraction of its value on the open market.

DONOVAN: There *is* no open market.

JACK: Oh, yes, there is. Quite a high one, too. I've found out.

DONOVAN: Your grandfather's will expressly forbids any sale.

JACK: No will can do that, Bags. You know that. There is always the excuse of urgent financial necessity.

DONOVAN: (*Scornfully*) What financial necessity?

JACK: Mine.

DONOVAN: You get an allowance.

JACK: If I pledged it all, it might just keep me at Manly for a week.

DONOVAN: But you don't want to live at Manly.

JACK: Prove that in court.

(*Pause*)

DONOVAN: My God, you're sinking pretty low this time, aren't you?

JACK: Or flying pretty high. It depends which way it's looked at. Four hundred and fifty thousand pounds seems pretty high to me.

DONOVAN: Is that what you're expecting us to pay?

JACK: Us?

DONOVAN: The family.

JACK: I questioned the word *us*, because the offer has been made to me, personally, and none of *you* really come into it.

DONOVAN: This is just blackmail. Nobody's made you an offer.

JACK: No single person. But a company has. It's called—let me remember—The Thames Valley Investments or something.

DONOVAN: The property developers?

JACK: They seem to think they could split up the park alone into over a hundred small estates. Over a hundred families where now there's only one. The thought of it warms my radical heart. It's progress, Bags.

DONOVAN: And you really think your mother's going to pay up half a million?

JACK: The family can offer me double, dear Bags—or treble if they like—but I won't accept it. Really, (*Quietly*) Can't you understand that in this I'm sincere? (*There is the distant sound of a gong*) Langham still beats that thing as if it were the last trump. Oh, look, there's Uncle George.

(*Jack, on his way to meet his uncle, appears to pay no attention. Donovan goes off with evidently more purposefulness than dressing for dinner. Jack embraces George*)

GEORGE: (*Happily*) My dear boy.

JACK: Uncle George. I'm so glad.

GEORGE: So am I, my dear boy. So am I.

JACK: You're just the very man I most wanted to see. Will you look at some drawings of mine after dinner? You know what I think of your opinion and I've brought them all the way from Paris to show you.

GEORGE: I should be delighted. Well, well. When they told me, I could hardly believe it. What have you come back for? Money, I suppose?

JACK: Yes.

GEORGE: How much?

JACK: Four hundred and fifty thousand pounds.

GEORGE: Four fifty thou ... ? How did you lose all that?

JACK: No. I don't gamble in those figures anymore.

GEORGE: Why do you need the money then?

JACK: I don't really. I think I'll give it away to charity.

GEORGE: Charity? Is that the name of that little thing you brought with you? I've just been chatting with her in the hall. How did you ever smuggle her past the customs?

JACK: Oh, in the usual way, Uncle George. I declared her as my personal baggage.

GEORGE: (*Chuckling*) My boy, I'm really delighted to see you. And to think I nearly put off this weekend because I thought it was going to be dull. (*He takes his arm*) Now tell me all about Paris and all you've been doing. (*They move off together*)

Fade

Evening.

Jack enters the so-called Tapestry Room and stops in surprise. Then he looks 'round in mounting anger. There

is a discreet knock on the door and Langham comes in,
exacting the immemorial butler's privilege of not waiting
to be told to come in. He is followed by a valet carrying a
tailcoat, white waistcoat and trousers on a hanger.

LANGHAM: (*Quietly outraged*) My Lord, whoever did
your packing has completely forgotten your evening clothes!

JACK: Oh. (*Bravely*) Well, I wasn't going to wear any,
Langham.

LANGHAM: (*Smiling politely*) Your Lordship thought
perhaps to find your house without guests? Very unlikely on a
summer "Friday-to-Monday." (*To the valet*) On the bed,
Masham. (*To Jack*) I have taken Masham from Colonel Donovan, my Lord, for the time being, and fixed the Colonel up with
one of our temporaries. (*Jack smiles. There seems no doubt*
where Langham's loyalties lie)

JACK: Where have you put Colonel Donovan?

LANGHAM: There are some rooms in the West Tower that
her Ladyship had done up for overflow use. They are perfectly
comfortable, although rather a long walk to the bathrooms. (*To*
Masham) Not *that* shirt, Masham. His Lordship prefers three
stud-holes. (*To Masham*) The pumps facing *outwards*, Masham.

MASHAM: Colonel Donovan prefers . . . .

LANGHAM: Never mind what Colonel Donovan prefers.
(*To Jack*) These are all your own clothes, my Lord. I would
doubt if you've grown out of them. (*Masham has finished his*
duties. He now stands "at attention" awaiting further orders)
Very well, Masham. His Lordship prefers to dress himself.
(*Masham slips out quickly. Jack looks at the clothes on the bed,*
beautifully laid out)

JACK: (*Looking at the bed*) Oh, Langham, do I *have* to?

LANGHAM: (*Refusing to be drawn*) Have to what, my
Lord?

JACK: Dress in these damn things again?

LANGHAM: (*Quickly*) Yes, my Lord. Now to remind
you—this is the bell for the housekeeper, and this for the maid.

This one is for the valet. No doubt your Lordship will ring it when it's time to do your tie. Would there be anything else, my Lord?

JACK: (*With a sigh*) No, thank you, Langham. (*As Langham is leaving*) Oh, Langham, what has my mother had done to this room?

LANGHAM: Your mother, my Lord?

JACK: Colonel Donovan, then. Where are the tapestries?

LANGHAM: In the Kent morning room.

JACK: (*Explosively*) Oh, my God, no! That's sacrilege!

LANGHAM: Yes, my Lord. It is a little unfortunate.

JACK: And my mother agreed?

LANGHAM: Her Ladyship has an agreeing nature. (*Bowing slightly*) May I say how very good it is to have you back, my Lord.

(*He goes out. Jack explores the room. He evidently knows exactly where there is a sliding panel—once tapestried, now covered in silk—and he opens it. Two or three steps lead upwards to another silk covered panel. From behind the door there are voices*)

LADY H: (*Off*) You are *not* leaving, Bags, and that's the end of it. If you go, then I go with you.

DONOVAN: (*Off*) Why not? Wouldn't that be best?

LADY H: (*Off*) And start the biggest scandal since Tranby Croft?

DONOVAN: (*Off*) There'll be enough scandal anyway when he gets sued for blackmail.

LADY H: (*Off*) Oh, Bags, darling Bags, why do you take him so seriously? He's the same Jack as he ever was—just a little boy showing off, throwing his favorite toy out of the window just to annoy his father. A word from me and he'll come 'round. Trust me. Oh, darling, do trust me!

(*Jack closes the panel abruptly. Then he goes over to the bed and sits down, looking at his impeccably laid-out evening clothes without appearing to see them*)

Bedroom Passage, Evening.

Lady H. comes out of her bedroom, followed by her maid, who is still making last second alterations to her toilette. She shoos the maid away, hesitates at the door of the next room, then knocks. At Jack's "Come in," she goes inside.

Tapestry Room. Evening.

Jack is having his tie fixed by the young valet, Langham's "promising" protege.

JACK: (*Seeing his mother*) Thank you, Masham. (*Masham leaves. Referring to his tie*) All right?

(*Lady H. comes forward to adjust it slightly, peering at it short-sightedly. Their heads are very close*)

LADY H: (*Looking up at him*) You still look very beautiful.

JACK: Thank you.

LADY H: I expected you to appear in floppy corduroy trousers and an open Byron shirt.

JACK: I meant to.

LADY H: Why didn't you?

JACK: Langham scared me.

LADY H: Of course. He scares *me* to death. But one must never allow Langham to scare one out of doing what one wants to do.

JACK: Like putting tapestries in the Kent room?

LADY H: What's wrong with that?

JACK: One of the most beautiful rooms in England, and some of the finest tapestries in the world, set to battle with each other and producing—what?

LADY H: You really do love this house, don't you? I suppose it's the only thing in the world you ever felt emotion for.

JACK: Do you really believe that?

(*Pause. They stare at each other. Lady H. suddenly gives a sob—controlled, of course, for it's far too late for her to disarrange her exquisite appearance—but nonetheless sincerely felt*)

LADY H: Oh, Jack, it's been so long! (*She embraces him, taking care not to crease her dress, or disarrange his tie*)

JACK: (*Smiling a little*) Yes, mother. It has.

LADY H: (*Releasing him*) What was the point in hiding away?

JACK: You know the point, mother.

LADY H: Anyway you're back now, thank heaven.

JACK: You shouldn't thank heaven.

LADY H: (*With an impatient gesture*) Oh, that's all too silly for words. It's typical little Jacko, showing off.

JACK: Throwing his favorite toy out of the window to annoy father?

LADY H: (*Glancing at the secret door*) Eavesdropping? Well, that's little Jacko, too. Isn't it? But I'm glad you heard that. It was quite true. Darling, we should go down. Although our little Crown Prince isn't anything, he gets in a pet if we don't treat him like little Willy Germany. (*She is moving past him when he suddenly grips her arm*)

JACK: Mother, I'm serious.

LADY H: (*As to a child*) Yes, of course you are, darling. Jack, you're hurting. (*He drops his hand*) Serious about what?

JACK: Selling this house.

LADY H: To Thames Valley Investments? For a quarter of what it's worth? Why, with your socialist principles, are you so determined to make millionaires of those shabby speculators? Your Fabian friends aren't going to applaud you for ruining a beautiful estate by transforming it into a hundred expensive homes for prosperous businessmen. And the house? Is that to be a great hotel making more millions for Thames Valley Investments? I don't call any of that very revolutionary, my poor little darling. Just vandalism for profit, that's all. (*Jack is, as ever, silenced by his mother's logic, also by her cool authority. Patting his cheek*) Poor Jack. You never could think very clearly about these things, could you?

JACK: (*With sudden rage*) Oh God, there are times when. . . .

LADY H: (*As to a child*) You could kill me, dear. I know.

JACK: You don't know! You can't begin to know. For you everything must come from here. (*He touches her head*) Nothing ever from here. (*He touches her heart*)

(*Lady H. instantly turns to a looking glass to see if her hair or dress has been disarranged*)

LADY H: (*Over her shoulder*) I've no heart?

JACK: None. All right, selling this house to a capitalist combine will harm rather than help the cause I believe in. That's from here. (*He touches his own head*) And I accept it. But here (*He touches his heart*) I *know* I'm right. It *is* wrong, mother, for a single family to occupy a house and land that could make homes for hundreds of others.

LADY H: (*By now satisfied with her toilette, smiling*) The heart has its reasons? (*Jack nods. Lady H. approaches him again*) But are they, little Jacko, quite the reasons you think?

JACK: I know myself well enough to be sure that my reasons are honest.

LADY H: (*Smiling*) Socialism, I'm sure, is an honest creed. It's based, of course, on envy—but why not? Envy's an honest emotion. But where, dear Jack, does jealousy fit in? (*Pause. The dinner gong goes*) Langham's really in form tonight. Extra loud for the owner of Manly. Put your coat on. (*She helps him into his tailcoat. She fixes his tie again*) You know, the best solution to everything would be for me to send a nice large check to Mr. Keir Hardie or Mr. Ramsey Macdonald for your *cause,* and you come back to Manly and live in it again.

JACK: As Bags' guest?

LADY H: As my guest.

JACK: In my house?

LADY H: How else could it be done? Your father's will was very brutal, but I'm afraid no solicitors can change that.

JACK: (*Quietly*) Mother, you must try to understand this. I am utterly and completely determined to dispose of this house —and its lands as I, its owner, see fit. You will neither wheedle me nor shame me into any kind of surrender. (*Pause*)

LADY H: (*With a sigh*) It'll mean a battle, Jack.

JACK: Or scare me either. (*She smiles and pats his cheek*)

LADY H: We'll talk later. We can't keep our wretched little Highness waiting.

(*She opens the door and indicates that she would like him to offer her his arm. He does so. They continue to walk down a seemingly endless passage*)

LADY H: (*Looking at him*) Yes, you look good. I'm proud you're my son. (*After a moment*) Shouldn't you say something?

JACK: (*After looking at her*) I'm proud that you're my mother.

(*Her voice and the image of the two of them walking formally arm in arm fade simultaneously*)

Night.

In whatever place is reserved at White Manly for such occasions, we see the house party and guests watching Mrs. Chappel's flame dance. There are one or two notable absentees from the company. Lady Margaret can be seen to slip away in the general applause.

Terrace. Night.

The terrace is deserted save for George, who is quietly sipping a brandy and smoking a cigar. Margaret comes on from the house, and is about to descend into the garden when Lord George speaks.

GEORGE: He's not in the garden.

MARGARET: Lord George. I didn't see you there. Who are you talking about? Freddy?

GEORGE: No, my dear. Not Freddy. Our host—as I suppose he is—is in the study waist-deep in archives. I've no doubt that he would enjoy an interruption—if it was provided by you.

MARGARET: Why on earth do you think . . . .

GEORGE: (*Impatiently*) I don't *think*. I *know*. Go and disturb him in the study and leave me in peace.

MARGARET: (*Perching on his chair*) Do you really think he wouldn't mind?

GEORGE: Huge bedazzled eyes, my dear—all through dinner and after it. He's yours if you want him. Do you?

MARGARET: Aren't we jumping?

GEORGE: (*Again impatiently*) We're jumping nothing. That's the situation and you must cope with it as only you know best.

MARGARET: He's talked to you?

GEORGE: Yes.

MARGARET: But what did he *say*?

GEORGE: (*Somnolently*) That your nose turns up—or down. Or stretches out for miles. I can't remember. Leave me in peace.

MARGARET: Has he ever done anything really bad?

GEORGE: Yes.

MARGARET: What?

GEORGE: Betrayed state secrets to a hostile power.

MARGARET: The Kaiser? He's not hostile.

GEORGE: He will be.

MARGARET: I meant that German woman. Why did she shoot herself?

GEORGE: Why don't you go and ask him?

MARGARET: It was for love, I suppose.

GEORGE: People don't die for love. I mean, it just isn't done.

(*Jack has come on*)

JACK: Have you looked at those drawings?

GEORGE: Yes.

JACK: What do you think?

GEORGE: I'll tell you later. We don't want to bore Lady Thingummy.

MARGARET: I wouldn't be bored.

GEORGE: (*Hoisting himself from his chair*) Then I would. Women have no place in serious discussions.

MARGARET: (*Innocently*) Where are you going?

GEORGE: I have two reasons for going where I'm going— one because you plainly want to be alone with my nephew, and the other because I need to go where I'm going. But please get your business over quickly, or do it somewhere else, because *that* is my favorite chair, and I shall be back. (*He goes off*)

MARGARET: (*Calling after him*) You're a filthy old brute.

GEORGE: (*Off*) I'm a brute and often filthy, but I'm not old.

JACK: He doesn't seem to want to talk about my drawings.

MARGARET: Has he taste?

JACK: The best. There's Berenson and there's George.

MARGARET: What he thinks will be important, then?

JACK: I didn't only come back to blackmail my family— I know that's already all over the house party. My most urgent reason was to ask Uncle George if I should continue as a painter or find another occupation. A bank clerk, perhaps.

MARGARET: Or a landowner.

JACK: (*After a pause*) No.

MARGARET: Why not? You love this place.

JACK: I'm selling Manly to Thames Valley Investments for the highest price I can get.

MARGARET: All right. But keep the house.

JACK: (*Outraged*) The house without the park and with

a vista of appalling fake-Tudor villas? (*His voice fades away. She is smiling at him. He smiles back.*) Yes. I gave myself away then, didn't I? Does Freddy love you very much?

MARGARET: When he thinks about it, yes.

JACK: And do you love him?

MARGARET: When I think about it, no.

JACK: Why are you marrying him?

MARGARET: It's very suitable, isn't it?

JACK: I suppose so. Have you ever loved anyone?

MARGARET: Yes. You—for a whole year.

JACK: That's an invention.

MARGARET: No. I met you at a dance and fell head over heels in love. I was a schoolgirl, remember?

JACK: I am remembering.

MARGARET: For a year after that I followed every tiny detail of your career with dreadful excitement. When I read that you'd fallen off your horse at a point-to-point I was sick for three days, and my mother had to get the doctor.

JACK: I don't remember that I hurt myself very much.

MARGARET: Ah. But you might have. That was what so upset my stomach. The thought of your dying, or worse still, marrying, was sheer physical torment. I said prayers for you every night.

JACK: They don't seem to have been very efficacious.

MARGARET: I'm afraid not.

JACK: What killed your love?

MARGARET: A report from Berlin.

JACK: The famous internment camp article?

MARGARET: No. That was later. I approved of that. Oh, yes, I know. The information you betrayed was privileged. You heard it in this house from the Prime Minister, talking confidentially to your father, and no one noticed the pretty little boy in the corner, in the Eton collar.

JACK: I was long past Eton collars.

MARGARET: But you weren't noticed. So the confidential information finds its way into the Berlin press and embarrasses the government. For heaven's sake, what's wrong with that? Governments *should* be embarrassed. What I mean was the other thing.

JACK: Yes, I see. The other thing.

MARGARET: What was she like?

JACK: (*After a pause*) An empty-headed and flirtatious little goose.

MARGARET: Geese aren't usually suicidal.

JACK: A very vindictive goose—especially if she knows she is going to die anyway—might be more than suicidal. She might be murderous.

MARGARET: I see. She must have loved you very much to do that.

JACK: Or hated me.

MARGARET: Hated you for not loving her in return. I can understand that.

JACK: I can't. I am and always have been out of my depth when people talk about those two emotions. I have never experienced either—only observed their outward manifestations in other people.

MARGARET: You don't hate Colonel Donovan?

JACK: Not enough.

MARGARET: Or love your mother?

JACK: I've been away from her for six years.

GEORGE: That's how you should know you love her. I'm interrupting, I hope. (*His entrance has been silent and unobserved. He lowers himself into his favorite chair with a sigh of pleasure*)

GEORGE: Well, are you two getting married?

MARGARET: I hope we are.

GEORGE: I like this girl, Jack. In my youth if a girl were asked a question like that, she'd faint dead away and you'd have to revive her with burnt feathers. Yes. If I were you I'd have her, Jack.

MARGARET: You're becoming embarrassing, Lord George. I'm going to bed. Good night.

GEORGE: Without telling him what room you're sleeping in?

MARGARET: He is my host, Lord George, and therefore that information would be superfluous. (*She bows to both and goes out*)

GEORGE: By gad, she carried that off pretty well. You know, that's quite a woman, Jack.

JACK: Yes.

GEORGE: You ought to marry her. It would solve everything, wouldn't it?

JACK: What about Freddy?

GEORGE: He's going for a soldier. In ten years' time he'll marry some dreadful Anglo-Indian girl and live happily ever after. This one's too good for him. But she'd make a good Marchioness of Huntercombe.

JACK: The drawings, Uncle George.

GEORGE: Yes. You can't tell much from drawings, you know.

JACK: *You* can.

GEORGE: (*Unhappily*) Yes. (*He leaves it at that. Jack breathes a heavy sigh*)

JACK: Are they as bad as that?

GEORGE: Oh, no. Very accomplished.

JACK: What you mean is that, as a draughtsman I'm the most talented Marquess you know.

GEORGE: I'm sorry, dear boy, but you begged me to tell you the truth.

JACK: Shall I give up painting altogether?

GEORGE: By no means. Keep it—as a hobby. Marry Lady Thingummy and settle down at Manly.

JACK: You were serious about that? How can I, with my reputation, settle respectably at Manly?

GEORGE: Much is forgiven a resident Marquess that is inexcusable in an exiled bohemian. You'd have to make a few minor concessions. For instance, that little appendage of yours. . . .

JACK: Amy?

GEORGE: You're not in love with this creature, are you?

JACK: No. Nor she with me.

GEORGE: Good. So it's all settled, and we won't have book-makers roaring the odds all over this very beautiful park. The nightmare has lifted.

JACK: It hasn't. You're trapping me, damn you! All of you!

GEORGE: Dear boy, from the day we're born we're all trapped into something. I was trapped into lechery and drink, and I've loved every second of it. You're trapped into being the seventeenth Marquess of Huntercombe, with the most beautiful house in England and a certain talent as a painter. Is that a tragedy?

JACK: Yes.

GEORGE: Well, it's not making *me* cry.

JACK: Anyway, I don't want to marry a girl called Lady Margaret Ballard.

GEORGE: What an appalling snobbish remark.

JACK: What makes you think she loves me?

GEORGE: She said so, and she's an honest girl.

JACK: And what makes you think I love her?

GEORGE: Because she looks as if she could have been your sister. (*As Jack frowns*) Work that out, dear boy, at your leisure. I need a drink.

A Sitting Room.

Jack goes into the house with George's glass. We follow him through open French windows into a small sitting room. There is a tray of drinks on the table. Jack replenishes George's glass, then takes one for himself. There is a knock.

JACK: Come in. (*It is Margaret. She is holding something*)

MARGARET: I've brought this to show you. I thought it might amuse you.

(*She hands him a gold card case. Jack puts down the two glasses and takes it. He opens it and takes out, first, a little sprig of white heather*)

JACK: (*He takes out another object*) Ah. (*He examines a photograph*) I remember this. *Illustrated London News?*

MARGARET: Yes.

JACK: And on top of it all, a sprig of white heather and a St. Christopher.

MARGARET: To bring you luck.

(*He closes the case and hands it back to her. She shakes her head*)

MARGARET: Keep it.

JACK: (*Taking it and opening it*) Just let me keep the white heather.

MARGARET: No. No. Take the case. I don't think the white heather would work without the rest of it.

(*He kisses her quietly, without passion.*)

JACK: Thank you very much. (*He slips the case into his pocket*)

MARGARET: Good night.

(*She goes out. Jack stares after her, then picks up the two glasses and rejoins George on the terrace.*)

GEORGE: Thank you, my dear boy. You were a devil of a time getting it.

JACK: You wouldn't have lied to me about those drawings, would you?

GEORGE: (*Shocked*) I'd lie to anyone about anything in the world, and frequently do—but never about art. What would be my purpose?

JACK: To save Manly.

GEORGE: My dear boy, Manly will have to go one day anyway. So will all the great houses when your scruffy friends come to power. By selling it, you only anticipate history by a few years.

(*Jack polishes off his brandy in one quick swallow*)

GEORGE: (*Angrily*) That's not the way to drink good brandy.

JACK: Dutch courage. It's one thing to make a firm decision, quite another to communicate it to the people most concerned. Where do you suppose my mother is?

GEORGE: The cricketers and other hooligans were singing songs and playing stump cricket in the Long Gallery. She won't be there, that's certain. It rather depends whether H.R.H. has gone to his bed. She wouldn't go to her own before.

JACK: My mother has a very nice sense of the proprieties.

GEORGE: You grow waspish, Jack.

JACK: Does she really love that oaf?

GEORGE: The evidence supports that view.

JACK: (*Passionately*) What can she possibly see in him?

GEORGE: He must have hidden qualities, Jack. Someone is calling you, I think. (*We hear Amy's voice plaintively calling "Jack, where are you?"*)

JACK: Oh, Lord. I'd forgotten all about her. (*Calling back*) I'm here, Amy. Up on the terrace.

(*Amy comes in from the lawn, rather breathless*)

AMY: I've been looking everywhere for you. Oh, you're with Georgie-Porgie.

GEORGE: (*Finishing his brandy*) This is good brandy. (*He gets up*) I shall take what remains of the bottle to bed with me. Good night.

AMY: He's a saucy old guiser, that. I could hardly sit down at dinner from being pinched. You were a bastard to leave me alone all night.

JACK: I'm sorry.

AMY: (*Taking his arm*) What have you been doing these last three hours?

JACK: In my father's study, reminding myself of things about this house.

AMY: You love it, don't you?

JACK: Yes, I did.

AMY: Do.

JACK: Do, I suppose.

AMY: I thought so. I told you what would happen if you came back, didn't I?

JACK: I didn't believe you. (*Turning to her*) Amy. . . .

AMY: I know what you're going to say, dear. Don't upset yourself by saying it.

JACK: Is that man I stole you from still. . . .

AMY: Oh, yes, I should think so. I could always go back to him. Anyway, there are quite a few others.

JACK: (*Very awkwardly*) Of course I . . . I should always see to it that you're. . . .

AMY: (*With sudden anger*) Shut up!

JACK: I'm sorry.

AMY: We had fun. But you aren't anyone's for life, Jack.

JACK: Am I not?

AMY: Well, there's one, the one you talk about from morning till night and say you hate and despise and all that— and you'll never get away from her as long as you live. But you can't marry her, Jack, because the Prayer Book says it's not on. But I shared a bit of your life for a time, and I'm glad, but (*Loudly*) I don't need paying off.

JACK: I'm sorry, Amy. I'm terribly sorry.

LADY H: I thought I'd find you here, Jack. (*She has come from the inside of the house, smiling, gracious and beautiful*) You're very naughty to have left me all alone to cope simultaneously with a set of rowdy cricketers and a very bewildered "Royal." (*Bowing*) Miss Sprott.

AMY: (*Bowing back*) Lady Huntercombe.

LADY H: I hope I'm not interrupting anything?

AMY: Oh, no. Nothing at all, really. Will you forgive me. I'm going to bed—that's if I can find it.

LADY H: You'll find Langham by the main stairs. He'll show you.

AMY: Good night then.

LADY H: Good night, Miss Sprott. (*She moves politely away when Amy kisses Jack*)

AMY: Good night, Jack.

JACK: We'll talk in the morning.

AMY: There's nothing to talk about, Jack. Really nothing. (*Kissing him*) Good night. (*She goes out*)

LADY H: You should marry that girl, Jack.

JACK: I have other plans.

LADY H: Have you? (*Stifling a yawn*) You must tell me.

JACK: Mother, I *have* decided to live in this house.

LADY H: Of course you have, dearest boy. It's the only sensible solution.

JACK: But not to live in it as your guest.

(*There is a pause. Lady H. becomes instantly alert.*)

LADY H: How, then?

JACK: As the *owner* of it.

LADY H: Yes, I know—but where's the money . . . ?

JACK: The estate pays for itself.

LADY H: The estate does, but the upkeep of the house and the gardens comes to nearly a hundred thousand a year.

JACK: As you and Bags keep it up.

LADY H: Your father left you nothing.

JACK: You may have inspired that or not. I don't know. I don't like to think about it.

LADY H: Jacko—how could you?

JACK: I'm not Jacko. I'm Jack. I don't like to think about how much you had to do with that will. Or that letter that Bags made me sign. Perhaps it was father's intention that you and Bags Donovan should have Manly.

LADY H: That Freddy should have Manly.

JACK: He must have known that what's Freddy's would always be yours, and what's yours would always be Bags Donovan's. Well, what's mine is going to be mine. What everyone seems to have forgotten is the wording of the entail—the house, the gardens, the park and the estate, and the contents of the said house. If the house can legally be sold because of the owner's financial necessity, how much more easily can the two Rembrandts, the three Velazquez, the five Gainsboroughs . . . There are sixteen Canalettos in this house. Did you know?

LADY H: You'll live in a house with very bare walls.

JACK: Oh no. I have a lot of painter friends in Paris. Mother, this isn't a bluff. I can live at Manly as its owner, not nominal but in fact—and *you* can live here whenever you like and for as long as you like, as my guest. You. Just you. No one else.

(*Pause*)

LADY H: Thank you. But I doubt if that arrangement would be convenient. Good night, darling.

JACK: (*Almost despairingly*) I know how you love Manly. Do you really love this man more?

LADY H: I love him more than anything in my life. I doubt if you'll understand that, and I doubt if you ever will. But then, of course, you've never understood, have you, how much I love you?

JACK: Did you say loved?

LADY H: No. Love. (*She kisses him*) Pleasant dreams. (*She disappears, leaving Jack staring uncertainly after her*)

Fade

Jack's Room. Morning.

Jack is in his room. He is by the window, staring out. He hasn't changed from his evening dress. It is daylight. There is a knock on the door. Jack doesn't reply. There is another, and after that Freddy cautiously peeps 'round the door.

FREDDY: Have you been sitting there all night?

JACK: Most of it.

FREDDY: I looked all over for you last night.

JACK: I was on the North Terrace.

FREDDY: Yes. I heard from Margaret just now.

JACK: What did she tell you?

FREDDY: Just about everything.

(*Pause*)

JACK: I'm sorry.

FREDDY: The one thing I want to know is—are you serious?

JACK: That's the one thing *I* want to know. (*Putting his hand on his shoulder*) I'm sorry, Freddy, I'm not being flippant. I am serious, I think, more serious than I've ever been in my life. Do you mind if I lie down? I didn't seem to sleep last night what with one thing and another. (*He lies down on the bed, and closes his eyes from sheer exhaustion*)

FREDDY: Margaret being one thing?

JACK: Only one of many.

FREDDY: (*Sitting on the bed*) She's rather more than that to me, you know.

JACK: Is she, Freddy? Honestly?

FREDDY: She doesn't take me very seriously. She's always saying I'm too young to feel. But surely you feel more deeply when you're young.

JACK: More deeply, perhaps, but for a shorter time.

FREDDY: I don't understand what you're doing down here.

JACK: Nor do I.

FREDDY: Do you really want this house?

JACK: Do you?

FREDDY: People are always telling me I don't. But people don't know.

JACK: People like mother and Bags.

FREDDY: Mainly.

JACK: And people are wrong?

FREDDY: Yes, they bloody well are.

JACK: (*More alert now*) But people say all you want is to be a soldier, and that you don't give a damn about anything else.

FREDDY: Let them just wait until I'm of age.

JACK: Was it you who's been reading those histories in father's study?

FREDDY: How did you know that?

JACK: It was either you or Bags, and Bags would have put them away more tidily. (*He sits up now, eyes open and fully awake*) Well, my little fourteen-year-old brother!

FREDDY: I'm not fourteen.

JACK: You are to me. Are you telling me you're prepared to fight?

FREDDY: Fight who?

JACK: Are you going to fight me?

FREDDY: About Margaret, to the death.

JACK: Good, Freddie. Will you fight me about Manly?

FREDDY: There's no point. Manly is yours if you want it.

JACK: If I want it.

FREDDY: Do you?

JACK: Last night I said I did.

FREDDY: Last night.

JACK: Go away and make your century.

FREDDY: A double one today. For Margaret. Anyway, it's only seven o'clock.

JACK: Oh, God. (*He struggles with his collar*) Help me off with this.

FREDDY: (*Doing so*) Is it all only for spite?

JACK: It might be for love.

FREDDY: (*Angrily*) For love?

JACK: Go on. Strangle me. It might be the best solution of all. (*Freddy rips the collar off and throws it and the tie away*) No. Not for love of your betrothed, not even for love of this house, my house. (*Angrily*) Which *is* mine, and which I *should* own. (*Recovering himself*) And not for love of a cause in which I do, most whole-heartedly, believe. But for another kind of love

—an unworthy love—of which I must rid myself forever or cease to live. Forgive me, dear Freddy, I'm very tired and very drunk. (*There is a nearly empty bottle of brandy on a table, which Freddy now glances at*) Our Uncle George's bad example. (*Rolling over in bed, Jack seems asleep. Freddy pulls a blanket over him. Then, quite coherently*) Fight those people, Freddy. Me included. Oh, and here's something that belongs to Margaret. She left it lying about. (*He takes Margaret's card case from his waistcoat pocket and tries to hand it to Freddy, but it falls to the ground. Freddy picks it up from the floor and puts into it its scattered contents*) Tell her it's not white heather I need. (*He is asleep before Freddy can ask him what he means*)

Summerhouse. Morning.

Once more we are at the cricket match. Lady H. is talking to the Crown Prince.

PRINCE: (*Pointing*) They are putting up the sticks again, I see.

LADY H: The stumps.

PRINCE: The stumps. How stupid. Does that mean the game will soon be beginning again?

LADY H: (*A little distraught*) In about quarter of an hour, sir.

PRINCE: Splendid. And continues until ... ?

LADY H: Six-thirty.

PRINCE: Imagine. But at least today one side will beat the other, no?

LADY H: Not necessarily, sir. Oh, dear, it's so difficult to explain.

PRINCE: I know it is difficult to explain. So many people have already tried to explain it to me. Never fear, Lady Huntercombe. Before six-thirty this evening, I shall have mastered it.

LADY H: I wonder.

(Donovan comes on hurriedly)

PRINCE: Good morning, Colonel.

DONOVAN: Good morning, sir. I wonder if you would forgive me if I appropriated our hostess for a few moments. I've a matter of business to discuss.

LADY H: Surely it can wait, Colonel Donovan?

DONOVAN: I'm afraid not Lady Huntercombe. It's very urgent.

LADY H: Would you forgive me, sir?

PRINCE: Of course.

(Donovan and Lady H. move away)

LADY H: *(Calling)* Oh, George. The Prince is alone and needs someone to explain the rules of cricket to him. *(Sharply)* George, do your duty. George!

GEORGE: *(Off)* By gad, you're a hard woman sometimes, Lettie.

DONOVAN: *(At length)* Jack's leaving this morning.

LADY H: Are you sure?

DONOVAN: Langham just told me.

LADY H: When is he going?

DONOVAN: Almost at once. Drops his bombshell and darts for cover. Brave little lad, isn't he?

LADY H: There's nothing lacking in his courage. Did you ring up your Mr. Larkin?

DONOVAN: It's no good, Lettie. He can do all he threatens. All he has to do is to go to court and plead financial necessity. If his solicitors have told him he can get judgment to sell his house in order to live, then he'll even more easily get judgment to sell his pictures in order to live in his house. No. I'm afraid he's not bluffing.

LADY H: I didn't think he was.

DONOVAN: Could you possibly win him 'round, do you think?

LADY H: Yes, I could, Bags, very easily. *(Looking at him)* And you know very well how I could.

DONOVAN: You haven't considered *that,* I hope?

LADY H: (*Evenly*) What kind of a woman would I be if I didn't consider it? My house, my whole way of life—my son, too—against just you, dear Bags.

DONOVAN: (*Smiling*) Do I pack my things?

LADY H: (*Not smiling*) No. I hope I'll never have to give you up, Bags, but if I ever do it won't be because of blackmail.

DONOVAN: Good. Now Larkin has a plan that he thinks could beat him—which is to put in various counter suits.

LADY H: I won't have it. If we are to be turned out of this house, my dearest, then let us face our eviction with the maximum of dignity and the minimum of fuss.

DONOVAN: That makes a good phrase, Lettie, but I, for one, am going to fight.

(*Jack strolls in*)

JACK: Colonel Donovan, may I speak to my mother alone, please?

DONOVAN: No, you may not. If it's anything to do with finance you will say it in front of me. I'm your mother's business adviser.

JACK: I'm perfectly aware of the nature of your relationship with my mother, Bags.

LADY H: Jack, this is no place for a scene.

JACK: Is saying goodbye to my mother a scene? (*Looking at his watch*) A rather hurried goodbye, too.

LADY H: Do you mind, Colonel?

DONOVAN: Very well. (*He walks away*)

JACK: *Colonel?* Even in front of me?

LADY H: In front of anyone, Jack.

JACK: Until you're married?

LADY H: That is quite right. You won't make me quarrel with you, Jack.

JACK: No. You know I won't. I've failed even to do that. The awful thing about me is that even as a failure I'm still a failure.

LADY H: What do you mean by that?

JACK: (*Kissing her on the cheek*) Goodbye, mother.

LADY H: When are you coming back?

JACK: Never.

LADY H: You don't mean that!

JACK: Yes.

LADY H: Jack . . . Jack, what trick are you up to now?

JACK: No trick, mother. No more tricks. Not ever again.

LADY H: (*Scoldingly*) Jacko, look at me. (*He does*) Last night you meant it all, didn't you?

JACK: Yes.

LADY H: Then what's happened since?

JACK: Well, you see . . . (*Pause*) I had a story carefully worked out to answer that. It would have been a lie, of course, but it would have made sense. I was going to tell you that George had looked at my drawings later last night and had told me I had great promise as a painter.

LADY H: What did he tell you?

JACK: It doesn't matter. But, mother, tell that story to Bags, please.

LADY H: Yes, I will.

JACK: And to Margaret. That's important, too.

LADY H: I'll remember.

JACK: So, goodbye.

LADY H: Jacko, what's really happened? (*No reply*) What's happened?

JACK: I don't know. I've lost, that's all. And I won't try again, because I know now I always will lose. So there's no point, is there?

(*Pause*)

LADY H: I wasn't going to fight.

JACK: I didn't think you would. But you see, I didn't want to win.

LADY H: (*Embracing him*) Jacko, you *will* come back, won't you? Just for a time?

JACK: Perhaps, if you invite me. But not when . . . not when *he's* . . . .

LADY H: No, of course not. You do know how much I love you, don't you?

JACK: Goodbye, mother (*He breaks free from her and runs away*)

LADY H: (*Following him*) Jacko, you must come back. Promise me you'll come back. (*There is a pause before Jack's voice comes to her*)

JACK: Yes, mother.

(*Lady H. stands, looking after him, not bothering to hide her tears from George who has come up to her*)

LADY H: George, he's never coming back.

GEORGE: Oh, I expect he will.

LADY H: No. I know it. And I love him. He doesn't believe it, but I do. George, what have I done that's so wrong?

(*George gives no reply, for there is none to give. He merely pats her shoulder comfortingly*)

(*We see Jack climbing into an open motor car of the period and joining Amy already ensconced in the back. The car drives off. Jack, with a tense, but now unemotional face, staring ahead. Amy has her arm through his*)

AMY: Sure you're doing right?

JACK: I've told you. I'm going to be a great painter.

AMY: (*She turns 'round for a last look at Manly*) I've got to admit it, it really *is* quite a place, this Manly.

JACK: Yes.

AMY: Well, as it's your last time, you might at least turn your head.

JACK: Never look back, they say. Don't they?

(*Amy looks at him, sees his grim and determined mood and settles for it. She turns 'round and hugs him contentedly*)

(*Last shots show Lady H. waving goodbye, Jack's unrelenting back as he is driven away in the open car, and then, and finally, Lady H. dropping her disregarded arm, carefully repairing the ravages to her appearance, and then walking back on George's arm to greet the assembling guests, once more a gracious, smiling hostess: a senior member of a family to which, it might be remembered, "Nothing ever happens"*)

Fade-Out

Maruxa Vilalta

NUMBER 9

*(Translated by W. Keith Leonard
and Mario T. Soria)*

Maruxa Vilalta

A leading modern Spanish language dramatist, Maruxa Vilalta appears in print for the first time in the United States with the inclusion of *Number 9* in *The Best Short Plays 1973*. Since its original production in Mexico City, the play has been widely presented throughout Mexico and in a number of foreign countries. At its premiere it was lauded in the press as "a short play of major significance" that is "a protest against the materialism that has invaded us" as "it sets forth the conflict between liberty and submission, between the passion and the surrender of contemporary man, and also echoes forth the anguished cry of the author to save our children because they must not grow in such an environment."

Maruxa Vilalta was born in Barcelona, Spain, but has lived in Mexico since 1939 where she attended school, earned her B.A. at the *Liceo Franco Mexicano,* and studied further at the College of Philosophy and Letters, National University of Mexico. A prolific as well as perceptive and imaginative writer, she has published several novels, scores of essays, short stories, and more than a dozen plays.

Since 1960, her plays have been performed with regularity on Mexican stages and in 1970 she was the recipient of the *Juan Ruiz de Alarcón* Prize, awarded by the Mexican Association of Theatre Critics for her "tragic farce," *Esta noche juntos, amándonos tanto,* named as the best play of the year.

The author also is a theatre critic and journalist for the *Diorama de la Cultura,* the cultural section of *Excelsior,* one of Mexico's most widely read publications. Additionally, she has gained prominence as a stage director in her adopted country and is a vice president of the Mexican Cultural Institute. Miss Vilalta lives in Mexico City with her husband and two children.

Number 9 was translated into English by W. Keith Leonard and Mario T. Soria. Mr. Leonard is a former chairman of the Hiram College Department of Speech and Theatre Arts. He has been active in the Latin American Theatre Project and the American Educational Theatre Association; presently, he is teaching in the Department of Theatre at Western Illinois University.

Dr. Soria, originally from La Paz, Bolivia, is chairman of the Foreign Language Department at Drake University. A Latin Americanist by profession, he specializes in the field of the theatre and has co-translated several Latin American plays which have been produced and published. He is the author of a book on *Armando Chirveches* and editor of an anthology of contemporary Bolivian theatre.

Characters:

MM099, CALLED 9
YX157, CALLED 7
A BOY

Scene One

Behind a large factory, a small yard which is surrounded by a cement wall. It is like the bottom of a sack, like a well with high walls which is lighted from far above. The only exit leads to another, larger, yard which in turn leads to the street and the factory entrance. In a very visible place, a loudspeaker. There is also a bench, a trash can, and some barbed wire on the floor. Everything produces the sensation of a gray and cold nakedness. If a cyclorama and set pieces are used, an effort must be made to maintain the impression of high walls and a locked-up feeling, a feeling of oppression.

A flute is heard as the curtain rises: worker MM099 is playing it. He's fifty years old. His overalls are as gray or grayer than the décor. On his upper pocket there is a badge which reads: MM099. His tune is a popular, sad one. After a while, worker YX157 enters. He is thirty-five. He wears the same type clothing with the appropriate badge on his overalls. He carries a paper bag in his hand.

SEVEN: Good morning.
NINE: Good morning.
SEVEN: Why are you playing the flute?
NINE: Because I'm old.
SEVEN: Why are you old?
NINE: Because I'm playing the flute.
SEVEN: But you are young.
NINE: Are you sure?
SEVEN: We can start all over again.
NINE: We cannot.

SEVEN: We cannot. (*Silence*) Who are you waiting for?

NINE: I'm waiting for the opportunity.

SEVEN: What opportunity?

NINE: The opportunity.

SEVEN: There are many opportunities.

NINE: Very few.

SEVEN: The opportunities are for the intelligent. You are intelligent!

NINE: You are intelligent!

NINE AND SEVEN: (*Together*) We are intelligent!

NINE: Let's cry.

SEVEN: Why?

NINE: Because we are intelligent. (*Silence*)

SEVEN: (*Showing his paper bag*) My wife packed some sandwiches for me.

NINE: I also brought my lunch.

SEVEN: You don't go to the dining room?

NINE: No.

SEVEN: At noon we can eat in this yard.

NINE: Yes, in this yard. (*Silence*)

SEVEN: You, where were you born?

NINE: Here. And you?

SEVEN: Here. How long have you worked in this factory?

NINE: Fifteen years. And you?

SEVEN: A year. Much less than you.

NINE: It's the same.

SEVEN: How, the same?

NINE: All you need is to get started. Afterwards, time means nothing.

SEVEN: The factory is very large.

NINE: Very large.

SEVEN: If they hadn't moved me to the machine next to you, we could have continued working here without getting to know each other. The factory is very large.

NINE: Very large.

(*A woman's voice comes from the loudspeaker. It is a stereotyped voice, falsely suave and sweet, mellow, like*

*that of an airline stewardess greeting the passengers, or
with a tone which is a mixture of superiority and benevolent condescendence)*

LOUDSPEAKER, WOMAN: The Sun of Your Life Company—
cleanliness and efficiency above all—one of the foremost factories
in the world of preserves and one of the most modern ones, wishes
its 1,384 Point 6 workers a good morning. The Sun of Your Life
provides for its personnel a clean, healthy and happy environment in which to work. We hope that today will be . . . *(She
pauses, adopting a sloganeer's tone which she will employ every
time the following phrase is used)* . . . a very profitable working
day!

SEVEN: We still have a few minutes.

NINE: Yes, when the sweet miss begins, there are still a
few minutes.

SEVEN: We can talk.

NINE: Let's talk. *(They remain quiet. A pause)*

SEVEN: Who do you think it is?

NINE: Who?

SEVEN: The Point 6 worker. The sweet voice says there
are 1,384 Point 6 workers in the factory. Perhaps there's been
some change. I would swear that on Tuesday there were 1,385
exactly. Is today Thursday?

NINE: Friday.

SEVEN: No, Thursday.

NINE: It's the same.

SEVEN: It's the same. *(Pause)* No! If it were Sunday it
would not be the same.

NINE: It would be the same as every Sunday. *(Silence)*

SEVEN: It won't be long before the whistle.

NINE: It won't be long.

SEVEN: What's the opportunity you're waiting for?

NINE: None.

SEVEN: What do you mean, none?

NINE: Or if you prefer, the opportunity to die without
making a sound.

SEVEN: Why without making a sound?

NINE: Why make one?

SEVEN: Why die?

NINE: Just to say, "enough!" Just to laugh at the whistle.

SEVEN: You're really something, 9. Can I call you 9?

NINE: Sure. I call you 7.

SEVEN: The use of numbers is just a custom.

NINE: Sure. Just a custom.

SEVEN: MM099. What is your real name?

NINE: Joseph.

SEVEN: Joseph.

NINE: Forget it. 9 is more original.

SEVEN: I didn't dare call you 9. Perhaps zero-ninety-nine, but just 9. . . .

NINE: It's my diminutive.

SEVEN: It seems too personal to me. You're older than I am.

NINE: It makes no difference. Here we are all the same age.

SEVEN: They use the code number because it's more practical.

NINE: Sure, because it's more practical.

SEVEN: How are they going to remember that you're Joseph and I'm Michael? There must be lots of Michaels here. On the other hand, YX157, I'm the *only* one. No one else.

NINE: No one else. (*A short pause*)

SEVEN: If you would like to, we could eat in the large yard.

NINE: We're better here.

SEVEN: There's less noise.

NINE: There's less noise.

SEVEN: Hardly anyone comes here.

NINE: Only that cute little speaker.

SEVEN: And us.

NINE: And the machines. I can see them behind the wall. They do not abandon us. They are near. They are *always* near.

SEVEN: Nearer than in the large yard.

NINE: Nearer.

SEVEN: It seems that the "Voice of Happiness" sounds weaker here.

NINE: You hear it well enough.

SEVEN: They've installed speakers like this everywhere. You hear them even in the johns.

NINE: They are well organized. (*Silence*)

SEVEN: I know a funny game.

NINE: Funny?

SEVEN: Voices and shouts of animals. I ask and you answer. The dog barks. What does the owl do?

NINE: I don't know.

SEVEN: Hooooo.

NINE: Ah!

SEVEN: And the magpie?

NINE: I don't know that either.

SEVEN: He chirps.

NINE: You're very well informed.

SEVEN: I saw it in one of my son's books. Now they teach many things in school.

NINE: Yes. They teach many things. (*Brief pause*) Now it's my turn. What does the raven do?

SEVEN: He croaks. It's my turn again. What does the stork do?

NINE: I don't know.

SEVEN: It cranks!

NINE: Well, it cranks very frequently. What do birds do?

SEVEN: What birds?

NINE: All the birds.

SEVEN: All the birds sing.

NINE: Are you sure? (*Unpleasant, persistent, the whistle of the factory blows. 9 and 7 look at each other*)

SEVEN: It's time.

NINE: It's time. You go in there and it doesn't let you go.

SEVEN: Who?

NINE: The machine. You go in there and you fuse yourself with her in a loving embrace. And for eight hours, you're one. You and the machine.

SEVEN: You know lots of things, 9.

NINE: I know nothing.

(7 *takes his paper bag and goes towards the exit. The whistle blows again*)

NINE: I can't get used to it. It happens every day and I can't get used to it.

SEVEN: To what?

NINE: Fifteen years. The sweet song of the sirens.

SEVEN: In all the factories of the world, I don't think there's a whistle as unpleasant as this one. We'll talk at noon, 9.

NINE: We'll talk, 7.

(*They exit*)

Scene Two

Inside the factory. The stage is empty except for the actors. A scrim with painted cobwebs separates the actors and the audience. Noise of machines working. 9 and 7 are standing. With automatic movements, they mark the time and the rhythm rapidly though not exaggeratedly. They lift an arm, they lower it; they stretch the other arm, they bring it back; they suggest taking something from one side and putting it in front of them; they push a lever, they pull another, etc., etc. When they have finished with the cycle, they start again. They do not do this in unison. The effect that must be achieved is that of the routine movements of the two men when they operate their machines. Without moving from their places or paying attention to the loudspeaker, they should continue this action throughout the scene.

From the loudspeaker one suddenly hears, in contrast with the monotonous sounds of the machines, very luminous and romantic music—Debussy's "Clair de Lune"

*played on a violin. The noise of the machines is heard in the
background throughout the scene. Suddenly the music is
interrupted.*

LOUDSPEAKER, WOMAN: The Sun of Your Life Company—
cleanliness and efficiency above all—offers you now, in the middle
of your working day, a musical selection. (*The music resumes
for a moment, then there is another interruption*) Remember, let
today be a very profitable working day!

(*Again, the music and another interruption. A man's
voice is heard through the loudspeaker. Impersonal and
authoritative*)

LOUDSPEAKER, MAN: Attention! Attention! Worker RR121
is asked to return *immediately* to his post. Attention! Attention!
RR121 is reminded that he should not talk with his fellow workers and he's asked to return *immediately* to his post. (*"Clair de
Lune" is heard and interrupted*) Attention! Attention! All workers interested in the dining room service that the company provides for its personnel's convenience are reminded that they
should sign up in the main office from 9:47 to 9:57 and from
4:47 to 4:59, a week in advance.

(*The music ends*)

LOUDSPEAKER, WOMAN: This has been "Clair de Lune" by
Debussy, brought to you by The Sun of Your Life Company—
cleanliness and efficiency above all—for the enjoyment and cultural enrichment of its workers. Tomorrow you'll listen again to
another masterpiece from the universal repertoire. Today we shall
continue working in an environment of happiness, cleanliness and
efficiency, thanks to the installations made by our technicians for
the most effective utilization of our machines and our men.

(*The noise of the machines increases. 9 and 7 continue
for a few seconds their working pantomime, now at a very
accelerated rhythm*)

(Darkness)

Scene Three

The yard. 7 is seated on the bench, with his sandwiches and a couple of bottles of soft drinks. He eats. 9 is standing.

SEVEN: Aren't you eating?

NINE: I'm not hungry.

SEVEN: (*Stretching out*) Ah! I'm dead.

NINE: Dead is saying a lot.

SEVEN: Well, I am.

NINE: Don't be so vain. Dead is saying a lot.

SEVEN: I guess you're right. I shall stick it out until the day's over.

NINE: Even when it stops, I keep on hearing it.

SEVEN: What?

NINE: The noise of the machines.

SEVEN: (*Stops eating*) Like hammers, like the pounding of hammers.

NINE: Like the pounding of a clock.

SEVEN: Like the squeaking of wheels.

NINE: Like the approach of a locomotive. You know it's coming. And you're there. And it ends by running over you.

SEVEN: Does it bother you?

NINE: What?

SEVEN: The noise of the machines.

NINE: It's part of me. I carry it with me everywhere.

SEVEN: What's worse is always having to do the same thing. One year!

NINE: Fifteen! And the day arrives when you no longer operate it. The machine operates you. You are the machine and she is the brains.

LOUDSPEAKER, MAN: Attention! Attention! (*9 turns around brusquely towards the loudspeaker. His eyes remain riveted to it. He is full of hatred both for the loudspeaker and its voices*) In twenty-nine minutes, fifty-three seconds, you will return to work.

In twenty-nine minutes, (*Brief pause*) forty-two seconds (*He underscores*) and a half, the whistle will blow.

SEVEN: Well ... (*He shrugs and resumes eating*)

LOUDSPEAKER, WOMAN: The Sun of Your Life Company—cleanliness and efficiency above all—gives its workers more facilities and more time to eat than other companies. May you enjoy your meal!

SEVEN: (*With the bottle in his hand, he offers a toast to the loudspeaker*) Thank you.

NINE: (*Looking at his hand which is affected by a nervous tremor; laughs bitterly*) Stop! (*He holds his trembling hand*) This rebel gets away from me sometimes. The doctor says it is a nervous tic. It's not serious. It only happens when I'm tired. (*Excited*) It's not serious, I already know that! How can it be serious if nobody cares? (*Silence*)

SEVEN: Aren't you eating? (*He offers him a sandwich*) It's one of yours. It looks good.

NINE: Yes, it looks good. (*9 takes the sandwich. He has gained complete control of himself. They eat, 9 without enthusiasm, 7 hungrily*)

NINE: (*Offering another sandwich*) You want one?

SEVEN: (*Who wants it*) No. I think not.

NINE: Come on, take it. This one's enough for me. I don't even know if I'm going to finish it.

SEVEN: (*Takes the sandwich*) All right, thank you. I'll tell my wife tomorrow to pack an extra sandwich for you.

NINE: Forget it. (*They eat and drink in silence. 7 looks up at the sky*)

SEVEN: Beautiful day today.

NINE: Yes, a beautiful day. And up there a smiling blue sky.

SEVEN: You said the same thing yesterday.

NINE: Did I? Then there must also have been a smiling blue sky.

SEVEN: Yes, there was.

NINE: But over there ... very high.

SEVEN: Do you think it was smiling for us?

NINE: Who?

SEVEN: The sky. Do you think it was also smiling for us?

NINE: Why not? For the stones and the worms. For the insects and the microbes. And for us, too. (*Silence*) No, I don't think I'll finish it. . . . Do you want it?

SEVEN: (*Accepting without hesitation*) You're wrong in not eating them. They're very good.

NINE: There's nothing clean about them.

SEVEN: No?

NINE: No. You can eat them without a worry. If you could have just seen how, at the street corner stand, the old man with his dirty hands picked up a dirty slice. . . . It's enough to make you lick your fingers. "Nothing canned," I tell him every morning. "Above all, nothing sterilized."

SEVEN: (*Offering*) You don't drink either?

NINE: I already have.

(*7 drinks*)

LOUDSPEAKER, MAN: Attention! Attention!! All workers who do *not* use our dining room facilities are reminded that alcoholic beverages are strictly prohibited. All workers who do *not* use our dining room facilities are reminded that alcoholic beverages are strictly prohibited.

SEVEN: And are those who *do use* the dining room facilities also forbidden to drink alcoholic beverages?

NINE: What for? They just don't serve it.

SEVEN: The dining room is very large inside there.

NINE: Very large.

SEVEN: Everything shines. The tables, the walls, the floor . . . the floor as much as the tables. Everything shines.

NINE: Everything shines.

SEVEN: Perhaps we could eat there some day.

NINE: Never.

SEVEN: It wouldn't be too expensive.

NINE: It would be very expensive.

SEVEN: Why?

NINE: The price would be that you could never again enjoy your sandwiches.

(*Silence*)

SEVEN: We haven't had many opportunities.

NINE: No.

SEVEN: Now they teach a lot of stuff in school. It will be different for my son.

NINE: It will be different for your son. (*He takes the flute from his pocket and starts to play the same tune he did at the beginning. 7 continues eating*)

SEVEN: Don't you know anything happier?

NINE: No. I'm sorry. (*He starts to play again*)

(*A Boy stops at the entrance. He is about ten years old. He is carrying a lunch box. He listens to the music without moving for a few seconds. He approaches 9, slowly, attracted by the flute. 7 smiles at him*)

SEVEN: Ah, it's you. How are you? (*The Boy advances, enchanted by the flute*)

SEVEN: (*To the Boy*) You're late today. You have to hurry or they're going to yell at you. (*9 stops playing*)

NINE: (*To the Boy*) Hello. Who are you?

BOY: (*Coming to*) Huh? What?

NINE: Hello. Who are you?

SEVEN: He comes here every day.

BOY: I bring my father's lunch.

SEVEN: And what are you doing here? You better hurry.

BOY: I heard the flute (*To 9*) Is it yours, the flute?

NINE: Yes. Do you come here every day?

BOY: I bring the lunch. (*As if repeating a lesson*) My father is a worker for The Sun of Your Life Company. I, too, shall be a worker for the company if I grow up fast and if they accept me. (*Silence*) Well, I'm late . . . (*He starts to leave, stops, turns to 9*) Perhaps afterwards you will let me play with your flute? (*He goes out*)

NINE: I wouldn't like it.

SEVEN: What?

NINE: To see you here for fifteen years, like me. To see the boy grow up and be here a year, like you. I wouldn't like to see it.

(*Silence*)

SEVEN: Have you finished eating?

NINE: I've finished.

(*7 gathers the papers and goes to throw them in the trash can*)

SEVEN: Cleanliness ... (*He collects the bottles and is about to put them in a corner. He stumbles on the barbed wire*) Damn it! (*He tries to free himself*)

NINE: (*Without looking at 7*) Can I help you?

SEVEN: (*Fighting the barbed wire*) No, thanks, I can do it alone. (*At last he frees himself*)

NINE: That's it. A barbed wire fence. That's the only thing missing in this happy and prosperous factory. A barbed wire fence all around. Electric, if they could. (*Silence*) I would have liked to help you, 7.

SEVEN: I know it.

NINE: I would have liked to help you free yourself from the barbed wire, but I couldn't. No one can. We must do it alone, do you understand? No one can help anyone, do you understand? We must do it alone.

SEVEN: I understand.

NINE: (*Laughs, indicating the wire*) Like a cobweb. They have us well trapped. (*Laughs*) Well trapped.

SEVEN: Enough! (*9 continues laughing, then stops. 7 looks unhappily at the hole that the barbed wire has left in his overalls*) Of course, they're torn. And they just gave them to me. Now I'll have to wear them patched. I hate patches!

NINE: (*Turns*) A fly! (*He laughs*) A fly in our sterilized factory! (*7 tries to swat the fly with his hand*)

SEVEN: It got away.

NINE: Good. (*Silence*) How long do you think a fly lives?

SEVEN: I don't know.

NINE: Two days in the life of a fly, how many days would

that be in the life of a man? Have you heard about flytrap plants?

SEVEN: Yes, I think so. I heard something about it.

NINE: (*Suddenly, very excited*) And did you know that there are plants that blend themselves with the earth, that take its color?

SEVEN: Like chameleons?

NINE: Like chameleons.

SEVEN: No, I didn't know that.

NINE: Did you know that certain plants, to defend themselves from other dangers, allow ants to live inside them?

SEVEN: No, I didn't know that.

NINE: Plants are wise. They have all their movements planned. Like machines.

SEVEN: And those flytrap plants . . .

NINE: Insectivorous plants, you should say. Insectivorous plants. They are as wise as our man-trap machines. The plant traps the body of the fly; the machine traps the brains of the man. They are exquisitely feminine.

SEVEN: Who?

NINE: The plant and the machine. I mean, they demand an absolute devotion from you. (*He begins to walk from one side to another, calculating aloud*) The insect trapped by the plant could last two days before being totally wrapped up by the tentacles and absorbed. Two days, or forty-eight hours in the life of a fly represent in the life of a man as much as forty-eight hours considered in proportion to the difference between the duration of man's life and the duration of a fly's life; that is to say, forty-eight hours multiplied by the result of the division between the duration of the life of a man and the duration of the life of a fly which means that the man who is trapped by the machine . . . .

SEVEN: (*Shouting*) It's all right! Shut up!

NINE: (*Ironically*) Does it bother you? Why? You don't have to be afraid of words. Above all, when words tell the truth, pure and clean, although not always sweet truth. You don't have to be afraid of the good and noble truth. I assure you that there isn't much difference between that fly and us. She's fighting to satisfy the needs of her digestive system, the same as us. She uses very little of her brains and very much of her honest legs. And her wings. We can only use our honest legs. The fly is better off. We have no wings.

SEVEN: But not everything is. . . .

NINE: (*Interrupts him*) Yes, yes, I know. Not everything is always that way. Let's not be pessimists. Let's try to have constructive thoughts. Thoughts that are educative, productive, depurative, communicative, seductive, sensitive, digestive, abortive, cohesive, copulative, operative, ponderative, lucrative and lubricative, imperative, volitive, incentive, and incisive. In any case, thoughts to live with. That's it! Above all, let's try to live.

SEVEN: Be quiet!

NINE: Pardon me. (*Silence. He pats his stomach*) Well, well. One more day that we have eaten, in spite of everything.

SEVEN: (*Unhappily*) Of course. Of course, for the fly or for the man it's the same thing.

NINE: (*Indifferent*) It's the opportunity.

SEVEN: The opportunity to die, isn't that it? (*9 doesn't answer*) I believe that it's better to live, nevertheless.

NINE: It's the same.

SEVEN: It's not the same. There are moments . . .

NINE: Yes, there are moments.

SEVEN: . . . that are worth everything.

NINE: There are moments.

SEVEN: Once when I was a child, they brought me a truck with real lights. Real big, red lights that shone in the darkness.

NINE: It must have been beautiful.

SEVEN: Very beautiful. That night I could not sleep. I got up in order to see how the lights shone. I was afraid that they might have been weakened or that they would go out forever. But no, there they were. And from that day on, I slept with the truck at the side of my bed. I guarded the lights. And each time I saw them shine, it was. . . .

NINE: It was a moment.

SEVEN: Yes, a moment. Like another time, I had a new woman. A completely new one. Like the toy truck. And all for me. (*A pause*) It was my only new toy.

NINE: The woman?

SEVEN: The truck.

NINE: Did it last long?

SEVEN: No, it did not last. I discovered that the lights did not really burn. They only glowed in the darkness. Besides, the truck was not for me. It was just borrowed.

NINE: And the woman?

SEVEN: She was also borrowed. It was like a lottery prize; it couldn't last. One morning, she went to make a phone call and she got married to the bank clerk. She could have called from another place. From the phone booth or a gas station. But she went into the bank and married the clerk. (*A pause*) She had soft skin . . .

NINE: Like the leaves.

SEVEN: Like what?

NINE: Like leaves in summer. When rain falls and trees bend. To the right and to the left. A soft skin . . . And trees bend.

SEVEN: What trees?

NINE: Whichever you like. Those out there in the street, for example.

SEVEN: They could have planted trees in this yard.

NINE: Yards must always be clean. Trees are dirty. They attract dogs.

SEVEN: I thought you liked trees.

NINE: I like them. But they're not for me. I know perfectly well what's for me and what isn't.

SEVEN: 9, can I ask you a question?

NINE: That's why we're talking. Those who talk, ask and answer each other. Or at least, they think they answer.

SEVEN: You, why don't you eat in the dining hall?

NINE: (*Indifferently*) It nauseates me.

SEVEN: The food.

NINE: Those who eat it.

SEVEN: They're like us.

NINE: That's why they nauseate me. They're *all* like me. They're nothing. (*Silence*)

SEVEN: Bessie's not the same. The other one had light in her eyes—more light than eyes. She had golden eyes, like her hair. Bessie also has a pair of eyes, but you don't even see them. Besides, she wears an apron. And a bank clerk would never notice her. But I married and . . . There are also the children. The oldest goes to school. Bessie's my legal wife. I put my insurance in her name.

NINE: You did well.

SEVEN: After all, working here has its advantages. The insurance and all those things. It has its advantages.

NINE: Yes, it has its advantages.

SEVEN: Even a department for the personnel's problems. You have a problem, you go there and you tell them.

NINE: And do they solve it?

SEVEN: I don't know. I never went there. You should know more about it than I do.

NINE: I never went there either.

SEVEN: You've been here such a long time. You must have had many problems.

NINE: Their Problems Department is open from 3:59 to 4:48 p.m. Tell me, what do I do if a problem turns up at exactly 8:30 p.m.? Tell me, what do I do?

SEVEN: Well, you wait.

NINE: There's the mistake. Problems don't wait. Problems never wait; that's why they're problems. They just appear. When you least expect them, they appear. They plant themselves in a corner of your brain, and they begin to torture you.

SEVEN: Yes, I suppose the Problems Department is not enough.

NINE: You tell them your problems and it's just like at the doctor's. You're no longer a man, just a case. "The case of worker MM099." It sounds important, don't you think so?

SEVEN: Yes, very important. (*Silence*) What did you do before coming here?

NINE: I was in another factory. And you?

SEVEN: I was in another factory. And before that I was a dispatcher. I dispatched rapidly, all day long.

NINE: Me, too, I must have done all of that. I must have dispatched and collected and nailed and painted and shoveled and covered walls with cement. Once, a long time ago, I must have done all of that . . . or part of that. I don't remember. It makes no difference. (*Silence*) You know, I feel as if I owe you something.

SEVEN: Why?

NINE: This talking, one pays for it, right? Talking so much with you, I feel I owe you something.

SEVEN: Don't you have anyone at home?

NINE: I have the landlady, but she is deaf. Sometimes I take some woman there, but it's not to talk. I had a brother, but he played the hero and died as a volunteer soldier in the war. It was a question of time. An error of a few minutes.

SEVEN: Of a few minutes?

NINE: A "small administrative error." Wars also have their administrative section. The order of cease fire was given but the announcement did not arrive in time and my brother died. Wars are great. Just "small errors" once in a while, but in general everything very well organized. Immediately they sent me a telegram. Very correct. An announcement, like the one that shouts "Attention! Attention!" through the loudspeaker. "Attention!" they wrote to me, "Urgent . . . We are very sorry to notify you that on Tuesday at four o'clock . . . (*Pause; then continues slowly*) We're very sorry to notify you . . . ." (*Silence*)

SEVEN: Well, that was a long time ago.

NINE: That was centuries ago.

SEVEN: During the war.

NINE: During the war.

SEVEN: Do you think they would call on us if there's another war?

NINE: Sure they would. All of us are good for wars. Not

for department heads. Not for sitting at a desk. Not even for bank clerks. Not for a soft skinned woman. But for war, yes. Even we are good for war.

(*The Boy has entered without either 9 or 7 seeing him. He discovers the flute that 9 has forgotten on the bench and takes it in his hands. Now he puts it in his mouth and makes a sound. 9 and 7 turn around*)

BOY: Hello. (*He gives the flute to 9*)

NINE: Hello. Do you like the flute? (*The Boy nods*) It's a good flute.

BOY: Can you teach me how to play it?

NINE: We'll see. Are you planning on staying around here?

BOY: Yes. I stay here until my dad comes out. I got permission as long as I don't go where the machines are. But I'll be able to hear them from here. And from the large yard, too. Is it true that they're behind that wall?

NINE: Yes, behind the wall.

BOY: How near!

NINE: Very near.

SEVEN: (*To the Boy*) Do you like the machines?

BOY: A lot.

NINE: More than the flute?

BOY: (*After a moment*) I think so . . . more than the flute.

SEVEN: Will you keep on coming to the factory?

BOY: Yes, every day. And when I'm just a little bit bigger they will let me be an apprentice. And I'll have a uniform! Like my dad's. (*To 7*) Like yours!

NINE: (*To the Boy*) No!! Don't ever wear a uniform! Now, go away!

(*The Boy, startled by 9's outburst, starts to go but trips on the barbed wire. He lets out a painful cry. 9 and 7 rush over to him. 9 takes the Boy in his arms while 7 frees him from the wire. 9 gently puts him on the ground*)

NINE: Did you hurt yourself?

BOY: (*About to cry*) No! (*He rushes out*)

NINE: *Not the children!* Leave the children alone! (*He takes the wire and angrily hurls it away. In the process, he hurts his hand*)

SEVEN: Have you hurt yourself?

NINE: Yes, I hurt myself. (*Silence*) It's nothing.

SEVEN: We'll take those wires away from here. We'll throw them away.

NINE: We'll have to ask for permission.

SEVEN: Perhaps they're used for something.

NINE: Of course they are. It's the cobweb. (*Pause*) I wish that it were over.

SEVEN: What?

NINE: The time they give us to eat. Each day, it becomes longer.

SEVEN: (*Imitating the woman's voice on the loudspeaker*) "The Sun of Your Life Company—cleanliness and efficiency above all—gives its workers more comfort and more time to eat than other companies." (*Silence*) No, they don't give us more time. What happens is that our sandwiches are eaten too fast. Those who eat inside take more time. In the dining hall they have music.

NINE: Yes, they have music.

SEVEN: In the dining hall everything shines.

NINE: Everything shines.

SEVEN: Tell me, 9, would you go?

NINE: Where?

SEVEN: To war. Would you go?

NINE: If they called me.

SEVEN: But you don't believe in war?

NINE: It might be the opportunity.

SEVEN: The opportunity to die?

NINE: Yes.

SEVEN: Death scares me.

NINE: It's because you're still alive.

SEVEN: And you're not?

NINE: I eat sandwiches, as you can see.

SEVEN: And that's being alive?

NINE: That and what you do with your wife at night.

SEVEN: Is that all?

NINE: Almost all.

SEVEN: But that boy who was just here—that's being alive, too.

NINE: Unfortunately. (*Silence*)

SEVEN: (*Triumphantly*) You missed something!

NINE: It could be.

SEVEN: You yourself talked about the rain and the leaves of the trees!

NINE: Oh yes, blessed nature!

SEVEN: I don't mean because of nature, but because of the moments.

NINE: Yes, the moments. The moment of leaving here, for example. The moment of leaving this place forever.

SEVEN: You say it as if it were a cage.

NINE: It is. Not a single bar is missing.

SEVEN: No one is stopping us from leaving here.

NINE: No one.

SEVEN: No one's helping us either.

NINE: We should go by ourselves, without help. And here we are, turning around.

SEVEN: Where would we go?

NINE: Turning around. Have you ever seen a bear turning around, tied by his chain? That's what we're doing, you and me. Number 7 and Number 9. First the work. Then the food. We run around with a cup, collecting coins. We still add a somersault or two to complete the circus act.

SEVEN: A year.

NINE: Fifteen. Until one day you free yourself, at last.

SEVEN: What day?

NINE: The day you die.

SEVEN: Have you thought about that day?

NINE: Yes, I have thought about it.

SEVEN: Do you fear it?

NINE: I wait for it. It's a great day. You must wait for it completely dressed up, with your best clothes on. It's an important day. You know how important it is and you wait for it. You speak about everything else and you pretend not to remember it, but you wait for it. You're always waiting for it. It's getting nearer. Nearer. You think you're irreplaceable. That the whole world will shudder when your day comes. But it comes. And people do not even notice it. And around four o'clock in the afternoon they bury you. A sunny afternoon, probably. (*Silence*)

SEVEN: You talk a lot about death.

NINE: One has to talk about something.

SEVEN: We could talk about life.

NINE: It's the same thing.

SEVEN: Why this yard? Why this factory? Who has done this to us?

NINE: They have. The other ones have done it.

SEVEN: The other ones?

NINE: Everyone and no one. The one who walks down the street, and the one who doesn't leave his house. The one whom you see, and the one whom you don't see. The one who is your friend, and that one whom you don't even know. They have done it. They have put us here, out of the game.

SEVEN: And they have forgotten about us.

NINE: We don't count. We don't get to play. It's they who pass by, out there. It's they who run, who go and come, who think, who fight, who triumph. And we just look at them. We don't get to play.

SEVEN: It's unjust.

NINE: I don't know.

SEVEN: It's unjust!

NINE: It is.

SEVEN: It's like a well. We shouldn't have fallen in.

NINE: We shouldn't have been born in it.

SEVEN: Why us?

NINE: Why not?

SEVEN: It's like a well. We shouldn't have been born in it.

NINE: We shall die in it.

SEVEN: Yes. Many things can kill a man. War, sickness....

NINE: Disgust.

SEVEN: Exhaustion, desperation, poverty.

NINE: Disgust. (*Silence*)

SEVEN: What did you do yesterday afternoon?

NINE: I bought bread and ate.

SEVEN: And today?

NINE: I shall buy bread and I shall eat.

SEVEN: And after you eat?

NINE: I shall sleep.

SEVEN: And tomorrow?

NINE: I shall sleep. And then I shall get up again, and I shall come to the factory. I'll get up. I'll eat. I'll sleep. I'll eat. I'll sleep. I'll get up. I'll come to the factory. (*Shouts*) No, I *will not come!* (*In a low voice*) I will not come. (*Silence*)

SEVEN: When you play the flute, do you dream?

NINE: Sometimes.

SEVEN: I also dream.

NINE: About leaving the trap.

SEVEN: About leaving here.

NINE: About leaving the trap. One of these days, without making a sound. Just to say "enough!" and leave the trap.

SEVEN: Do you want it so much?

NINE: In the beginning, each day, each minute, I always thought about leaving here. I always wanted to. Now, only at times, but with more intensity. I want it with my teeth clenched. Counting the days and seeing the nights escape from me. I long for it as one longs for a woman. With the body tensed. And it's not to leave in order to go to another factory, do you understand? Nor is it to go to dispatch or to nail or to shovel or to cover walls with cement. It is to finish with all of this once and for all, do you understand? It's not to play in the game anymore, and not because they've put me at the side, but because of my own will. It is to choose at last for myself the role that I am going to play and stop doing what the others have told me to do!

SEVEN: I'll also leave here. (*The factory whistle*)

NINE: Do you see? You can't leave. Everything goes on as usual. Everything always goes on as usual. The world turns, conscious of its responsibilities. Dogs, mules, and camels are whipped in every latitude, from the arctic to the antarctic. The ice is melted. The river rechanneled. The mountain tunneled. The worm crushed and the chicken digested. And you're no different. You get up and you come to the factory. And they make their whistle blow. But one day you make up your mind. It is just a matter of making up your mind, and one day, one marvelous day, you stop spinning, just stop. And how you laugh at their whistle and their factory and their industries and organizations! How you laugh at all of them! The opportunity. It's a matter of one, single, small opportunity.

SEVEN: I'll also leave here. When my opportunity comes.

NINE: Your opportunity will come.

SEVEN: No, 9, not death. *Life*.

NINE: It's the same thing.

SEVEN: Let's go. (*He leaves brusquely*)

NINE: But one day, you make up your mind. You stop spinning, just stop. (*He exits*)

(Darkness)

Scene Four

The yard. 7 *is seated on the bench. His expression reveals a deep sadness.*

SEVEN: I would have sworn that he was laughing. "The opportunity," he said. I would have sworn that he was laughing. (*The Boy comes running in, with the flute in his hand*)

BOY: Look, he gave me his flute! Before going in, he told me, "Here, for you," and he gave me his flute. (*Silence*) How good the machines sound!

SEVEN: I would have sworn that he was laughing . . .

LOUDSPEAKER, MAN: Attention! Attention! Worker YX157 must report *immediately* to the main office.

SEVEN: . . . As he wished, without making a sound. They didn't even stop the machines.

BOY: Why are they calling you?

LOUDSPEAKER, MAN: Attention! Attention! Worker YX157 must report *immediately* to the main office.

BOY: Aren't you 157?

SEVEN: Yes, I am.

BOY: Why do they want you?

SEVEN: He was my friend. I was near him. He was my friend.

BOY: Is it true that he is dead?

SEVEN: Yes, it's true.

BOY: Why's he dead?

SEVEN: (*Brusquely*) Because he wanted to kill himself!

BOY: Why did he want to kill himself?

SEVEN: For nothing.

BOY: For nothing?

SEVEN: For nothing.

BOY: And how did he kill himself?

SEVEN: The machine. He let the machine trap him and . . . (*Suddenly shouting*) Get away! He said for you to go away! Do you understand? To get away!

BOY: (*Retreating, frightened*) He gave me his flute.

SEVEN: (*After a moment*) Forgive me. (*The machines are still heard*)

BOY: (*Pause*) What was his name?

SEVEN: Joseph.

BOY: Didn't he have a number?

SEVEN: Yes, he had a number. He is dead. Now his name is Joseph!

BOY: Poor Joseph.

SEVEN: (*Cries out*) No, 9, not death! Life!

LOUDSPEAKER, MAN: Attention! Attention! Worker YX157 must report *immediately* to the main office.

BOY: Why don't you answer? They're calling you. Aren't you going to the main office?

SEVEN: No, I'm not going!

BOY: Why? If you don't go, they'll fire you.

SEVEN: They will not fire me. I shall leave by myself!

BOY: Where?

SEVEN: I shall leave the trap. I shall go away from here.

BOY: Where to?

SEVEN: Of course, there's Bessie and the children. . . .

BOY: Aren't you going to the main office?

SEVEN: (*Laughs; a laughter that has a strange resemblance to that of 9's*) Like a cobweb. They have us well trapped.

BOY: Aren't you going to obey?

SEVEN: One year. Fifteen. Yes, I suppose that I'm going to obey.

BOY: I always obey. And when I'm a worker for the company, I'll also obey.

SEVEN: (*He now begins to resemble 9 more and more. He repeats in the same tone as 9 did:*) Not the children! Leave the children alone!!

(*He takes the wire and angrily hurls it away, just as 9 did. And as it happened to 9, he hurts his hand. He continues speaking with the same words that 9 used, while the Boy repeats the words used earlier by 7*)

BOY: Have you hurt yourself?

SEVEN: Yes, I hurt myself. (*Silence*) It's nothing.

BOY: We'll take those wires away from here. We'll throw them away.

SEVEN: We'll have to ask for permission.

(*The factory whistle blows. The machines stop*)

BOY: It's time to leave. I'm going to look for dad. (*He starts to go, turns back to 7, and holds out the flute*) He gave me his flute. (*He leaves*)

LOUDSPEAKER, WOMAN: One more working day has ended

in The Sun of Your Life Company—cleanliness and efficiency above all—one of the foremost factories in the world of preserves and one of the most modern ones. The Sun of Your Life provides for its personnel a clean, healthy and happy environment in which to work. We hope that today has been a very profitable working day!

(*When the voice is heard, 7 turns sharply towards the loudspeaker and stares at it as 9 did before. His hand trembles as 9's did. He holds it*)

SEVEN: No, 9, not death! *Life!*

(*He slowly goes towards the factory. Exits. The noise of the machines can be heard again. It grows progressively louder as:*)

The Curtain Falls

Stanley Richards

Since the publication of his first collection in 1968, Stanley Richards has become one of our leading editors and play anthologists, earning rare encomiums from the nation's press and the admiration of a multitude of devoted readers.

Mr. Richards has edited the following anthologies and series: *The Best Short Plays 1973; The Best Short Plays 1972; The Best Short Plays 1971; The Best Short Plays 1970; The Best Short Plays 1969; The Best Short Plays 1968; 10 Classic Mystery and Suspense Plays of the Modern Theatre; Best Mystery and Suspense Plays of the Modern Theatre; Best Plays of the Sixties* (the latter three, *Fireside Theatre-Literary Guild* selections); *Best Short Plays of the World Theatre: 1968–1973; Best Short Plays of the World Theatre: 1958–1967; Modern Short Comedies from Broadway and London;* and *Canada on Stage.*

An established playwright as well, he has written twenty-five plays, twelve of which (including *Through a Glass, Darkly; Tunnel of Love; August Heat; Sun Deck; O Distant Land;* and *District of Columbia*) originally were published in earlier volumes of *The Best One-Act Plays* and *The Best Short Plays* annuals.

Journey to Bahia, which he adapted from a prize-winning Brazilian play and film, *O Pagador de Promessas,* premiered at The Berkshire Playhouse, Massachusetts, and later was produced in Washington, D.C. under the auspices of the Brazilian Ambassador and the Brazilian American Cultural Institute. The play also had a successful engagement at the Off-Broadway Henry Street Playhouse and later was presented in repertory by the New York Theatre of the Americas. In September, 1972, it was performed in a Spanish translation at Lincoln Center.

Mr. Richards' plays have been translated for production and publication abroad into Portuguese, Afrikaans, Dutch, Tagalog, French, German, Korean, Spanish and Italian.

In addition, he has been the New York theatre critic for *Players Magazine* and a frequent contributor to *Playbill, Theatre Arts, The Theatre, Actor's Equity Magazine,* and *Dramatists Guild Quarterly.*

As an American Theatre Specialist, Mr. Richards was awarded three successive grants by the United States Department of State's International Cultural Exchange Program to teach playwriting and directing in Chile and Brazil. He taught playwriting in Canada for over ten years and in 1966 was appointed Visiting Professor of Drama at the University of Guelph, Ontario. He has produced and directed plays and has lectured extensively on theatre at universities in the United States, Canada and South America.

Mr. Richards, a New York City resident, is now at work on a collection of *Ten Great Musicals of the American Theatre* and *The Best Short Plays 1974.*

Each year several hundred short plays are submitted to Stanley Richards by authors, agents, publishers, college and university drama departments, and theatrical managements. Richards personally reads and carefully evaluates every play.

According to Richards, a creative editor does more than collect plays, paste them on manuscript pages, and dispatch them to the printer. He has certain obligations to both his authors and his audience. His foremost responsibility to his authors is to present their plays to the reader in the best possible form. Sometimes he suggests additional work or changes. Often, in the case of a rejection, he still retains a "special interest in the author and his future works for I firmly believe that there is nothing more rewarding for an editor than to discover and maintain a professional vigil over the development of a gifted new dramatist."

An editor of plays also has an obligation to his audience to present as widely appealing an assortment as possible—"for a collection of plays to be effectual it must have strong appeal and areas of involvement for a wide category of readers."

Many reviewers have paid tribute to Richards' talent as an editor:

"Richards has made an impressive selection of the very best, most vital and most representative plays . . . there isn't a bore in the batch. . . ." —*Publishers' Weekly*

"Stanley Richards . . . shows a real understanding of what is meant by the best of something and manages a selection of short plays which is truly astonishing in that each and every one may be described as a winner."—*Drama*